TWICE LUCKY

TWICE LUCKY

My life in motorsport

STUART TURNER

Foreword by Jackie Stewart, OBE

Haynes Publishing

First published in October 1999

British Library Cataloguing in Publication Data:
A catalogue record for this book is available from the British Library

ISBN 1 85960 602 4

Library of Congress catalog card no. 99-73265

Jacket illustrations
Front, clockwise from top left: Timo Makinen, Escort, World Cup Rally; Rauno
Aaltonen, Mini, winning 1967 Monte; Formula Ford, France; Didier Auriol,
Sierra Cosworth, winning 1988 Tour de Corse. Back, from top: Donald and
Erle Morley, Austin-Healey 3000, winning 1962 Alpine; François Delecour,
Escort Cosworth, winning 1993 Portugal; Ron Gouldbourn, TR2; Mark
Lovell, RS200, 1986 Lombard RAC Rally.

Haynes Publishing, Sparkford, Nr Yeovil, Somerset, BA22 7JJ.
Tel: 01963 440635 Fax: 01963 440001
Int. tel: +44 1963 440635 Fax: +44 1963 440001
E-mail: sales@haynes-manuals.co.uk
Web site: http://www.haynes.com

Haynes North America, Inc.
861 Lawrence Drive, Newbury Park,
California 91320 USA

Text typeset by J. H. Haynes & Co. Ltd., Sparkford
Plate section designed and typeset by
G&M, Raunds, Wellingborough, Northants
Printed by J. H. Haynes & Co. Ltd., Sparkford

Contents

A sort of foreword

To   Jackie Stewart, OBE
From   Stuart Turner

Dear Jackie,

Although we have exchanged rude letters at regular intervals over the years, this is not just another in the series. From which you will gather that I need a favour.

I have just written an autobiography and the publishers feel that a foreword by you will help the sales. I don't see it myself – I think it will just hasten the book's plunge into remainder shops throughout the land – but, as a starving author, who am I to argue with a publisher?

I won't insult you by offering you money to write something but I promise that, provided whatever you say is suitably glowing, I will delete all references in the book to your total ignorance of the noblest branch of motorsport, rallying. Further, I won't even mention that when you did your one and only rally, starting in Glasgow, you failed to find the first control. Clearly, for a single-seater driver, finding Edinburgh Castle would have been something of an intellectual challenge.

I wouldn't dream of putting words into your mouth, but if phrases like 'an outstanding and charismatic team manager' . . . 'the book sparkles on every page' . . . or 'the best book I have read since (fill in whatever you like here)' . . . strike any chords, well, I am sure you will find the right things to say.

Your obedient servant
Stuart

To   Stuart Turner
From   Jackie Stewart, OBE

Dear Mr Turner
I address you in a formal manner because, although I have not yet read the galleys for what can only be a thin and insubstantial work, no doubt when my lawyers have seen it they will again be charging me incredible sums to protect my reputation.

I cannot possibly use any of the phrases suggested by you (how would 'The best thing I have read since *The Plumbing and Central Heating Guide*' help the book anyway?) but what I *can* put on record is that I have known you for far too many years and have been exposed to abuse by you at public gatherings, race tracks and in correspondence on a continuous basis since we originally got to know each other.

Our first unfortunate meeting was at Silverstone on 4 November 1964. You brought along a few very unfit-looking specimens that you called rally drivers who attempted to find their way round the British Racing Drivers Club's excellent track at Silverstone in broad daylight in one of the peculiar little vehicles that you called a Mini. They seemed very nice chaps who were clearly being led by what could only be described as an incompetent team manager. I will not be drawn into your crude attempt to drive a wedge between race and rally drivers by arguing about who was quickest . . . but I still have the timesheets for that day if you wish to see them. Your keenness for safety in those days – there was only Silverstone Sid and his ambulance on parade – was clearly less than it is today with the work you are doing with the Motorsport Safety Fund.

The wonderfully successful season that Ken Tyrrell and I had in winning the European and British Formula 3 Championships in a BMC Cooper was in some way part of your domain. I remember endlessly trying to reach you by telephone to ask if you would lend me a Mini to drive down from Scotland to the Earls Court Motor Show, because in those days I couldn't afford a car. Your answer was 'no', which has a very great deal to do with the fact that I have been so rude to you ever since.

I unfortunately suffered you not only through your BMC days but also when Ford, through poor judgement, employed you as Competitions Manager. They thought that they were putting you in as head of motorsports. Little did they know that the only thing that you had even the slightest knowledge of, and I use that word sparingly, was something called rallying. (Your lack of understanding of the racing world is illustrated by the assumption in your note that anyone in Formula 1 would be 'insulted' to be offered money.)

I will finish by saying that very little has changed over the years between us other than the fact that your long-suffering wife Margaret must surely be 'in waiting' for a Sainthood in the next Honours List. Therefore, in the interest of trying to boost her meagre housekeeping allowance, I will gladly allow this letter to be used to introduce the reader to the works of Stuart Turner, great worker for safety in all forms of motorsport, extremely poor team manager, excellent after-dinner speaker, and a very good friend. Hopefully, this will help when the book is read by the few unsuspecting members of the public who stumble upon it in discount stores.

Yours ever
Jackie

Introduction

WHEN A FRIEND heard that this book would cover nearly 50 years in motorsport, rather unkindly he suggested that it should be called *Anoraks 19.50 to 19.99* with the cover designed as a sales tag. However, as you probably noticed on the way in, I've called it *Twice Lucky* instead. Why? Because I joined the British Motor Corporation just as the Mini Cooper was coming on song, then later, Ford as the Escort was starting to shine; and you can't get much luckier than that.

I worked with John Thornley at BMC and Walter Hayes at Ford when they were both way ahead of their times in management style – they believed in appointing people then leaving them to get on with things, only stepping in when battles were to be fought with the bureaucracy you sometimes find in big companies. I shall always be grateful to them.

As I shall be to Cliff Gaskin for firing my enthusiasm for cars ... to John Bedson for getting me involved in motorsport . . . to *Motoring News* and Castrol for happy interludes in the series of hugely lucky breaks that, placed end to end, constituted my career ... to Flora Myer, my editor at Haynes, for being so gentle with me ... and to Jane French and Annie Hallam for launching me into yet another career, in public speaking.

I'm also very grateful to the following, many of whom have dug into long-forgotten files, for photographs: British Motor Industry Heritage Trust, Peter Browning, Bob Burden, Christabel Carlisle, Paul Easter, Ford Motor Company, Martin Holmes, John Hopwood, Brian Horne, Bob Howe, John Jago, Geoff Keys, Mike Moreton, Donald Morley, Peter Rowney and *Safety Fast* magazine.

It has been said that an autobiography reveals nothing bad about a writer except his memory. Well, this book shouldn't fall into that category because Graham Robson has allowed me to draw on his encyclopaedic knowledge of dates and places, for which much thanks. I am grateful to several former colleagues who have checked relevant chapters; however, I will not mention them by name in order to protect the innocent because errors and embellishments are all my own work.

One person I simply can't thank enough is the one who made it all worthwhile, my wife Margaret, not least for keeping me sane over the years, although I suppose sanity can only be a relative term in connection with someone voluntarily electing to spend his life in motorsport.

Stuart Turner
Chipping Norton, Oxfordshire

Chapter 1

Warm up

ALMOST ANYONE WHO has written a book will tell you the same thing – the hardest part is getting started. You arrange pencils on your desk according to colour . . . then rearrange them by size . . . untangle piles of paper clips . . . watch raindrops running down a window . . . *anything* to avoid the moment of truth when you have to put words on to a page. If you are using a computer then there are even more distractions. Have you ever got Solitaire out five times on the trot? I have. When starting this book.

In desperation, you even stare at the walls for inspiration and doing that actually solved my writer's block because I realised that the two trophies, two paintings and two posters, which are all that decorate my study, really sum up what this book is about.

The oldest item is a theatre poster for a variety show featuring Jill Summers who, as you will read, meant so much to me over the years. The poster reminds me of many evenings spent watching what, although I didn't realise it at the time, were the dying days of variety. Can you imagine the thrill for a young teenager of watching shows featuring nudes, then going backstage to meet the 'artistes'? It was all quite decorous of course because the girls were not allowed to move (well, not while on stage at least), but do kids today really get the same sense of fulfilment from the Internet I wonder?

Motorsport involvement comes with the first of the two trophies – the *Autosport* Award given for the winning navigator in the British Trials and Rally Drivers Association's Gold Star Championship. The award is in the shape of a map and I always think how fetching it looks on its revolving plinth with the strobe lighting. With drivers like Ron Gouldbourn and John Sprinzel, I spent endless nights on flat-out rallies competing against people like Tommy Gold, Mike Wood and John Hopwood who have remained friends to this day. Everyone regards 'their' days as the good old ones perhaps, but the '50s probably saw the best of road rallies with flat-out, night-long, virtual road races. I count myself lucky to have been involved during that period.

The first painting is a watercolour by the master, Michael Turner, and features Paddy Hopkirk and Henry Liddon on the Turini on their way to their 1964 Monte win in the Mini. It was presented to me by Castrol, who were our oil suppliers at the time. It was a win that led to Alec Issigonis joining us in Monte Carlo for a dinner party that included none other than Fangio. If the editor knows what's good for her, there will be a shot of the occasion in this book because it's my favourite photograph. If ever I feel like moaning about my lot in life, I just remember that *I once had dinner with Fangio*. And my gloom goes. The Michael Turner (no relation, as you'd know if you saw my daubings) painting also reminds me just how much I enjoyed running the BMC Competitions Department as well as working with people like John Cooper and Ken Tyrrell.

The second painting came six years later. It is by Dion Pears and was also presented to me by Castrol, this time to celebrate the Escort win on the 1970 *Daily Mirror* World Cup Rally by Hannu Mikkola and Gunnar Palm. Like the Monte, that also was an event to cherish: the slog over 16,000 miles from London to Mexico still makes it one of the toughest rallies ever held. We didn't actually move mountains but we moved among them often enough with a 57-hour stage (not a misprint) in the Andes. Endless air flights . . . bullet-proof windscreens scattered across South America as spares . . . mechanics in Santiago instructing drivers as they worked on their own cars in parc fermé behind bars (the best place for some of them) . . . time for a trip in a reed canoe on Lake Titicaca 12,500 feet above sea level . . . a rally to remember.

It was just as well that Ford won because I hadn't really got a proper budget for it; if we'd lost I suspect my career would not have lasted long enough to justify this book.

The second of the two posters on the study wall means a fast-forward to 1990 because it is a copy of the advertisement run by Ford to celebrate the first success, in prototype form, of the Escort RS Cosworth. I sent the car on the Talavera Rally in Spain as a way of adding spice to the launch of a new Escort. Never heard of the rally? Maybe not, but it was a vital step in getting production approval because, after all, how can a company cancel a new car when it's already been advertised . . .?

The second trophy on display is a Benedictine After Dinner Speaker of the Year award. Never heard of that either? It doesn't matter. And how can you judge between one public speaker and another? I don't know, and that doesn't really matter either because the award looked good enough on my cv as a speaker to turn a hobby into yet another career.

So, pausing only to re-arrange the pencils once again (I think they really look best sorted by colour) those are just some of the things that this book is about.

But apart from actually kick-starting the project, there is another problem in writing an autobiography: how to avoid people getting fed up with reading 'I'. I can't think of a way round this because, for better or worse (don't jump to conclusions just yet) the book is about me. Let me just stress that success in motorsport very much depends on a *team* effort. It is no coincidence that eight of the last ten business conferences at which I've spoken have used Formula 1 pit stops as a perfect illustration of teamwork.

Any success I had at BMC and Ford was because I had marvellous teams of mechanics, engineers and back-up staff to help me; I was just the fortunate individual fronting the teams at the time.

Happily, I don't think this book has turned out to be a history of one rally after another. That aspect of the period has already been well covered in some excellent publications. I've tried to look behind the scenes, to the business aspects of what was going on, because internal battles can often be as exciting as those on a race or rally itself. Certainly just as tense.

Mechanics, engineers, back-up staff . . . I'm sure there are some other people I've forgotten. Oh yes: drivers. Since navigating for umpteen different drivers a year on rallies in the '50s (my sense of self-preservation was less keenly developed then) I've been privileged to know and work with people like Paddy Hopkirk, Timo Makinen, Erik Carlsson, Donald Morley, Rauno Aaltonen, Hannu Mikkola, Pat Moss, Stirling Moss, Graham Hill, Jackie Stewart, Jody Scheckter, Roger Clark, Carlos Sainz, Jimmy and Colin McRae and many others, literally too numerous to mention. But if you're expecting lots of scurrilous stories and juicy gossip about them, you're going to be disappointed. I'm sorry but there aren't any. There are strong personalities in motorsport, of course there are, but I found it a delight to work with such people. So . . . no dirt. Anyway, this isn't a politician's autobiography.

I hope it says something about my relationship with drivers that I never had a legal contract with anyone. A friendly but never legally binding exchange of letters, often just a phone call, was enough.

Perhaps one memory encapsulates just how lucky I've been. While testing the Ford RS200 sports car, Jackie Stewart asked me to get in, and when I saw him grin at John Wheeler, the car's engineer, I knew what was going to happen: he took me for several laps of the MIRA handling course at what for him was probably only seven-tenths but for me seemed supersonic. If he was hoping to scare me, he failed, because I would cheerfully have spent all day being driven round.

The next day I sat in the same car with rally driver Stig Blomqvist as he hustled round the rally course at Ford's track at Boreham. So I was driven, at speed, by two World Champions within 24 hours.

'Twice Lucky'? The understatement of the age.

Chapter 2

Early years

I HAD THREE different mothers – my own, and two stepmothers – before I was out of my teens, plus a father who was not actually my real father, so today I would probably qualify for permanent 24-hour counselling from Social Services and at least two Safari holidays a year in Kenya. But it didn't seem all that complicated at the time.

I was born in Stoke-on-Trent on 14 January 1933. I've reached the point where I pause when I say that so that people can gasp 'You don't look your age', but it's a silly habit really because they never do. The family moved briefly to Huddersfield, after which we settled down at Stone in Staffordshire, just south of the Potteries, when my father went to work as an electrician at a nearby Royal Ordnance Factory. Stone would be my base until the RAF claimed me in 1951.

Although we were certainly not wealthy, ours was a loving household, and almost all my childhood memories are happy ones. I was an only child and got a lot of attention; as an example, our semi-detached house was called (are you ready for this?) 'Stuart House' – I promise the book won't all be this cloying. I was flattered to be told recently that there is now a plaque outside the house; less flattered when I found that it said 'Hydrant 20 feet'.

There was no motoring connection at this stage because we didn't have a car. In those days in the 1930s, I'm told, you didn't really aspire to one until you were in the managerial classes and father wasn't one of them. There were only about 1.5 million cars in the UK at the time compared with over 25 million today so the roads were pretty empty. My only fragmented memories of vehicles include seeing blue and white steam-powered Sentinel lorries (they were made in Shrewsbury) owned by Lyons Tea, pulling up by a local stream to refill their boilers, and the exotic lorries of the travelling circuses that visited regularly. No animal rights protesters turned up in those days, although the magic didn't work for everyone even then: I had a friend who was born in a circus but ran away when he was seven to live on a housing estate.

Progressive education methods had not yet become fashionable, so I learned to read and write fairly quickly. From my primary school, Christ Church in Stone, we were occasionally taken to the railway station to watch, with some reverence, the King going through on the Royal Train. It didn't have quite the right effect on me and left me rather jaundiced about the whole thing; I find all the bowing and scraping we still see today quite absurd – Bernie Ecclestone is only human like the rest of us isn't he?

Regular treats were for father to take me to Stoke to see 'The Potters' – Stoke City – playing football, where I had the joy of watching Stanley Matthews ('The Wizard of Dribble') playing in his prime out on the right wing; his sheer genius and total sportsmanship has left me with a very low threshold of tolerance for some of the alleged talent donning England shirts today. Then I was sometimes taken to the Old Trafford cricket ground, south of Manchester, to see great players like Len Hutton and Cyril Washbrook, and even, for light relief, to Hanley Speedway to have grit and cinders thrown in my face.

Next door in Stone, in the other half of our semi-detached house, lived the conductor of an important choir in Stoke-on-Trent, and I remember Sir Malcolm Sargent coming to noisily rehearse; not surprisingly the teachers wouldn't believe my excuse for poor homework. Later, during the war, there was even noisier (and for me, more exciting) disruption from the fleets of USAAF Flying Fortress bombers that filled the skies. The Luftwaffe seemed to have plans to redesign the landscape of the Potteries (not in itself an altogether unworthy cause) because I can remember being ushered into Anderson shelters or huddling under the stairs, waiting for the 'All Clear' to sound on the sirens. Blackout material was fitted to all windows, the glass had sticky tape put on as a safety measure, while cars had shields fitted over the headlights, which must have made driving interesting to say the least.

At one point we had evacuees descend on us from London. In a house our size that made it a real squeeze, but no one seemed to complain; it was all taken as normal for the time because, after all, there was a war on. The evacuees had the spare bedroom and soon became part of the family.

Rationing of clothes and food was in place of course and chicken was actually seen as a luxury. I remember a travelling shop calling and sugar being weighed into blue paper bags, and bars of soap being cut in two if money was tight; clearly there weren't Health & Safety inspectors lurking around every corner, although I don't remember the Black Death being a particularly significant problem. Not in our street anyway.

A bunch of us used to play cricket in a nearby cul-de-sac, using the 'pig bin' as a wicket – scrap food was collected in dustbins to feed pigs as part of the war effort. Although we were coached by Bert Shardlow, a league player who lived in the avenue, I never became a classic batsman because I was too distracted by a family of beautiful sisters who lived in a house overlooking the pig bin. One of them once sportingly offered to show us her knickers for two pence. The tragedy was that although we all rummaged among the conkers and sticky toffees in our pockets, we couldn't raise the two pennies, and old pennies at that. (I'm sorry if this is unduly distressing for you, but it does rather show that youngsters today don't know what real hardship is.)

My maternal grandfather ran a dancing school and for a time a cousin made valiant but unsuccessful efforts to teach me tap dancing. I was very careful to keep quiet about that later while I was in team management, I can tell you. And, like most lads at that time, I went . . . er . . . trainspotting. Go on, have your little chortle, I'll wait – but if you haven't stood on Crewe Station with a curling cheese sandwich for lunch, logging 'Royal Scot' 4-6-0 class locomotives as they steam off for quiveringly exotic places like Preston and Morecambe . . . well, I'm sorry, but the rich tapestry of your life will for ever have a bare patch.

Good grief, the memory of Crewe Station is making me quite emotional. You carry on reading, I'll catch you up in a minute.

I had an uncle, Cliff, who was a very close friend of the family (you'll see how close shortly) and who was a doctor in Wolverhampton. He had parents near Newcastle-under-Lyme and would regularly pick me up to spend weekends with them, going to Methodist Church, going for long walks and, most importantly, learning to play bridge, chess, and a mean and vicious game of Monopoly.

Above all – and this is something for which I will always bless Cliff and his parents – I learned to enjoy books; their house was stuffed full of them. They were great readers, and encouraged me to do the same; I caught a disease that has never been cured. Those were the days when Boots the Chemist had libraries where you could pay pennies to borrow books for a week or so. Regularly I would get through up to seven books a week, usually taking out a book on a Saturday morning, reading it (now, I suppose, you'd call it speed reading) and going back to change it before the shop closed at the end of the afternoon.

Uncle Cliff's job as a doctor sounded so glamorous that there were times when I later thought I should take up medicine myself. I must say I always liked the idea of nurses, crisp uniforms, black stockings and so on, but when I found that you had to train by cutting up things that sometimes bled, I rather lost interest . . . even today I hide behind the sofa whenever medical programmes crop up on TV. I do wish they wouldn't use those noisy drills and saws.

In 1943 I got a place at Alleynes Grammar School in Stone. Results of the Special Places Examination were listed in order of merit – no fudging to avoid hurt feelings in those days (equal second if you must know). My parents must have been impressed because they kept a school prospectus, which I still have; I notice we had to pay a fee of four guineas (nothing so plebeian as pounds) a term. Also: 'Homework is compulsory in the Main School, it is set on five nights a week'. So no debate there.

I realised that ours was quite a poor family when I and another boy were revealed as the only two kids in the class to pay less 'dinner money' than the others; a tactless teacher made it clear that because our parents were not earning enough, our meals were subsidised. If there was anything guaranteed to make me slightly left-of-centre, I guess that was it: it certainly put me well to the left of Tony Blair. But then, isn't everyone?

Alleynes had classes of between 25 and 30. Some things stick in my memory – reluctant admiration for a Physics teacher who hit me, unerringly, with a science text book thrown from 20 feet because I was talking in class (today I suppose I'd be taking him food parcels in prison for doing that), and a Miss Higham who reinforced my love of books and reading and encouraged me to write essays. That, I guess, was where the first germs of my being an author began – without her encouragement maybe I would never have gone on to edit a motor club magazine, which led to a job at *Motoring News*. And without *Motoring News* would there have been a move to BMC, then to Ford, and would I have any excuse for writing this book? See how much money Miss Higham has cost you ...

Sport didn't play a very big part in my life at this time. I didn't know anyone who played golf and, mercifully, I never took any interest in (yawn) tenniszzzzz ... Although I played for the house football team, our best result was to be beaten only 3-0 (if ever we got a corner, we did a lap of honour). Anyway I lost interest in ball games when I found that they could be dangerous. Having been hit on the left nostril when playing cricket, and the left testicle when playing football, both within a few weeks, I decided to switch to cross-country running, which at least wasn't a contact sport; I briefly captained the school in one cross-country competition but only because two other people who were better than me were ill on the day. I enjoyed making and flying model planes and, like every other kid at the time, I used to draw big American cars like gangsters drove in films, but this was the nearest I ever got to cars; motorsport didn't feature at all.

There were other compensations, though. Alleynes went co-educational while I was there. Just as well that, as a doctor, Uncle Cliff had earlier been given the task of telling me all about the birds and the bees. After an initial misunderstanding about how two such disparate creatures could actually mate, it all seemed fairly straightforward, although I remember it killed a lot of my interest in trainspotting.

But by far the raciest and most clandestine thing to do at the time was to listen to Radio Luxembourg on 208 Metres. Like everyone else from that generation, I know how to spell Keynsham, K.E.Y.N ... and so on, because that was where Horace Batchelor based his football pools tipping service; he advertised on Radio Luxembourg several times an evening, and always laboriously spelt out the name. You can date almost everyone in the country by whether or not they know that.

By then I had also discovered the glamour of show-business, because Uncle Cliff was involved ('courting' they used to call it ... it makes me feel very old to realise that a book like this almost needs a glossary) with Jill Summers, who was a successful stage comedienne. Later Jill would become a great *Coronation Street* TV character, the blue-rinsed Phyllis Pearce.

This meant that by the time I was in my very early teens, almost every Saturday Cliff would pick me up in cars like his Standard Flying Nine, Morris Ten, or an early upright side-valve Ford, and take me to theatres around the country to watch Jill perform.

She spent a lot of the time touring with her brother Tom (the act was billed as 'Tom F. Moss and Jill Summers') who had a sensational voice, not unlike that of Mario Lanza. She would come on as an usherette and interrupt him, they'd go into a comedy routine, then finish with a duet. Later her voice broke and went all gravelly, which is how people knew her on 'The Street'.

It was at this time that I also got to see and often meet legendary stars of variety like Max Miller, Frank Randle and Jimmy James. I sat mesmerised as they worked an audience. I didn't realise it at the time but I was watching John Osborne's *The Entertainer* being enacted in front of me because those were the dying days of variety. Knowing something of the financial struggles involved in putting on such shows has left me very jaundiced about the shrieks from the luvvies today if, say, opera doesn't get enough subsidy. Call me a philistine if you wish (there's no need to shout) but if, at the prices charged, a show can't put enough bums on seats to be viable, then maybe the bums on stage should lower their fees.

Weekdays at school were perhaps less exciting although still enjoyable. I've come across one report (from Summer 1948, when I was in the Fifth Form) in which my Maths master wrote that 'It is a pleasure to teach him . . .', which probably explains why I was so good at compiling inventive motorsport budgets in the future. But whoever wrote under Physical Education that 'He has shown enthusiasm and interest throughout the term' had me mixed up with someone else.

However, in spite of getting good School Certificate results (the equivalent of O levels today) and having started the first couple of terms in the Sixth Form, working towards Higher School Certificate exams (A levels), I left. In those days it was less automatic than it is today to flow through from school to university (only about 2 per cent of pupils did) and I was under no great pressure to do so.

My decision was probably influenced by complications in my family relationships. My mother, Edith, a lovely lady whom I still remember with affection, had died from a cerebral haemorrhage in 1944 when I was 11. This led to a succession of housekeepers looking after my father and me. Some were nice but there were some real dragons who couldn't cook except for fry-ups; they probably arrived sizing up my father and hoping to marry him. Although I wasn't unhappy (at least I don't remember it that way), it was a fraught period.

Before long, though, my father re-married, but that was a tragically short relationship because my new mother died following an operation when I was 15. The platitudes the parsons used by way of comfort after losing two mothers within four years left me agnostic, at best.

When I was 18, and still living at home, my father married for the third time, which meant that I inherited my second stepmother, Gertie, but this time she had a fully fledged family as well, for there were four stepsisters and one stepbrother.

Father and I moved in with my 'new' family, to the Crown & Anchor pub in the centre of Stone. Gertie was a tremendous matriarchal character and it all worked well, for they were a great family and made us very welcome. They had a small garage and taxi business next to the pub, with long-chassis Austin Eighteens, a Triumph Renown with a glass division, and a Vauxhall 14 hearse. There was no debate about whether to double de-clutch with that lot – you had to.

But things then got slightly more complicated, for it was gently revealed to me that the favourite Uncle Cliff that I had been close to for many years (and was still meeting regularly), was in fact my real biological father. Perhaps this was not the easiest information to give to a teenager who had already lost two mothers, but I don't think the news sent me into shock; maybe subconsciously I was expecting it. Cliff duly married Jill Summers and she became very close to me until she died.

When I left school I found a place in the County Treasurer's office in Stafford, which made me a trainee civil servant although certainly not a trainee millionaire because my starting salary in 1950 was £135 a year; £2.60 a week. I was the lowest form of civil service life at the time. My appointment letter stated that '. . .it may be necessary to vary your lunch hour as Junior Clerk in order to provide for the office being kept open from 1.0pm to 2.0pm, and you will be expected to remain after 5.0pm as the occasion arises, until the post has been despatched . . .'

My main task it seemed was to leave the office at 10.30am every day to buy the doughnuts for the typing pool and I also remember joining NALGO (the civil service trades union), the only time I was a member of a union.

It was Uncle Cliff's father, who was the Town Clerk at Stoke-on-Trent, who had the idea that I should be steered into the County Treasurer's office. The family's aim was that I should eventually become an accountant although there was even talk of my going into politics (that shows how little they thought of me). However, before I delved too far into double-entry bookkeeping, the nation had other plans. One day in 1951 my call-up papers arrived, summoning me into the Forces for two years of compulsory National Service; there were various ways of avoiding the sentence but I decided not to try.

It was a *real* upheaval. One week I was living in Stone, surrounded by a family. The next I was off to serve my country and was marched, to ribald comments from the locals, through the streets to go to Padgate in Lancashire (it's now a young offenders' prison, I believe ... make what you like of that) to do my square-bashing and be indoctrinated into the RAF as Aircraftsman G. S. Turner 2513562. No one ever forgets their service number; I certainly haven't because it is burned into a shoe brush that is still in perfect condition today, which says something about the quality standards of the purchase people then.

I was scared. This was the first time I had been away from home for long. I certainly hadn't slept in wooden huts before or had to tramp a hundred yards to get a wash, and I didn't quite know what to expect. I don't think any of us – my new 'muckers', to quote Forces slang – knew either.

Mind you, it wasn't a conventional start because soon after I started square-bashing I had to spend a couple of months in hospital with sinusitis, which meant that when I rejoined with a new intake of recruits I was two months ahead of everyone else on the square, which was handy because 'getting some service in' was seen as a bizarre badge of honour.

On joining up I ticked the appropriate boxes on various forms so that the RAF could decide what to do with me. Finally, I was told that I was going to the Far East and was kitted out with tropical kit. I said fond farewells to everyone I knew, milking the moment for all it was worth, because I thought I was off to Singapore.

Three days later I ended up in Bodmin, Cornwall. This was because one of the boxes I had ticked indicated that I was interested in languages so I was sent on a one-year Russian language course; it could have been Arabic instead but the RAF chose the language for me.

It was a Joint Services School for Linguists, with a Lt Colonel Thompson from the Army in overall charge, with RAF and Naval admin officers. Every morning we were marched on to the parade ground to be drilled by Regimental Sergeant Major Dawson from the Army, fierce voice and all. Three different colours of uniform, all on the parade ground at the same time – it was a bit like line-dancing with attitude. People later became concerned about the Berlin Wall, but our drill was more reminiscent of Max Wall and if they shook in Moscow it can only have been with laughter. Bodmin had an asylum as well as the Russian language school – sometimes I wasn't sure which we were in!

We were supposed to keep our kit clean but couldn't afford much blanco on 24 shillings a week (£1.20 today) so we watered it to make it go further. A fellow airman, Eric Lowe, reminds me that I was on parade next to him when the RSM, after the daily smack in the balls from his stick, asked him why his small pack was paler blue than those of the airmen around him. Eric replied that he had watered it the night before, at which the RSM bawled, 'It's a small pack, not a f . . . ing geranium'.

On another occasion a Lieutenant Commander told us on parade that there had been a reported case of theft. Someone had pinched another serviceman's bun and, in his opinion, stealing another man's bun was 'worse than buggery . . .' This left me with rather mixed views about the priorities of the Senior Service.

RSM Dawson was a traditionalist and I recall that he was once apoplectic when a Naval man, wan after a heavy night, asked him if he could tell us to stop our ridiculous heel-clicking as we collected our pay. The noise. And all those people.

Dawson retired while we were in Bodmin and we all affectionately pulled on ropes to tow his car off the camp in what I was told was a traditional Army ceremony. It could of course simply have been a pilot for a new get-you-home service.

We were on an intensive language course. We were put in small groups of four or five with one Russian tutor (often a political defector) teaching us to speak Russian, and then we'd get together in bigger groups for grammatical work from a British professor. That was about all we did all day.

A rather dour Estonian tried to use humour to get us to grips with the Russian language (something of a contradiction in terms really) and once laboriously explained that 'After a Russian woman makes love, she says "You have possessed my body, but never my soul". An American woman says "What was your name again?" And an English woman says "Do you feel better now love?"' All that in half-understood Russian. Gosh, how we laughed.

Because we'd been selected for a language course, we all thought we were desperately clever although we weren't really because the bright ones were doing a similar course in Cambridge where the project had been developed. Nevertheless we were given a certain

amount of leeway by the officers – after telling us in a pep-talk that
'you are all 18 now so ten years ago you were 8', the Commanding
Officer took it well when we gave him a standing ovation for such
mathematical wizardry. It was in this fairly relaxed environment that I
started writing, quite literally, on lavatory walls. What's that? Everyone
finds their own level? I quite agree; in my case it was a mickey-taking
news bulletin that was pinned up in the ablution block every week. I
also wrote articles for the camp magazine (*Teapot & Samovar* – part of
which was in Russian, in Cyrillic script, no less), and around this time I
had a poem published in *London Opinion*, a popular magazine of the
day:

> One thing makes me homesic
> At a picnic.
> And that's
> Gnats

It still seems unfair that I've never been on the list of candidates for
Poet Laureate.

While in Bodmin, I had my first exposure to motorsport when a
group of us spent some time pushing Prince Bira's ERA racing car up
and down a runway to get the damned thing started. Bira in Cornwall?
He and Prince Chula had been living at Rock, near Padstow, for some
years and I guess a local airfield was the nearest place he could
exercise one of his racing machines.

This was a truly bizarre year in my life. A year in Cornwall, learning
to speak a foreign language at His Majesty's expense, knowing that I
probably wouldn't use it in later life.

I suspect that it was a very 'camp' camp at times because it had a
rather earnest theatrical group specialising in obscure Russian works.
However, I do want to emphasise that although I was indeed learning
Russian, I did *not* go to Cambridge and I was *not* the fifth man in any
gay spy ring – I couldn't even make twelfth man in the camp's cricket
team.

The majority of us turned for entertainment to Bodmin town where
at the local dance a sign reading 'NO JIVING IN AMMUNITION
BOOTS' was perhaps not the aphrodisiac we were seeking when
convinced, as we were, that we were secretly being given bromide to
protect the local maidens.

One afternoon a week was devoted to sports but apart from some
cross-country running (I'd have done more but the Military Police
kept fetching me back) this mainly consisted of hitch-hiking to Jamaica
Inn for a pint. Thumbing a lift back one day, a few of us jumped into
the back of a lorry and were alarmed to find a dead donkey; and even
more alarmed when the lorry seemed to be heading perilously close to
our cookhouse.

Not long ago when I was in Bodmin I called in to the local museum and also contacted the Duke of Cornwall's Light Infantry to find out more about the camp – how many people had been involved and so on. I was reminded that the paucity of material was probably because we had all signed the Official Secrets Act! (I'm all for a quiet life, so just to be on the safe side would you mind tearing out this page and eating it when you've read it?)

After Bodmin we were posted to Wythall, south of Birmingham, now as Junior Technicians, to learn all about radios. If nothing else, the entertainment level was higher there than in Bodmin because we were able to hitch-hike to the Birmingham Hippodrome every week to see, among others, a teenage Shirley Bassey.

The final step in the Government's master plan for the protection of the nation was to send us to Germany where we were to monitor what Russian aircrew were saying over the air.

Because of my spell in hospital, which counted towards my two years National Service, I was only in Germany for a few months, but I was there to celebrate my 20th birthday on Hamburg's (in)famous Reeperbahn. More delicate readers may now like to gently turn the page because, as a present, some RAF friends persuaded one charming lady in a night club to lift her skirt; they placed matches in a particular area, which they then lit while singing 'Happy Birthday to You'. It looked more like an inverted Christmas tree than a birthday cake but I suppose the thought was there. Very character-building, National Service.

As you can see, it wasn't a conventional two years. Was it all worth it? I'm not sure. I got reasonable marks at the end of the Russian course (76 per cent) and I spent a lot of time in Germany with earphones strapped on, with nothing much happening. But nowadays almost all my Russian has gone. I can still recite a couplet by Pushkin in the original but, frankly, it's not easy to work it into general conversation, not in the Cotswolds anyway; I've also remembered enough to shout 'Save me' if they ever invade. The radio instruction course didn't stick because I can't even programme a video recorder today. But at least it left me with a love of Cornwall so it wasn't a total waste.

Today, people argue that National Service could be a cure for loutish behaviour and all society's ills. All I can say is that National Service didn't seem to do any harm. With growing youth unemployment and an ageing population with time on its hands, perhaps they *should* bring it back. For the over-65s.

During my service I still found time to keep in touch with Jill Summers, who by that time was the comedienne in shows with memorable titles like 'No Nudes is Good Nudes', 'Bareskins and Blushes', 'Evening Nudes', 'Passions and Peaches', and so on. I was actually going out with one of the 'peaches' for a time; her signed glamour photograph by my bed in the barracks enhanced my standing amongst fellow servicemen immensely.

Many of the shows were run by Paul Raymond who, at the time, also did a mind-reading act on stage. When I came towards the end of my RAF Service in May 1953 and was looking for a job, I was faced with a choice. Because of Jill's links with 'the business' I could either have had a job with Paul Raymond, and spent my life surrounded by stunning showgirls, or I could have chosen accountancy. I chose accountancy, which eventually led to motorsport.

We all make mistakes.

Chapter 3

Motorsport – catching the bug

IT WASN'T A case of 'put out more flags' when I was demobbed and returned to Stone. They didn't put out any and, frankly, didn't seem to have noticed that I had been away. I was now 20, fitter and stronger than ever thanks to the RAF, and more worldly wise but . . . what next?

In theory I was all set to be an accountant and started a correspondence course to this end. I still couldn't afford a car and I didn't fancy the dreary bus journey to and from my previous employers in Stafford, so I joined a subsidiary of Triplex (the glass-making company) called Quickfit & Quartz in Stone. Yes, there really *was* a company called that; I suspect some of the lewd misspellings we got on correspondence were deliberate. The company made laboratory glassware and I was hired as an Audit Clerk, this time at £5 a week, which was a considerable advance on anything that had gone before. But it still wasn't much because in those days a new Morris Minor cost £583.

Although I've called this book *Twice Lucky*, I reckon it should be at the very least *Thrice Lucky* because I found myself working in the same office as a girl called Margaret Tabernor. I now know that Margaret didn't think much of me at the time because she has just told a close friend, 'Although I changed my mind later, I didn't like Stuart very much when he first came to work alongside me. I thought he was arrogant, cocky, big-headed and rather rude to people.' How misleading first impressions can be . . .

Eventually we got married, she became part of my life and now, along with our two smashing daughters, she *is* my life. She only half jokes that if, heaven forbid, the British Grand Prix was held in our front garden, that would be the day she mowed the back lawn because although she won a rally navigator's award at one point, she has never been a raving motorsport enthusiast. I've always been very, very grateful for that because the sport is marvellous as a job for 8, even 18, hours a day. But not for 24.

Although I'd been to the Isle of Man to watch TT motorcycle races, seeing heroes like Geoff Duke racing, I never had any great ambition to own a bike. I tried one briefly but kept falling over on corners until someone pointed out that the sidecar had been pinched.

Apart from Bira's ERA, my only other early memory of a motorsport machine is seeing a Tojeiro racing sports car (LOY 500) parked on a trailer in Stone High Street one day. My introduction to rallying came quite by chance. One of my step-sisters, Jean, had a boyfriend called John Bedson who collected her one Sunday to do a North Staffs Motor Club Sunday afternoon rally. He asked if I'd like to sit in the back. At one point I took over the maps and found that I could cope with this newfangled thing called navigation.

Whether it was because of the accuracy you needed as a would-be accountant I don't know, but I loved every minute of it – and this was in a Rover 14. I got the motorsport bug and it's been downhill ever since. I later took (and passed) my driving test in that Rover (failing the first time when the gear lever came out in my hand as I reversed) and I owe John a lot for getting me started.

He later built a Rover Special and I did the Measham Rally with him in it and this kindled my interest in special-building. Incidentally, I'm convinced that Britain's current supremacy in Formula 1 can be traced back to those days when young enthusiasts like Colin Chapman were building specials, making and mending and using their ingenuity.

I joined the North Staffs Motor Club in 1953 when it had 200 or so members. Minutes of its inaugural meeting in 1950 record that 'already there are 300 clubs in the country' and '386 events in the sporting calendar of which 180 are speed events'. The subscription was set at two guineas and, daringly, 'it was decided to allow ladies as members'. It was a relatively prosperous club with a powerful committee of bankers, solicitors and factory owners, mainly potters. The club had a strong competition programme, including an annual race meeting at Silverstone and, perhaps equally important, a Ladies Committee that ran regular and lively social functions (television was not a competitor of course in those days). In many ways it was just about the perfect club to join. It was a sign of the end-of-the-Millennium times that the club faded out later, eventually winding up in 1991 because of a lack of interest.

Anyway, I got the rallying bug and started competing regularly. On the way to the start of one event, John and I actually broke down in the rain, in his open special, under a big road sign that said 'Welcome to Wales'; even that didn't put me off and I got progressively more involved, first of all with people like 'Mac' Mackintosh, Tommy Gold, Ron Gouldbourn and Clive Rogers.

Within a year I had become totally immersed in motor club life. I started to edit the club bulletin, and turned it into a monthly magazine, known as *The Potters Wheel*, later just *The Wheel*. I tried to keep my tongue in my cheek when writing it, and although we never got sued it must have been close once or twice. Margaret had relatives who were printers and with their help we managed to get the magazine out regularly on the first of every month – I believed (and still do) that good communication is vital to the success of any organisation like a motor club. I was careful to send the magazine to the local newspapers as well as the motoring magazines and I was flattered at one point to see it described in *Motoring News* as 'exotic'; for a moment I thought they'd said 'erotic'.

I started writing a series of articles to fill the space – 'How to go rallying', that sort of thing – and the result was that G. T. Foulis, which was *the* motorist's publisher in those days, invited me to write my first book *Rallying*, really as a spin-off from those articles. You may still come across a copy if, like me, you spend hours browsing in second-hand bookshops (well, early Barbara Cartlands have become so hard to find, haven't they?). I dedicated the book 'To my bank manager – for his continuing interest', which was appropriate because the £200 or so that came in for many years in royalties helped to keep him from my door.

I won the 'Roy Taylor Challenge Trophy' (Roy was one of the Club's founders) for six consecutive years, 1955 to 1960, as best club navigator, which proves, I suppose, how seriously I took club life as motor cars, and motorsport, became all-consuming interests. I also went to Aintree in July 1955 to see the wonderful Moss-Fangio battle in the two Mercedes-Benz W196 cars in the British GP. I remember standing in awe, looking through the wire mesh fence, watching Herr Neubauer managing this result. (I was at a function with Stirling only recently at which he said he never knew if Fangio let him win.)

As well as navigating, I began organising events. The first I tackled for the club was a treasure hunt for which the first clue was 'Pieces of Eight'. This was because a friend and I were jogging along a section of road in running kit with 88 on our backs (the things one does for one's Art). When they found us, competitors were given a slip reading 'Personally, I'd look at tonight's Evening Sentinel', then when they bought a newspaper from a supplier we had standing along the road and looked in the Personal column, their next clue read 'Encore Gracie, encore Sid, to the northwest you are bid'. Why? Because there was a village called Morefields, and Gracie Fields and Sid Field were household names then. Some people even found the checkpoint.

One particular year I ran eight evening rallies for the Club and we *averaged* 35 entries for them. I also started marshalling at race meetings. On the first occasion, at Oulton Park, I happened to have a brush in my car and solely on the strength of this awesome piece of equipment I was nominated a 'Sector Marshal'. It wasn't long after the terrible Mercedes-Benz crash at Le Mans in 1955 and by pure chance a 300SL, driven I believe by Jonathan Sieff, came off the road near me and hit the bank. Soil shot everywhere and that was when I realised I wasn't particularly brave because I thought the car had exploded and by the time it came to rest I was just south of Carlisle. And still accelerating. A pitiful case of premature evacuation.

I was just glad afterwards that I hadn't admitted to having a tin of Elastoplast in the glove-box otherwise I might have been made Chief Medical Officer.

My other lasting memory of Oulton Park in those days is watching Stirling Moss drive in five races at one meeting and win three of them. His cars gave trouble in the other two so he went into the pits. But he didn't then hide in a hospitality unit to phone his stockbroker, he had the cars fixed and went out again *to entertain the crowd*. In one race he held his nose and pulled an imaginary chain to indicate his opinion of a car, and the circuit rocked to a sound you perhaps don't hear enough in motorsport nowadays . . . laughter.

Perhaps I wasn't a lucky marshal because not long after the Mercedes incident at Oulton, I was marshalling at Silverstone when Jack French (a legend in the 750 racing movement with his 'Simplicity') tipped his car over in front of me at Becketts so I had to haul a concussed Jack to safety. I also recall waving a flag at Colin Chapman, who took absolutely no notice of me – something I came to expect of him in later years.

Incidentally, if you think that stretching the rules and inventive homologation were all new in the 1960s, let me remind you that those were the days when Chapman was causing controversy with his ingenious de-siamesing of the inlet ports of engines and other ways of getting round the 750 Club's rules.

Those were also the days when almost any car could be used on rallies such as those run by North Staffs. Tuning was minimal – in fact the height of engine preparation seemed to be to fit double valve springs. But at least it meant that invariably one was competing against identical cars. In fact, moving ahead only a year or two, I can remember starting serious National-status rallies in a TR3, and finding up to 50 otherwise identical TR2s or TR3s in the entry list! No exaggeration – that's the way it was in the late 1950s, and it ensured that the best *crew*, not the driver with the most powerful car, usually won.

And before you dismiss the drivers' exploits in those days, consider this: which is more difficult – to beat eight or nine (ten on a good day) other works cars on a World Championship rally today or beat 49 absolutely identical cars on rallies in the '50s? Let's be charitable to today's drivers and say it's a 50/50 call.

Many navigators, and drivers, took wakey-wakey pills – Benzedrine,

Drynamil or Dexedrine usually – to keep them going all night (the same generation are probably taking Viagra today for much the same reason). Race drivers of course didn't need such stimulants because, apart from anything else, if you risked one of the circuit snack-bars in those days, you simply had to be prepared to run 100 metres in under 10 seconds.

Pills were legal and doctors gave prescriptions quite readily. A tablet taken at 10pm kept you alert through to the greasy breakfast the next morning, although the pills did make rally crews talk a lot. But then what else is new? I thought the pills had made me hallucinate on one event because I was sure I'd seen kangaroos leaping along the road in front of our TR2. In Staffordshire. When I sheepishly recounted this at breakfast I was much relieved to find that there were actually wild wallabies in the area.

Around this time I made a big mistake. I read a book called *Building and Racing my 750* by Patrick Stephens. I thought then, and still think, that this is one of the best motoring books ever published although a mildly dangerous one because it encouraged almost everyone to think that they could do the same – build their own 750 special and go racing.

This, I thought, was the way for me to have my own car for the first time and to get into motorsport as a driver. I bought two Austin 7 Chummies, for a total of £5, and duly took them apart but never got much further – a familiar story in special building. Instead I moved on to a 1937 Model C Ford 10, which had been shortened and made into a semi-special with an Aquaplane head and twin Solex carbs. After competing with it for a spell, I took the body off then Alfie Price, a local blacksmith, welded on a frame of electrical conduit on to which I fixed aluminium panels. He was also an undertaker; not an inappropriate occupation considering the way the car handled.

Just across the road from the Crown & Anchor in Stone lived a man called Cliff Gaskin, and I became great friends with him. He had also built a special, but a much more sophisticated device with a tubular chassis and Morgan front suspension. It was powered by a Catalina Flying Boat engine (not the engine that drove the propellers, of course, but the 500cc flat-twin auxiliary unit that powered various systems) to which he mated an Austin 7 gearbox and transmission.

Cliff worked at Joules Brewery in Stone as a cooper and hand-beat the radiator cowl for my special from an aluminium fermenting vessel. The car's maiden voyage was nearly its last because the bonnet catches came adrift and the bonnet flew up and trapped my fingers, but I survived and later used the car on what were then called driving tests.

Then I moved on to Anglias, then to a Rochdale GT (all glamorous stuff you'll note, but that was the way many of us progressed in the 1950s). When I picked up the Rochdale body shell from the factory (for £140), the Olympic was there in prototype clay form. That looked incredible to me at the time and it later got such rave road-test reports that I was surprised it was never taken up by a major manufacturer. However, as Richard Parker, the designer of the car, told me recently, the fibreglass probably put them off.

This was the period when go-karting (we never forgot the 'go' in those days) was drifting across from America and the ever-ingenious John Bedson built a 98cc motorcycle-engined machine, the wheels of which were RAF-surplus aircraft tailwheels. A yellowing newspaper clip lists John and me as joint builders but in fact my only contribution was to suggest the name: The Dustkart. Perhaps we weren't taking karting entirely seriously because another North Staffs member, John Phillips, called his machine the 'Horsankart'.

By 1956 and 1957 I seemed to be rallying almost every weekend and this was the period in which I was driven (not drove) in a seemingly endless variety of cars – MGAs, Standard Vanguards, 8s, 10s and Pennants, Austin A40s, Anglias, A30s, A35s, Hillman Minxes, Morris 8 Tourers, Austin-Healey Sprites, Fiats, Morris Minors, Riley 1.5s, specials and every possible permutation of TR. Eventually I settled down mainly to navigate for Ron Gouldbourn in his TR2s and TR3s, finding out the hard way that you couldn't get out of the early TR2s if parked near a kerb because of the ultra-low doors.

The best events – the London, the Rally of the Dams, the Knowldale CC's Mini Miglia, the Jeans Gold Cup, the Yorkshire and the Plymouth – attracted entries on their own merits but as many of them were in the BTRDA Gold Star Championship, Ron and I made a serious attack on that.

Like many of the most successful drivers at that time, Ron was no spring chicken and he certainly didn't have any sponsorship. He was already 42 when we won our first BTRDA Gold Star in 1957 and all the money had to come from his own resources as a used car dealer. Most younger enthusiasts simply couldn't raise the money to prove how good they actually were. A familiar story? Sure. But nobody said motorsport is fair.

Except that he was so successful, no one in rallying seemed to know much about Ron at the time. He was a big, burly, well-set-up bloke, but not the most popular person in the North Staffs Motor Club because he had a rather dour sense of humour, but he was respected because he got results.

Ron's business was in a big tin-shedded showroom at Hartshill between Stoke and Newcastle, with about 20 cars on site at any given time. I don't know whether this is an apocryphal story, but I believe someone once bought a car from him, discovered a faulty light bulb on the way out of the door, told Ron, and was politely directed to a garage just along the road!

He was not easy to get to know, but was *very* competent in a rally car, very precise in driving tests and very canny too – he thought a lot about his sport. Look at photographs of TRs on driving tests in those days and you'll often see just one with a blanket or coat stuffed into the radiator grille to keep the engine warm. Ron's TR. Did it make any difference? I don't know, but it often psyched the opposition, which can be the cheapest form of tuning there is.

There was a particular Morecambe Rally that ended at the Midland Hotel in the town, with a series of driving tests on the promenade on the Sunday morning, including a long and glorious 'Monte Morecambe'. Of all the front runners, Ron was possibly the only one who noticed that there was no time at which one *had* to report to do the tests.

Others, at least one of whom had beaten us on the road, rushed out after breakfast to tackle the tests in the pouring rain. Not Ron. I couldn't find him for ages, not until the test was completely dry. He then appeared, was much faster than anyone else and we won the rally. The event begins when the regulations arrive. . .

Ron and I rallied together for four years and maybe the hours we spent in his small office discussing tactics helped contribute to any success we had, but I always got on better, for instance, with his club-mate Tom Gold, who was a load of fun and very quick in Sprites and TRs.

It's a measure of the strength of the North Staffs club that in 1958 Ron and I were BTRDA Gold Star Champions (that was our second series win) while Tom, also driving a TR3, was the Silver Star winner.

There was fierce rivalry between North Staffs and the Knowldale Car Club in particular, which had members like Derek Astle, Ken Walker, Mike Sutcliffe and Don Grimshaw. I even had car stickers done saying 'Help stamp out Knowldale' to try to wind them up. But it was all hugely amicable and the clubs co-operated on a joint trophy, the KANS (Knowldale and North Staffs), to be given to the best team from the two clubs.

Through navigating for Ron I went on to win the *Autosport* Rally Navigators Trophy for the Gold Star Championship for three consecutive years – 1957, 1958 and 1959. Mike Wood had his name on the trophy for two earlier years. At the end of the 1959 season I suggested to *Autosport*'s legendary editor, Gregor Grant, that there was a tradition – in England at least – that if you won something three times on the trot you got to keep it. I don't think Gregor had heard of the custom but to his credit he agreed and it's still in pride of place at home.

As I was guest speaker at the 1999 British Rally Championship awards dinner, I thought I'd better find out who were the first winners of that series. To my surprise, Colin Wilson at the MSA told me that the first year the RAC Championship was run (1958) the winners were Gouldbourn/Turner and in 1959 Sprinzel/Turner. I'd genuinely forgotten, which shows how little impact the championship made compared with today. Bill Bengry then won it in 1960; I'd seen something of his determination when I navigated for him once in his VW Beetle.

There was nothing complicated about rallying at that time, at least not in the *real* events held in Wales, the Midlands and the North. Sometimes the navigator got the route, defined by map references, an hour in advance, but often only as we left the start line ('plot and bash' is what we christened it). The navigator's job was literally to find the way, the driver's job being to get there as quickly as possible. I reckon that when a driver is going well and a navigator is on song on the maps, rallying is the finest sport there is. Mercifully, I was never car sick so in later years, at BMC, I really admired Pat Moss's partner, Ann Wisdom, who was sick yet always kept going: a real heroine.

There was no nonsense with regularity or hunting for controls in the sort of rallies we did, which at least made them good training before tackling International events. I never had ambitions of being a rally driver although I took enough interest in driving to become a member of the Institute of Advanced Motorists (the 'Great I AM') in 1956; I dropped out the moment they started to take themselves too seriously with, would you believe, twee covers to put over the car badge when a non-member was driving.

Rallying was not reported well in those days – *Autosport* concentrated on motor racing, while *Motoring News* was still a trade paper – so Ron and I didn't get much publicity when we won the Gold Star for the first time, but things bucked up when we won one of the most significant rallies of 1958, the Bolton, because the first prize was a brand-new Speedwell-modified Austin A35. Navigators held sway in those days and I was often able to negotiate the terms with drivers under which I would crew with them. On that occasion I was able to prise 47.25 per cent of the A35's value out of Ron. Since he was a second-hand motor trader the negotiations were long and arduous. I was quite proud of that.

There was criticism of the Bolton Le Moors CC for offering such a huge prize, and I remember writing to *Autosport* defending their right to do so. It certainly got excellent publicity at the time both for the organisers and for us. I've got pictures of two occasions – both the Mayor of Llandudno *and* GP driver Tony Brooks shaking hands with Ron in front of the prize car. There was every reason for the fuss, of course, because in late-1990s currency that must have been the equivalent of £10,000 and I still don't have a clue as to how the Bolton Le Moors Car Club managed to finance it.

In the meantime, as the North Staffs magazine editor, I had been cultivating the local press – even today I would recommend anyone to do that. If you become known locally, in however small a way, and you need time off for motorsport, you're more likely to get it if your boss has read a bit about you.

I was so keen to learn more about rallying that I actually wrote to

Monte-winner Maurice Gatsonides for advice about map boards and timing equipment. He was renowned for his precision with the latter, although if I'd known that his interest would eventually lead to the Gatso speed camera I'd never have written. I was mulling over this only the other day when one flashed me a cheery greeting.

The first International rally I did was the RAC of 1956, with 'Mac' Mackintosh, in a VW Beetle; he was a VW dealer at Newcastle, near the Potteries, a staunch North Staffs member and a great friend. We finished second in our class, behind another Beetle, and somewhere there is a picture of the car on the Otterburn ranges where I can't be seen because I was out of sight, clutching the seat with my head buried well down in it – this not only got the centre of gravity down but most appropriately meant that I was in a praying position.

At the same time as rallying with North Staffs drivers, I was also competing regularly with Geoff Keys, a talented engine-tuner in Stone, noted for always presenting immaculate cars. He was not active in the North Staffs but concentrated on events run by the clubs in Stafford and Congleton, which meant that I could often cram two events into a weekend. Geoff and I mainly used an A40 Sports but won a '56 Winter Rally in a Fiat 600 with the only clean sheet. Through links with Fiat, Geoff borrowed cars for us to do a couple of Mobilgas Economy Runs. Run by the Hants & Berks Motor Club, this event was taken seriously by the press and was heavily advertised; to protect its integrity it had rigorous scrutineering and you had to carry observers to see you didn't freewheel to improve economy. They were allocated by ballot. The year we entered in a Fiat 600, we drew the heaviest man for the section in the Lakes; we weren't very quick up the Wrynose and Hardknott Passes but, ye gods, we were quick down them from what I can remember of the odd moments I had my eyes open.

Putting all the events together meant that I was doing between 50 and 60 rallies a year in 1959, sometimes two in a weekend when events like the *Birmingham Post* and the London were on a Friday night and I could squeeze a local club event into the same weekend.

I had a few enjoyable and successful outings with John Sprinzel including one in a works-owned Alfa Romeo, but the truly Golden Age of night rallying, when we could still drive fast on public roads without annoying people, was coming off the boil. In the 1950s, for instance, when events like the *Express & Star* were held in deepest Wales, Tom Gold and I won the rally in his Sprite, lost 4 minutes on the schedule yet were flat out *all* the way.

I wasn't always rallying with men either because through my BMC connections (described in the next chapter) I'd got to know Pat Moss. The approach came from Pat and Marcus Chambers at BMC (this, I guess, was the first time he and I got together). For me, of course, this was a great thrill as Stirling Moss was one of my all-time heroes (still is for that matter), Pat is his sister and I soon got to meet him.

You can argue for ever about who were the top women drivers of all time but in the 1950s and 1960s Pat was totally supreme. She wasn't just the quickest girl, she was one of the fastest drivers and I know that every other 'works' driver – BMC or not – respected her as that. One mark of top drivers is whether other drivers instinctively look at their stage times. They always looked at Pat's.

I enjoyed sitting alongside her, and can't remember a single moment when I was frightened. I was *always* impressed. It's a pity she was called Moss because some people suggested that she got her place through favouritism. Nonsense. If she'd been Mabel Satterthwaite instead (sorry Mabel, but you see what I mean) she'd still have been quick. As her navigator (and, later, team manager) I found that the way to motivate her was to say casually, 'No one is likely to do this section on time'. And then sit back in awe as she did.

There was only one totally feminine trait that she never conquered and she admitted it cheerfully: at some time in an event she usually managed to leave her handbag behind and a mechanic had to be sent off to meet her further ahead to get it back to her.

I did several British rallies with her in a Morris Minor (NMO 933, known by everyone in the business as 'Grannie'). No sooner had the front-wheel 850 Mini been announced in 1959 than Pat and I shared victory in the Mini Miglia rally, which put a lot of TR drivers' noses out of joint! Although we won by about 10 minutes, my lasting memory is of Pat complaining all night how slow the car was and of me sitting in the car with my feet in about 3 inches of water; *all* Minis leaked in those days.

Then, in 1960, we tackled the Hopper National in one of Marcus's A40s, an event that dug its way all around the muddy tracks of Kent and finished, crazily, with a few daylight sprints around Burnham Beeches; Pat, more skilful than most, and certainly a lot braver, was amazing and we won that one too.

Margaret had been very patient with me because, except at work, we couldn't have been seeing all that much of each other. Eventually, though, we looked at our diaries, found one weekend date that I had free – the only date, as I remember – and we eventually made it! We were married in March 1960 and it was the best day's work I ever did.

But I still wasn't ready to be totally domesticated. I wanted to move on to International rallies.

Chapter 4

Co-driver's seat –
home and abroad

UNLESS SOMEONE ELSE was paying I could not afford to compete in overseas events, but fortunately Ron Gouldbourn was a persistent character and coaxed support from the local Standard-Triumph dealer, then caught the attention of Ken Richardson, who was running the Standard-Triumph works team. Ken's policy seemed to be to use a wide variety of drivers on a one-off basis so we were not overly optimistic about our long-term prospects, but I remember being thrilled when he asked us to do the 1958 RAC Rally in a works Standard Pennant, our team mates being Tom Gold and Paddy Hopkirk. Starting from Blackpool and finishing in Hastings, we almost won that – Peter Harper beat us in his Sunbeam Rapier and we finished second overall, having led at half-distance.

This was advertised as the 'Rally of the Tests', but it developed into a real endurance event, particularly in Wales and the Lake District where many of the hills were blocked with snow; not many crews visited every control. The marking system was screwy because even though we were not one of the 15 crews who scrambled over the Hardknott and Wrynose Passes (which meant that we missed a control up there), we still finished ahead of all but one who did.

There were 196 starters, but many retired. Ron did a great job in keeping our modified car on the road, all three Pennants made it to the end, Standard won the Team Prize, and we also won the Blackpool starters' award.

Ken Richardson seemed to like us after that because we immediately went off on the Tulip Rally, using a works TR3A; this was the first time a factory paid me to go rallying. Not enough to order a yacht – it was £52.50, ie £7.50 a day for seven days living expenses – but when I got the call from Richardson I was so excited that I thought he meant I had to pay and asked who I should make the cheque out to.

We ended up clean on the road, won the class, and finished tenth overall.

If nothing else, that event proved how important teamwork was because although Keith Ballisat and Johnny Wallwork, in the other TRs, were quicker than Ron on some tests, they both lost time on the road. If Keith had not stayed ahead of Ron on the final test at Zandvoort, we would have finished even higher up, but there were no team orders . . .

It was on Tulip Rallies that I first realised how beneficial it can be for an organiser to take trophies seriously. The Dutch have it made with clogs, tulips and windmills to feature as awards, but it must be possible for any motor club to do better than some of the tasteless tack one often sees. But I digress. The Tulip Rally was also where I first met Rob Slotemaker, a Dutchman with theories about cadence braking on slippery conditions. We watched his demonstrations with foolish derision and in effect said 'Don't call us, we'll call you', not realising that he was way ahead of his time in seeing the value of anti-lock braking systems.

Either Ken Richardson wasn't impressed by our class win or he didn't believe in giving people regular works places because after those two drives – successful drives – Ron wasn't offered another full works outing! No, I don't understand it either.

The first Monte Carlo Rally I tackled was in 1959 with a Standard Ten. It wasn't a true works car (though we were in the team entry so Ken Richardson hadn't shut us out totally), but because we'd had more success locally, Ron Gouldbourn again turned to the local Standard-Triumph dealer, Tom Byatt, to help to get us into a suitable 'ex-works' car.

Everything went fine until we got to Monte Carlo, then on the Mountain Circuit a broken throttle connection lost us 20 minutes. But what I really remember is that we were in the Tip Top night club along with most other crews within minutes of the event ending. Those were days when rally drivers knew how to enjoy themselves. One evening in Monaco a delightful lady, possibly working to put grandchildren through college, was about to give what was called an 'exhibition', at which point a driver – nobly trying to inject an element of culture – moved to a piano to provide her with musical accompaniment. The hotel manager rushed out, shouting, 'Monsieur, stop, stop. No music after 11 o'clock!' Well, that's what I'm told anyway.

After that Monte I got a lift back to England with Eric Mather and Ian Hall in Ted Lambert's Morris Minor, which had been entered for the prestigious *Concours d'Elegance*. This was taken quite seriously in those days and the Minor had leopard-skin seat covers and almost everything else, plus a lavatory (I promise you – read the magazines of the day if you don't believe me) in the back. I hold the record for travelling the furthest across France (from Monte Carlo to Boulogne) sitting on a lavatory seat. It left a lasting impression on me and I thought it was unkind of the man to laugh when I phoned to discuss a tentative entry in the *Guinness Book of Records*.

I also got together with John Sprinzel for overseas events at about this time; he was getting support from BMC, usually by being loaned cars but sometimes by being a co-opted team member. We began by doing the Sestrière Rally in February 1959 in an A35, then took a Sprite on the Lyon-Charbonnières, followed by an MGA Twin-Cam on the Tulip. Such events included things like doing five brisk laps of the old Nurburgring at night, happily with co-drivers on board. Memorable.

Suddenly I was getting more visibility because John got a lot of coverage in the motoring press, not only because he co-owned Speedwell Performance Conversions and Graham Hill was one of his co-directors, but also because he lived in London and hob-nobbed with the magazine editors at the Steering Wheel Club and other watering holes. All very cosmopolitan and sophisticated for an innocent lad from the Potteries.

John was a great wheeler-dealer, or fixer, very alert to all the angles and a great character – marvellous company. Nowadays we would call him hyper-active but he was a sometimes emotional man who could get very excitable. One of the jobs, maybe one of the key jobs, of a navigator/co-driver is to watch over the driver like a mother hen and if there is any tendency for them to start puffing and snorting, or for their eyes to come out on stalks, to calm them down. I did that, quite a lot, with John.

He and I tackled the '59 Liège-Rome-Liège in John's own Sprite (PMO 200), which was really a forerunner of the Sebring Sprites that followed. That Liège was something like 92 hours long with no breaks and I can't remember ever being so tired; Lord knows what it must have been like for John because I was not a confident driver and he did the lion's share. Coming back through Germany towards the finish, we were definitely hallucinating. Of the 97 cars that started, only 14 finished, and somehow we dragged ourselves back to a class win and 12th place. There's a tendency to think that close finishes are unique to today's rallies. Not so – we'd have moved up two places if we'd been 10 seconds quicker, and that after 92 hours flat out. There are pictures showing us at the finish actually smiling, but I can't think why, or how we had the energy to do that. It was absurd yet so tough that people still remember it with nostalgic awe and affection.

Maurice Garot, the chief organiser, once said that his ambition was to run a Liège where no one finished! One of his methods was to set times between controls then list a span of times at which each control would actually be open. The two did not tie up: by sticking to the sector timings, you would eventually arrive at a control that would already have closed and you would be eliminated.

One year Maurice announced sorrowfully that the police had demanded that he must position secret speed checks along the route. He then silently held up a card with the locations of the secret checks written on it ...

A month later John Sprinzel and I did the German Rally in a works TR3A, and won the Manufacturers' Team Prize with two other TRs, but that was to be another one-off drive; John later criticised Ken Richardson's cars severely in his splendid book *Sleepless Knights*, and perhaps as a result wasn't asked to drive for Triumph again under Ken.

I suspect that John and I were getting a bit carried away at this time. First of all we talked about founding an Association of British Drivers but then drew up regulations for an exclusive body of up to 50 drivers, to be called Squadra Cinquanta, with membership by invitation only. There was to be a badge, which John's silk-screen printing company would manufacture, and all of them would be numbered.

All a bit pretentious and it deserved its come-uppance. It got it when members of the Stockport Motor Club, John Hopwood and Roy Fidler (who was a fishmonger), waved two fingers at the whole idea and set up Ecurie Cod Fillet instead, which was much more democratic (using the word in its loosest sense). They had the charity, at least, to invite me as a member, which I'm still proud to be, as Cod Fillet continues to prick the pomposity of motorsport today. Vital work. Looking back, I guess John and Roy needed a keen sense of humour because for a time they rallied a Buckler, which leapt about so much I remember it was always very difficult to pass them.

In 1959 the German Wolfgang Levy, who was a friend of Pat Moss and Erik Carlsson, invited me to do the RAC Rally with him in a works Auto Union 1000 SP Coupé, a shatteringly noisy little car that had a 98lcc three-cylinder engine and front-wheel drive.

Wolfgang spoke almost no English and I had no German. My Russian wasn't going to help, and anyway I'd forgotten most of it by then, but we agreed via interpreters that I would shout 'attack' if we needed to be flat out. We 'attacked' a lot that week, I remember.

I'd never even sat in a car with him before the rally started and I certainly didn't know anything about Auto Union DKWs, so I really don't know how to rate Wolfgang – I don't think he was quite as fast as Erik Carlsson but then who was? – but he certainly pressed on well, and we never went off the road even in the snow and slush.

It was the first of Jack Kemsley's routes with lots of mileage, lots of night navigation, and some special tests, which was fine by British co-drivers like me. Wolfgang was in the lead before we found the road blocked by snow drifts over the mountain near Tomintoul; we were 50 minutes late in reaching the Braemar control and were placed eighth.

As Peter Garnier wrote in his *Autocar* column: 'Levy had put up fastest time of his class in pretty well all the tests, and had incurred no further penalty points on the road sections. Therefore, without the Braemar penalties, he would have won the Rally hands down . . .'

After the event Auto Union protested about the blocked section but then returned to Germany leaving me to handle the appeal in Pall Mall before the Stewards of the RAC, an august body comprising Lord Shawcross QC, Col William Short and Lord Brabazon of Tara.

I produced maps and loads of evidence and to my shame had to argue against Jack Kemsley, who was and remained a good friend. Don't forget that the war hadn't been over all that long and to be arguing for the Germans against British interests was not a comfortable experience. The Stewards eventually found against us but said, 'We do this in the cognisance that there is a higher court of appeal.' In other words, 'Take it up with Paris if you feel strongly about it.' Auto Union declined to do so and let the appeal drop.

Early in 1960 Triumph asked me to do the Monte with Keith Ballisat in a Herald. In a fit of stupidity I fell asleep in France while driving, crashed the car and put us both in hospital. It left me with a mission to tell people *never* to use rigid material to rest a map on because my board broke Keith's pelvis when it jammed against the dash. I remember that the wine in the French hospital, fed intravenously, was of a very good year. As we left by ambulance we were told that my two broken ribs would heal quickly but that Keith's pelvis would need six weeks; English doctors disagreed because he was back at work the next week. Mind you, I suppose it could have been because they were short of beds . . .

Although I was doing 50 or 60 rallies a year at home and abroad, whenever Margaret and I had a spare weekend we would drive off to Wales, Derbyshire or somewhere to go 'white-roading' – looking to update my knowledge of the roads and the navigating challenges that might be thrown at me in future.

If the weather was fine on those weekends, it was really very pleasant sitting up some isolated track in Wales eating our sandwiches, but only if we weren't stuck with the car up to its axles. Amazing how often we met other so-called 'amateur' co-drivers doing the same thing.

At that time I had the patience to worry about details – should I use a soft pencil (and how soft?), should I use folded or flat maps? How should I mark up the tricky bits on the maps? I kept my maps until they were very tatty, because it used to take hours to transfer all the markings to a new sheet.

Those, incidentally, were the days when there was no gulf between world and club rallies – drivers would get back from a continental rally and cheerfully do a minor event the next weekend.

All this hyper-activity meant that I couldn't really find time to do justice to a correspondence course in accountancy, so it wasn't long before I had to make a choice between that and motorsport. It wasn't a difficult choice, although my decision was eased when I took 'Economic Aspects of Industry and Commerce' in one accountancy exam and failed. Six months later, without having opened a book, I took the exam again, flannelled . . . and passed. The experience reinforced my belief that there are really only two valid economic theories: 1) for every economist there is an equal and opposite economist and 2) they are both wrong.

So it was no contest – I chose motorsport.

But I had a problem. I still didn't see how I could make a living out of rallying because very few drivers got any fees or contracts from teams and no co-drivers got more than just expenses. For that matter, in those days most British works *drivers* were either motor traders like 'Cuth' Harrison, who were well off, or true gentlemen – a gentleman farmer in fact – like Jack Sears. Another driver, John Gott, was actually the Chief Constable of Northamptonshire.

Looking ahead a few years to the 1960s, it wasn't until my early BMC years that I started offering fees to co-drivers. When Timo Makinen won the Monte in 1965, with the drive of a lifetime, his co-driver Paul Easter was on expenses plus a miserable £50 an event. It took a stunning victory like that to make me realise how valuable such people were and to increase the fee.

For me, salvation came from an unexpected source. After writing on lavatory walls in the RAF then producing a motor club magazine, I'd started doing rally reports for *Motoring News* and *Autosport*. In one letter I sent with an article to *Motoring News*, I added a PS saying, 'If ever you need anyone for a permanent job, please give me a call.'

To my relief, an offer came by return.

Chapter 5

Motoring News – *and 'Verglas'*

THE LETTER THAT landed on my doormat in May 1960 was from Wesley Tee, the proprietor of a printing and publishing group that included the long-established monthly magazine, *Motor Sport*. A decisive man, without even meeting me he offered me a job on *Motoring News* at £756 a year; there was also to be a 'worthy and suitable' company car (those were his words in my appointment letter). I didn't actually meet Mr Tee until the day I walked into 15-17 City Road in London to start work.

This was a real breakthrough for me. I had no master plan for a career but it seemed a logical step, not only to progress in motorsport but to get away from accountancy, which I was finding boring. I would be earning more than I had ever done before, I would be provided with a car for the first time (it was an 850 Mini, this time one that didn't leak), and I would be able to carry on rallying and to write about it.

In personal terms it was going to be a major upheaval. Margaret and I (newly married) would have to move from Stone, which we knew well, to somewhere in London, which we didn't know at all and which mildly scared us; for us yokels it was going to be quite a thrill of an evening to stroll and watch the traffic-lights changing. I would have to get used to commuting (which I hadn't done for years and even then only a short distance by bus), and I would have to learn about newspaper and magazine production as well as writing the words. We took the plunge and I'll always be grateful to Margaret that we did.

We went down to London one weekend, looked in newsagents' windows for flats to rent and found one in Catford, where we had to share facilities with the flat downstairs. Fortunately that didn't last long because the 'rallying mafia' swung into action and Stephen Clipston, a motor club member and an estate agent friend of David

Seigle-Morris (someone else I'd navigated for) found us a flat in Bromley, close to Bromley South station. Margaret and I commuted into London and as I went to City Road, she went to work at Aquascutum, just a step from Piccadilly Circus.

It was almost the perfect time for anyone to start their career at *Motoring News*, in fact perfect for anyone starting his career in motoring journalism. John Blunsden, who later went on to be a book publisher, was the Editor, Darryl Reach, who is now an Editorial Director at Haynes, who are publishing this book, was the Assistant Editor (and also the layout man), I was made Sports Editor, and that was it on the writing side. Paul Smith sold the advertising space with a secretary called Brenda Clyde – and that was the total staff, five people running *Motoring News*, which then had a circulation of around 18,000 a week. Mike Twite was also involved, but only occasionally, on loan from *Motor Sport*.

Motoring News was still a very young paper in those days. It had been founded in the 1950s as a motor trade publication and it was only in the last two years that it had begun to cover motorsport of any sort. Except for reports from contributors like Graham Robson, Val Domleo and me, it had really had very little rallying content and none at all on the ground.

There were no union rules at News Publications – Wesley Tee simply wouldn't have allowed it, and would probably have closed the place down first – so we would go off to events during the weekend (race, rally or whatever), come back home, write the copy, send it down to the printers, check the galley proofs when they came back, paste them up on the page, OK the final proof, then watch the paper being printed. Pasting things on paper must sound crazy to modern journalists but it was the norm at the time. And *Motoring News* was always at the forefront of technology anyway; for instance, we moved from quill pens to ball points weeks before our rivals at *Autosport*. The first time in my life I pressed the button on a camera was at Prescott hill-climb where *MN* had sent me to cover a meeting. I played safe and went to a corner where cars were virtually stationary and fired away. That print appeared in the paper the following week. In effect we did virtually everything except go out on the streets to sell it. Bliss!

Slave labour? Maybe, but whenever I meet up with an ex-*Motoring News* staffer at a function today, we invariably go into happy reminiscent mode.

Hard work? No, it didn't seem like work at all and I loved every minute of it. If I had an ambition at all, it was to earn enough so that Margaret wouldn't have to go out to work. How attitudes to women staying at home and men being the bread-winners have changed since then, especially with the growth of feminism; I was only saying this to Margaret the other day as she was cleaning my shoes.

I think it's important that an author is honest with his readers so I'd better mention that I used to write 'Readers' Letters' if there weren't enough genuine ones. I would produce controversial correspondence (I was I. J. Smith for a time) attacking cherished institutions – anything criticising the Institute of Advanced Motorists or caravanners netted shoals of letters, but it was cruel really because they were such easy targets.

There was also the glamour of operating next door to that famous monthly, *Motor Sport*, the bible at the time. Bill Boddy was the lofty editor whom we revered, although we rarely saw Denis Jenkinson, the Continental Correspondent, because he spent most of his time wandering around Europe posting his copy back to London from wherever he was on that particular day.

(Jenks, incidentally, had a cavalier attitude to punctuation. He once said, I believe, that he never worried about that – he was only writing the facts and that 'there is someone back at the office with a pepper pot full of commas and full stops which they can shake all over my copy. . .')

Boddy and Jenks regarded *Motoring News*, I think, as something of an upstart publication; they were benevolent to us, but not much more.

On Monday and Tuesday Darryl Reach and I would travel up to the *Herts Advertiser* printing works in St Albans to actually produce the paper. *Motoring News* went on the presses between the *Church of England Newspaper* and a pop music paper called *Disc*, so you can't say we didn't keep good company. If when we were assembling the paper we found that a promised race or rally report hadn't arrived, we could – and often did – make a panic call back to John Blunsden in the office to say, 'Help, we've got this problem, we need 1,000 words to fill.' By the next messenger (no faxes or e-mail then, of course) an elegantly written 'think piece' would arrive on something like 'Whither sports car racing?' or whatever; John could turn out beautifully crafted pieces at a moment's notice.

I've always been fascinated by great characters like Old Man Tee. He's no longer with us but all ex-staffers remember him, mostly with affection; I always got on well with him. He could be difficult to work for and because he was The Boss he always wanted his own way, but he could pick his people and I have to say that although he was an eccentric in many ways, he was a great proprietor. I guess he was rather like Lord Beaverbrook, owner of the *Express*. It is said that when his lordship wanted to fire an editor, he would send him on a world cruise to soften the blow. One such editor is alleged to have got back to Southampton to find Beaverbrook on the quay shouting 'Go round again' because he hadn't found a replacement. Old Man Tee might have done something similar although I suspect it would not have been a cruise but a tube ticket to allow the departing editor to travel round the Circle Line.

He was a forceful and frightening driver and years later when I was at Ford I noticed that strange things used to happen along the A12 most evenings. Birds would huddle in the trees . . . dogs would whimper in corners . . . mothers would hurry their children indoors . . . drivers would nervously watch their mirrors . . . and then the Old Man would hurtle past like Toad of Toad Hall on his way home in TEE 10 (he went too fast for me to recognise the make of car).

He rarely bothered to influence the contents of the publications – I don't remember him ever coming into the editorial offices. (Someone who did was a young lad from New Zealand called Eoin Young and we helped him a bit. I wonder if he ever made it in motoring journalism?)

Mr Tee encouraged me to expand our rallying coverage because although he knew nothing about rallies he could see that it was good for circulation, which had started to rise. The only battle I ever lost with the Old Man was over a promotional idea. I suggested that if, say, we were covering a Chester Motor Club rally we should mention as many names as possible, put a picture of the event in the report, then direct mail a copy of *Motoring News* to every club member; for every 100 members I was convinced that we would get 25 new subscribers. He wouldn't agree and I wasn't sorry when it dawned on me who would probably be writing the address labels.

I started a gossip column called Rally Round-up under the by-line 'Verglas' (using the road sign for icy roads), which was originally just an excuse for putting in all the bits and pieces that arrived in my postbag. I used to do write-ups on rally equipment such as map reading lamps and, before Political Correctness became the rule, I wrote at some length about the charms of the lady rally driver Ewy Rosqvist.

We started to get readers sending in news and oddball comments. One wrote that he had recently been on a rally in Lincolnshire and had come across a signpost pointing 'To Old Bolingbroke and Mavis Enderby'. Underneath someone had tenderly written 'the gift of a son'. (Look it up on a map, near Horncastle, if you don't believe me.) The column discussed rally safety quite a lot and I lobbied that there should be 'no timing at all before 11pm or after 6am – if organisers can't sort a rally out in 7 hours they should stop running rallies'. Complaints against rallies were growing although a reader wrote in 1960 that 'for the last 10 years people have been predicting rallying is about to be stopped'. Plus ça change.

At times the 'Verglas' column became surreal, for instance with an attempt to prove that Offa's Dyke in the Welsh Marches was actually named after an ancient auctioneer who, when asked by the tribal elders how he wished to be known, cried 'make me an Offa'.

Where were things like the Booker Prize when we so richly deserved them?

As the paper began to build up a rapport with the clubman, I persuaded Wesley Tee to let me set up a new series, the *Motoring News* Rally Championship, offering our publicity and a bit of organisation but very little money. Money? I got on well with the Old Man but not well enough to ask him for any of that.

I arranged a discussion meeting for the *MN* Championship in the Imperial Hotel, Blackpool, in November 1960, the day before the start of the RAC Rally. Erik Carlsson sat in on the discussions, as did key people like John Brown, still an inventive organiser today.

We launched the Championship in the first issue of 1961 and within a year 'the *Motoring News*', as everyone called it, became the premier rally series in Britain and, I believe, for several years genuinely played a part in developing drivers. The rallies were the sort I liked to do – fast, tough, plot-and-bash events. The Championship developed drivers and navigators and everyone seemed to like it.

In 1961, as in later years, competition was tight. Bill Bengry (driving a VW Beetle) won the Drivers' series, while Brian Melia (mostly co-driving for Don Grimshaw in an ex-works Austin-Healey 3000) won the Navigators' title. By that time I had already moved on to my new job at BMC but my successors kept it going, developing it further, and it was a success for well over ten years.

I was also sent off to report on events where no one else was able or willing to go. I first met Alec Issigonis when I covered the Television Trophy Trial and he presented the awards, and I even covered the Le Mans 24-Hour race, in 1961; as a rally co-driver I suppose they could trust me to stay awake all night. That was memorable because I spent much of the night talking about pace notes with Denis Jenkinson. He'd had his famous record-breaking drive with Stirling Moss on the Mille Miglia in 1955 – his report on that was the finest piece of sustained motoring journalism there has ever been – but he said that on that event his pace notes had been to warn about bumpy level crossings and the like. He told me that when they got to the twisty bits (where a rally co-driver would be starting his notes) he simply sat and watched the Maestro at work.

Jenks mentioned that they'd developed hand signals because they felt that if you are at an absolute 100 per cent concentration level an intercom chattering in your ear can take a slight edge off your total commitment. Timo Makinen wouldn't use intercoms for some years for a somewhat similar reason – he even thought a constant sound could affect eyesight.

I wrote an occasional piece for *Motor Sport* and fondly remember the reaction to a road test of an Austin-Healey Sprite in which we commented '. . . what a pity it's such a poor courting car . . .'. The letters came in by the sackful, telling us how to take seats out, use the bonnet and so on. These were all put into perspective by a one-line letter that subsequently arrived from a reader saying, '*I've* had it in a Morgan three-wheeler.' I suspect it came from a musician because, as

Confucius should have said, 'Man who can make love in Morgan three-wheeler can play trombone in telephone kiosk.'

Around this time I auditioned as a TV race commentator. I went to Mallory Park and thought I'd done quite well until somebody gently pointed out that the car I had been talking about as the leader for the last few laps had actually been lapped early in the race . . . Another career path closed.

It was while I was at *Motoring News* that I had a real stroke of luck. Through navigating for Pat Moss, who was already very close to Erik Carlsson (she married him later), Erik asked me to do the RAC Rally in 1960 in his Saab 96, which was kind of him when you consider the protest pantomime in which I had been involved a year earlier with Auto Union. Erik himself was the 1959 European Rally Champion.

The week before the rally Erik and I went up to northern Scotland to have a look at the strange, narrow and bumpy roads – we honestly didn't go to practise, which was not allowed, and in any case we hadn't a clue where the event was going.

After flying up to Edinburgh we hired a Minor 1000, not a Saab (they were still rare in the UK), and drove around, just looking and recce-ing likely roads. After the event all sorts of scurrilous stories circulated. As I wrote in my rally report: 'One of the rumours at the finish had it that Erik practised the [Monument Hill] stage 84 times. In actual fact, we recce'd it once, and once only, in a very slow, standard, Minor, which stopped half-way along with flooded electrics . . .'

Later, on a narrow road north of Skaig Bridge, we met a fish lorry coming the other way. If I'd been driving we would have hit the lorry, but not Erik – he just drove off the edge of the road, which didn't have hedges or walls. I *hope* he realised that he would only roll down a bank; he was certainly cool because even while we were rolling he switched off so that the electric petrol pump wasn't ticking when we came to rest.

Back at the hotel that night, Erik suddenly stood up, rubbed his back against the wall, and said, 'I think I break ribs . . .' – and you could hear his ribs crunching. The next day, at the hospital in Inverness, they kept us waiting so long that Erik walked out. Pat Moss and I then went shopping in Boots, strapped Erik up in bandages, and that's how he won the RAC. (On the rally itself, marshals near the spot warned us to be careful because 'someone went over the edge last week'.)

There was no question of seeding and we started at No 178, three hours behind the Morley Twins' Big Healey, which carried No 1. Surrounded by Minis and Renaults we were only seven from the back, so I could see most of the cars leave the start in Blackpool before I had to go to work. It was a typical RAC of the period, like a long British night-navigation rally, but with a few special stages, the first time such things had been included. All four of the stages were held in Scotland; I'm still not sure how Jack Kemsley managed it, but some of them were on public roads which had been 'closed' for the occasion.

Mind you, even without the stages it would have been a difficult event, for some of the road sections were very tight and there were only seven clean sheets (out of 172 starters) after the first night, and it didn't ease up after that. At the end of the event only six people (including Erik) were clean on the road, so at least I contributed one-sixth, but Erik was also fastest on the key stage – 2 miles up and over Monument Hill, near Dalmally, in Scotland.

When we arrived, almost at the back of the field don't forget and in the dark, we heard that no one had beaten the target time of 3 minutes for the 2-mile stage; Ian Walker had managed 3min 4sec in his Ford Zephyr and the Big Healeys of Peter Riley and Ronnie Adams were both under 3min 10sec.

Erik just grunted, pulled his belt up tight, and unleashed the Saab. I couldn't do anything for him because we genuinely had done no more than drive once over the track before that day so I had no notes. When you think that the Saab probably had no more than 60-70bhp, a three-speed steering column gearchange, and four-wheel drum brakes, you have to marvel at what he did – 2min 58sec, by far the quickest on that one stage – which was enough to win us the event as all the other special stages could be done within the target times. Afterwards Erik didn't seem to know what the fuss was all about, because this was the sort of thing he did in every Scandinavian rally, but there's no doubt that it had shaken a few people.

I'm still asked what it was like, but apart from making the quip that I missed everything because my eyes were closed, all I can remember is the sparks flying out of the back as the Saab's undershield hit rocks. Even though he already had a reputation for being 'pa taket' (the Swedish for 'on the roof') he never gave me a moment's worry; he had a wonderful feel for a car. Incidentally, the mark of a good roll in those days was not to damage the roof-mounted spotlight.

Maybe it was that sort of experience that convinced me never to have any ambitions of being a rally driver. You have to sit alongside such people and realise how brilliant they are to know you could never do the same. If Erik had told me he was going to drive up Everest I would have gone with him without a qualm. Down Everest too for that matter. The final stretch of the rally was chaotic because we all got trapped in Friday evening traffic. Erik claims that I urged him to break speed limits and go the wrong way down one-way streets, but I honestly don't think I did, officer. Anyway the control was cancelled after all that.

For the first time the RAC excelled itself with a real 'showbiz' prizegiving, a black tie affair at the Talk of the Town, just off Leicester Square, London, with Eartha Kitt doing the cabaret. Following the final tests at Brands Hatch, Erik got the Saab through scrutineering, then at the appropriate moment we – car, Erik and I – came up through the stage, on a lift, to a fanfare and a splendid tune. It was a charming melody but Erik asked about it afterwards because, whatever it was, it wasn't the Swedish National Anthem.

When we were laying out *Motoring News* for the following week, someone actually set a front-page banner headline 'WE'VE WON THE RAC'. There was much debate before I won my case for a more modest and restrained 'IT'S "ON THE ROAD" CARLSSON' – a play on Erik's 'on-the-roof' reputation.

Despite this RAC win, I was brought down to earth during the winter of 1960/61 because when John Sprinzel and I wanted to do the Monte in a modified Austin A40 he had borrowed from Marcus Chambers, we had to find some way of funding the trip. This, by the way, was the first ever Monte to have special stages, five of them on the Common Route down from Charbonnières through Die and Gap to Monte Carlo.

To solve the funding crisis, we did a recce at our own, mainly John's, expense and completed a set of reconnaissance notes, including what were simple pace notes for the stages. These were then sold to Castrol for them to give to their runners. Not many drivers at that time would have had the wit to do that but, as I've already said, Sprinzel was a great ideas man.

Although this was perhaps the first really professional use of pace notes, and much as I'd like to claim the glory, we didn't really invent notes like that – we'd been using a simpler form of notes for some time. John Gott, when he was 'Captain' of the BMC team, had already been grading and analysing sections for some years but perhaps we took them further than ever before.

That was the notorious Monte (odd, isn't it, how often those two words came together over the years?) where there was a handicapping system that involved a car's weight and its engine size. Even before the start we all saw that this handed victory to Panhard (who had never won before and would never win again) so in the end John and I were really quite happy to finish third in our class behind a French DB and Pat Moss in another A40.

Wesley Tee was very generous, giving me a lot more time to go rallying than I guess I deserved, because almost immediately after the Monte, Erik and I went off to drive a Saab in the Canadian Winter Rally in Quebec.

It was a strictly navigational-and-time-keeping event – not the sort of thing that counts as a 'real' rally in my book. To me, rallying should have two people in a car, working together and going quickly, not playing party games. Mind you, I really should have known what was in store when at the pre-rally briefing the Clerk of the Course said, 'Last year, we know, some of you cheated by using binoculars to check the clocks before you rolled into the controls. This year we're going to hide them so that you can't see them until you arrive ...'

Even so, we could still have won the event; in fact we should have won but I made a cock-up, not by a few seconds but by 10 *minutes* at one point. After that we were leading the event on the road so whenever we reached a secret check, Erik would get out one of the emergency flares we compulsorily had to carry, put it in the snow and light it so that everyone else would know where the secret checks were.

It was always a joy to go rallying with Erik (we even went marshalling on Eppynt to help out on one event), but to my regret I never managed to persuade him to drive for BMC. I tried hard enough, believe me, but in the end Pat Moss left us, to marry Erik, and eventually to join him at Saab.

I've never lost my respect for his ability. Over the years it's amazing how often I have been watching an RAC Rally, only to have a hand descend on my shoulder and for this unique voice to boom in my ear: 'I think we can still beat them, Stuart, don't you?' I suspect he could still be in with a shout!

It's impossible to relate one generation of drivers to another, so we'll never know whether Erik was as quick as Carlos Sainz or Colin McRae. One thing's for sure, however: he always tried just as hard and prepared just as hard as they do. And he was backed by some splendid Swedish mechanics who were well up to speed on innovations – Erik's full-bucket, personally tailored seat, for instance, was one of the first seen.

Because he stayed on at Saab, as a world-wide ambassador – and what an ambassador – for many years after he had stopped rallying, he used to go out on test sessions with young bloods like Stig Blomqvist, and always matched their stage times. Apart from the big grin afterwards, there was always the same comment: 'Not bad for old man ...'

In 1999, nearly 40 years later, Saab put on a splendid party for Erik's 70th birthday and I felt privileged to be invited to Trollhätton for it. The evening included a 'This is Your Life' on Erik, and listening to him (with a Swedish interpreter alongside me) talking about his career, and chatting to people like Per Eklund and Stig Blomqvist, was like a master class in rallying. On the TV programme someone always comes on near the end from some far-off place; with the Saab version for Erik I was honoured to find it was me. In an article afterwards I think I was right in describing Erik as 'The Colossus of Roads'.

A great driver, and a great personality.

I suspect at that period I probably needed psychiatric help because I would navigate in anything, with anybody. As an example, Anne Hall rang me at work from Greece when she was doing the Acropolis to ask if I'd like to do the 1961 Mille Miglia with a friend of hers in a works-loaned Mercedes-Benz. Would I like to do the Mille Miglia? In a Mercedes? I would have walked to Italy if necessary.

I had mild second thoughts when I met the driver, a Kenyan called John Manussis, in Brescia and found that he'd had quite a few serious rally shunts. There were maybe 8,000 bends on that Mille Miglia; I reckon I shouted 'Slow down' on all of them.

Incidentally, before you build up a picture of an open Merc and a crew in goggles, I'd better mention that we were in a saloon – winning the 2,500cc touring class – and the event was really a rally by that time, although the locals didn't seem to know that because there were straw bales on roundabouts in towns where we were supposed to be obeying speed limits. And the fact that it was 'only' a rally hasn't stopped me from carefully displaying my Mille Miglia Club badge ever since.

I relished doing any event. Only one never seemed very lucky for me: the Alpine Rally. This was perhaps the greatest of them all and anyone counting himself a motorsport enthusiast should see the Shell film of the 1958 event (with Denis Jenkinson, no less, driving one of the camera cars) to get a feel for the majestic scale of it.

Erik and I broke down before we even got to the start of an Alpine. I got a shade further on another with John Milne in a works MGA Twin Cam but then he hit a post. As we waited for rescue, John – a Scottish barrister – and I discussed tactics for a court case he was flying back for. He may have been (perhaps was) winding me up, but he claimed that he had to defend a woman accused of persistently using a public lavatory without paying. We concluded that the only hope was to claim that she had squatter's rights.

A third attempt at the Alpine, this time with Les Leston, resulted in our TR3 breaking down. While waiting for recovery that time we were reduced to going round the local cemetery for something to do. As a hardened jazz enthusiast, Les was aghast when I insisted on buying a record of local music as a souvenir of our time in the village. Strange, really, because I thought what a jolly little polka it was, delightfully played by an accordion trio.

Time flew for me at *Motoring News*, but then in the summer of 1961 came the most unexpected approach of all, from the British Motor Corporation. Marcus Chambers, it seemed, had decided that seven years in charge of the famous Competitions Department was quite enough. Opportunity was knocking again.

Chapter 6

BMC Competitions Manager – the big challenge

MANAGER OF THE BMC Competitions Department? A dream job and the timing seemed perfect. The BMC team was respected, the Austin-Healey 3000 was a proven outright winner (and there was more to come from it), and although the 850 Mini wasn't very quick, the much more promising Mini Cooper was just about to be launched.

I found out later that the approach came because the then BMC Competitions Manager, Marcus Chambers, had recommended me for the job; he himself had decided to go as Service Manager with an Appleyard's garage in Bradford, and had been asked to recommend a successor well before leaving to ensure a smooth transition. Apparently he'd put me forward to John Thornley, the boss at MG where Competitions was based, as the only candidate. When John queried whether a mere 28-year-old could do the job (remember that this was all before 'yoof' became an absurd business obsession), Marcus reassured him that I could. Thanks Marcus.

At the time I wasn't really a regular BMC team member. I'd had occasional drives, most recently in a Big Healey with David Seigle-Morris in the 1960 German rally (when we won the GT category) but nothing at all so far in 1961. But John Sprinzel was always a semi-detached team member and he and I had spent a lot of time with other BMC members on events, so I guess Marcus and I knew each other fairly well. And I cheerfully confess I'd done all I could to increase my 'profile'; it's not immodest to tell the media about any success, just common sense because it can help you to get known and, not least today, find sponsors.

At the time I couldn't see why Marcus had had enough of the job after only seven years because it looked very glamorous from the outside, as many jobs do, and it was only when it was my turn to leave BMC that I could understand better the sheer hard grind and even repetitiveness. In my time at BMC I travelled overseas so many times that Manhattan might have been Manchester – how world-weary can you get?

Partly at my suggestion, Marcus called his own book *Seven Year Twitch*. He laid bare his thoughts about me in that book, written only months after he had moved out and, with totally false humility, I'd like to quote some of them here: 'I always thought that as gamesmanship was to Stephen Potter, so rallymanship was to Stuart. Some of his critics at the time decried his methods, which could be pretty ruthless . . . Stuart was one of the new generation of professional rally drivers.

'I didn't feel that Stuart really thought that his methods would bring him into prominence so quickly, and he paraded a somewhat bewildered air, rather like a professor who found himself being publicised on the discovery of a new process. I was sure that he would make a success of his job as my successor at BMC, and I wished him lots of luck . . .'

When I told Wesley Tee about the offer at the end of July 1961, he was fully supportive of my move. He said he was sorry I was going, because he felt that the gentle rise in the circulation of *Motoring News* was because of the extra emphasis on rallying, but he also told me that there would be kudos for the paper if one of its employees moved on to such a high-visibility job.

After just a brief interview with John Thornley, I left *Motoring News* a month later and ran in parallel with Marcus until he left at the end of September; my successor as 'Verglas' was John Brown, and he took over from me in more ways than one, for in November he went on to navigate Erik Carlsson to his second successive RAC Rally win.

On the personal side it meant moving near to Abingdon, and I was beginning to feel quite well off by this time, because BMC proposed to pay me £1,250 a year plus a company car; it also meant that I could realise one of my ambitions – that Margaret wouldn't have to go out to work any more. And we could afford to buy our first house, for £2,500.

Looking back, I don't think I was frightened by the challenge of managing the BMC team, maybe because there was so much to do in the changeover that I really didn't have time to brood. Anyway, I was inheriting a good team at Abingdon and I knew most of them from the rallies I had done with them.

The 'Comps' foreman, Doug Watts, was really the key to why the cars were so good. He was everything that was right about the place – wrap him in a Union Jack, hand him some roast beef, and you had the archetypal Englishman. Before I arrived I'm sure that John Thornley had Doug up in his office to tell him to keep a fatherly eye on me! He did.

Doug plus Doug Hamblin, Tommy Wellman and Den Green were at the core of everything, while Bill Price was always in charge of homologation, and deputised for me in many ways. Along with them and with guidance from long-term secretaries like Diana Kirkby, I couldn't go wrong.

We really didn't have an 'engineer' as such at Abingdon; all the development was done as a joint effort between the drivers, Doug Watts, and – at arm's length – by Alec Issigonis and Geoffrey Healey.

Cliff Humphries would do engine work, we had Syd Enever just a few yards away if we were running MGs or needed any specific advice – and of course we had John Cooper continuously stoking us up, and calling me with 'Stuart, why can't we have . . .?' conversations.

However, by not mentioning all the others I'm really demeaning their efforts. Any success was a team effort and the mechanics and, not least, Neville Challis the storeman played a part. Neville was always cheerful and had a good sense of humour. I was suitably impressed when he told me once that he'd got a blue at Oxford, until he added that if someone hadn't jogged his arm he'd have got the pink and the black as well.

Reporting to John Thornley helped enormously. He was 'Mr MG' in so many ways and had a real aura about him. He was a natural leader and motivator with that invaluable asset – enthusiasm – which really rubbed off on people. Perhaps most important of all, he had the skill (and it *is* a management skill that more should learn) to know when to leave people to get on with things. Absolutely nothing to do with this book – if an autobiographer can't digress, who can? – but when I was talking to the chief executive of a successful company recently about *involving* people, he told me that he'd rather his staff come to him for forgiveness than permission. Wise man.

John had lived and worked at Abingdon in an MG environment since 1930, and could see all the benefits of motorsport. He didn't have to be convinced that BMC needed to be competing. However, John didn't present me with any high-flown Visions or Mission Statements (why do most of them today seem so bland, smacking of apple pie and motherhood?). All he said was that he hoped I would enjoy myself and that he would always be available to support me. I inherited the balance of a year's programme that had been agreed at the previous Competitions Committee meeting many months earlier.

At the time John Gott was 'Team Captain'. That perhaps sounds old-fashioned now but with a lot of drivers involved, as BMC had then, having a 'senior' one made sense. I had always admired John's attention to detail, and I'm sure some of that dedication rubbed off on me and on how I prepared for events. Later on, people used to talk about the 'Turner Bibles', the pre-rally briefing documents issued before big events, but I'm happy to acknowledge that John had pioneered the concept.

My first experience as 'probationary Competitions Manager', as you might say, was to go off to Yugoslavia with a service crew on the Liège-

Sofia-Liège. My lasting memory of that event, where the roads were incredibly dusty, was of holding our Team Captain's head under the water from a village pump. My glee is perhaps understandable if you consider that, at the time, John was Chief Constable of Northamptonshire ...

Although we got on well, he was many years older than me and sensed that we would be coming at things from different directions. As a result he soon retired from the Team Captain's role but was always there if I needed advice; also, we would lend him cars for specific events like the International Police Rally; subsequently he bought a works Big Healey and raced it successfully for some years. A gentleman.

When I took over from Marcus, I inherited a successful but large and varied team of drivers. On the one hand there was Pat Moss, not just a first-class lady driver but also a formidable competitor and winner, along with David Seigle-Morris and Peter Riley; on the other hand there were the gentlemen, the *very* professional gentlemen, but amateurs for all that – the Morley twins, John Gott and Bill Shepherd.

I never under-estimated any of them, particularly Donald Morley, who was the fastest of all the Healey drivers until Timo came along, and of course the gentlemen proved that they could also be killers when the need arose. But although I was not aware at the time just how significant the shift actually was, we were moving to younger, professional drivers who could make rallying their living, and work virtually full time at it. As an example, I could never get Donald and Erle Morley to do a Liège. Why? It clashed with harvest time and as major farmers they had their priorities properly in perspective.

When Marcus left there was fortunately only one other big event to complete the 1961 season, the RAC Rally. I entered six cars, three Big Healeys and three MG Midgets, and if Erik Carlsson hadn't inconsiderately won the event for the second year running, Pat Moss would have been the outright winner in her Austin-Healey 3000. A six-car entry would be crazy for a work's team today, especially comprising two totally different models, but remember that preparation was simpler then.

This, by the way, was the first of the all-special-stage RAC Rallies with 24 stages totalling more than 200 miles, mainly on Forestry Commission tracks. If nothing else it proved that BMC's sports cars were perhaps not ideal for that sort of going. Second and fifth overall, the Ladies' trophy, two class wins and two class seconds was a good result, but not good enough. However, the Mini Cooper was on the way and this had a bonus because it brought a link with John Cooper who was involved with a team for saloon car racing, working with Ken Tyrrell. Much of what they would learn would rub off on how we prepared rally cars. To be working with John, already twice World F1 Constructors' Champion, and Ken was marvellous – they were both racers and highly competitive people.

Over the years, of course, John certainly delivered. Mini Coopers with drivers like John Rhodes, John Fitzpatrick, Warwick Banks and John Handley were always spectacular on the track. Down on top speed, maybe, but rarely matched in handling.

Except for an annual Competitions Committee meeting, usually held at Longbridge, there was never much formal monitoring of our progress, not even on the budget front; I suppose it helped that Norman Higgins, MG's financial controller, eventually became godfather to my eldest daughter . . . As an aside, quite a few drivers became godparents to other drivers' children. Because of this family atmosphere, I was not popular when I suggested that wives should not travel on events, like the Alpine Rally for instance, which meant a delightful spell at La Ciotat, because we needed to be concentrating on the events. It amuses me that the 'sex before competing' debate still rumbles on in sport today. I believe it's fine for a competitor but only if you don't keep the scrutineers waiting (you know how tetchy they can get).

Despite the merciful absence of a hugely formal control structure, John Thornley was fully in touch with what was happening because one of the delights of my spell at Abingdon was to lunch with John, Syd Enever and Reg Jackson et al in the wood-panelled MG boardroom. It was like dining with history. They were legends – Reg, the chief inspector, had been a riding mechanic with Nuvolari for instance. Here was I, a young upstart, messing about with Minis in their beloved MG sports car factory, yet they could not have been more helpful. Although Syd Enever and I were never particularly close, he was always ready to give us engineering guidance.

The octagon was everywhere – if it had not been anatomically inconvenient, I'm sure the lavatory seats would have been eight-sided. We got back after one Monte win with the Mini to find the flags flying. When I said how nice it was to see the Mini finally being recognised, it was explained that the flags were aflutter because an MG had won its category on the same event!

When I sat back to consider the works set-up, I couldn't find much wrong with it. The cars were certainly well-developed and prepared, and a lot more was on the way for 1962. Although Marcus had cut down on the variety of cars in use towards the end, perhaps too many different types were still being used. However, remember that in those days there were *two* battles on each rally: one to win something on the event, the other to win the advertising battle between manufacturers in the newspapers afterwards. Space had to be booked well in advance so sometimes, after a poor result by a manufacturer, the advertising agency had to make a third in class seem a major triumph. The wider the variety of cars, the more chance of *something* to advertise.

As an extreme example, for the 1962 Monte I was still in an experimental mood, and entered eight cars – six for 'real' crews, and two for important journalists (Robert Glenton of the *Sunday Express* and John Cotter of Independent Television News). Apart from two Mini Coopers, there was an 850 Mini, a Midget, an Austin-Healey 3000, an MGA 1600 Coupé, a Riley 1.5 and an Austin A110. Actually, looking at that list again, 'experimental' isn't quite the right word. 'Deranged' seems more fitting – for instance, would you care to load a service car with spares for that lot? At least the Midget, MGA and 3000 took class wins and Pat, in a Mini Cooper, the Ladies' prize – but she was down in 26th place and not overjoyed after a throttle cable had broken.

If there was another weakness, it was that BMC had always been very loyal, maybe too loyal, to British drivers. As far as I could see BMC had *never* used an overseas driver in its works rally team. My old North Staffs Motor Club friend, Tommy Gold, once graphically described the Scandinavians as 'beady eyed, Coca Cola-drinking bastards' (he couldn't possibly have met Timo Makinen by then). I realise that I'm on delicate ground here because enthusiasts waving Union Jacks may maintain that the *British* Motor Corporation should have been using only British drivers. But hang on. If you want to sell a car in Finland, who is going to get you most publicity there: a Finn or a British driver? No contest if you think about it. There would be no debate about nationality today, but then the subject came up quite often at our Competitions Committee meetings.

Anyway, by a series of happy coincidences, the team was about to become more multi-national. I didn't go out, cold-bloodedly, to find any beady-eyed Coca Cola-drinking Scandinavians, but within a year they – and Paddy Hopkirk – had found me, almost by chance.

I already knew about Rauno Aaltonen because in August 1961 Derek Astle (the rally world was crushed when he was killed on a Tulip Rally a short time afterwards) and I had been competing in the Polish Rally in Derek's own Austin-Healey 3000. Rauno was co-driving for Eugen Bohringer in a works Mercedes-Benz 220SE. On one stage, on the loose, Eugen moved over and Rauno drove the car – we were shaken by his quick time.

As a digression (it's not that my mind's wandering, it's just that so much happened then) I saw one of the coolest put-downs of all time on that Polish Rally with Derek. He had an impish sense of humour and as we approached the Polish border on our return, he hurtled towards the customs post and brought our red 3000 to a quivering halt about a metre from the guard's foot. The guard didn't say anything. He just knocked off his machine-gun's safety catch . . . (Just one more of the blue tablets, nurse, then I'll carry on with my main theme.)

Still in Mercedes-Benz cars, Rauno also won the 1000 Lakes, and (with Bohringer) finished second in the German Rally later in 1961. He was very ambitious, very astute, we got together, and he joined BMC from the start of 1962.

On his first event for us, the Monte, we nearly lost him when his Mini crashed, turned over and caught fire, but co-driver Geoff Mabbs dragged him clear of his safety belts, hauled him away from the car and undoubtedly saved his life. After that, Rauno did no wrong for us and was perhaps BMC's most valuable team member for the next seven years.

Paddy Hopkirk was next to arrive, but it was Paddy who approached me for a drive, not the other way round. I'd known him for years, first at Standard-Triumph and later, as a rival, when he was driving Sunbeam Rapiers for the Rootes Group, and although I knew he was having a hard time at Rootes, I didn't know that he was ready to leave them.

At the time the Rootes team of Peter Harper, Peter Procter and Paddy Hopkirk all seemed to be encouraged to compete against each other. Team orders? No, and if there had been, I doubt if they would have taken a blind bit of notice.

Paddy wasn't happy and realised that the Rapier wasn't going to be competitive for long, but the final straw came when he discovered that there would be no Rootes entry in the 1962 Alpine. The first thing I knew about this was when he wrote to me, telling me that he wanted to join a winning team, and that he wanted to get his hands on a Big Healey. His letter said, 'I do want to drive cars which are capable of winning rallies outright, even if I'm not!'

That was fine by me, but it wasn't long before he found out, as Pat and the Morley twins already knew, that the Healey was a beast that could, and often did, bite back. Paddy later insisted, far too modestly, that the Big Healeys frightened him but, as we all know, he came to love the Mini, and finally made his name, big time, in those cars. Drivers, incidentally, were not rich men in the 1960s – I recall that we only paid Paddy £1,500 a year at this time.

I knew nothing about Timo Makinen until the autumn of 1962 when Raoul Falin, a charming man who looked rather like Eugen Bohringer, and who was the Morris dealer in Helsinki, came to Abingdon and told me, 'I've got this young Finnish driver, Timo Makinen, you won't know him, but I've sometimes lent a car to him for Finnish rallies. He's quick – I think you might be impressed – and it really would help me in Finland if you could find a car for him to drive in the RAC Rally.'

We 'found' a 997cc Mini Cooper for him (actually 407 ARX, which Rauno had already used in the Alpine and the 1000 Lakes), put John Steadman (from Bristol) with him and sent him out on the RAC. Timo didn't speak much English at that time, and I think we even needed an interpreter (maybe Rauno) to tell him to 'just plod round, and if you can get a class win, that will be marvellous'.

That was the RAC Rally where Erik won for the third time in a Saab, where Paddy and Pat took second and third places in Big Healeys, and where Rauno was best Mini in fifth place. Timo, just 'plodding round', with a co-driver he didn't know, took seventh place, won his class, was a member of the winning team, and immediately convinced me that I needed him on a contract for 1963. He was a wild man then, and a wild man later, but in view of his pace I decided that I could put up with a lot of that.

The first of the legendary Makinen drives followed immediately. We had already put in a 1963 Monte Carlo Rally entry for Christabel Carlisle as a small 'thank you' for her sterling efforts racing a Mini prepared by Don Moore (one of the finest engine tuners I've ever known – as he proved with his Jaguar engines for the Archie Scott Brown Listers). Entries for the Monte had, crazily, to be in before the RAC Rally finished and we'd just entered 'C. Carlisle, Austin-Healey', the intention being for her to have a gentle drive to Monte Carlo in a Sprite with a cousin as her co-driver. After Timo's RAC Rally effort, I persuaded Christabel to go with him instead, as his co-driver, in a Big Healey! In the worst weather of all time Timo, who had never even rallied a Healey before this, won the GT category.

Christabel has said that if she had been able to get through on the phone after the first night of the recce she would have come home, then she realised that the Finn knew what he was doing. On the event itself she even said 'faster' on occasions. To Makinen, in a Healey, on ice. Brave girl. His GT win became more understandable when we found out later that Timo had been racing a D-Type Jaguar in Finland ... on ice.

As you read further, you may accuse me of writing too much about Timo, because he was not everybody's favourite person, but later he did a hat-trick on the RAC Rally in Escorts, and he seemed to lead nearly every rally he ever started. For all his faults (and there were many) I had a huge amount of respect for him. If I made any contribution to his career, it was by making sure that he usually took a calm British co-driver along to control him, although that was always a relative term.

As an aside, putting British co-drivers like Tony Ambrose and Paul Easter with the Finns worked in two ways: it helped to bring the disciplined 'UK navigator' approach to the crew and it made for a more integrated team. It also ensured that English was the common language. I took Timo to a Knowldale Car Club dinner and in my speech said he had been learning English specially for the occasion. It brought the house down when Timo then stood up, simply said 'BMC builds to win', and sat down.

It has been purloined by all and sundry since, but I would like to put my hand up and claim to have coined the phrase 'Flying Finns' at around this time. Not a lot to be remembered for though, is it?

Incidentally, way back then and through to today, Finns – while deadly rivals on events – have always been quite ready to suggest up-and-coming drivers worth watching.

Having Scandinavians in the team helped in several ways – they were at the forefront of knowledge on studded tyres for instance, and while not all the British drivers were enthusiastic about left-foot braking, at least the debate encouraged drivers to *think* about the issue and driving in general. They also thought about the cars, Rauno in particular being a great one for designing sump guards. Many is the time I've brought back paper table-cloths from French restaurants covered in designs drawn up over meals with him.

At the end of 1962 my driving line-up looked very different from the one I had inherited in October 1961, and it stayed remarkably stable for the next five years, for really it was only Tony Fall who arrived to make the team even more formidable. In a way Tony was unlucky in that he was often overshadowed by Paddy and the others, just as Russell Brookes was by Roger Clark later. It's just bad luck if your time in the sun happens to fall when there are other great people around – presumably in the 1990s there was another British sprinter quite close to Linford Christie, but his name doesn't exactly spring to mind, does it?

Tom Trana, who was quick, also drifted in and out of the team, often in Swedish-supported Minis. He stayed in our bungalow near Abingdon one night and clearly didn't approve of English heating systems because the next morning we found him sleeping fully clothed with the rug off the floor over him!

When David Seigle-Morris and Peter Riley both received offers to join Ford in 1963, the pressure on our driver line-up eased, but I was genuinely relieved that they were still going to be involved in the sport.

On the other hand, everyone at BMC was concerned when Pat Moss decided to head for Ford as well. Pat, after all, had been with BMC since 1955 and had just given the works Mini Cooper its first outright victories in 1962. Everyone at Abingdon liked her and she was a huge asset to us in publicity terms. Not surprisingly, when we were faced with her departure, the implications were discussed all the way up to the Competitions Committee. Originally I was only authorised to 'bid £1,500 and endeavour to obtain agreement to her exclusive use of BMC products', but that was never likely to be enough.

Things dragged on for weeks until her father, Alf Moss, eventually called me, telling me that Ford had made a big offer. I took a deep breath, raised my offer for 1963 to £4,000, only to be told that Ford was offering £7,000. I didn't attempt to match that because it had been agreed at a Competitions Committee meeting that now the Mini Coopers were winning, Pat's presence as a headline-grabber was no longer quite as important. We parted as friends.

Pat's long-time co-driver Ann Wisdom, having married Peter Riley, had retired to have a family and was no longer available so when I hired Val Domleo as a co-driver to accompany Pauline Mayman it cornered the only two senior British co-drivers Pat might have wanted with her at Ford. That, I guess, was rallymanship and I know that Pat was not best pleased at the time ...

I've referred to a Competitions Committee a few times so perhaps this is the right moment to spell out just how BMC's motorsport policy was agreed. Once a year John Thornley would fix a meeting where he and I would face up to the Chairman, Sir George Harriman, Alec Issigonis and Brian Turner (who was BMC's publicity chief), to talk about cars, events and drivers, what the opposition was going to do, and how much money I needed to run a programme. The Committee was fairly ad hoc and John Cooper (always on my side) and Donald Healey would usually be there too.

Beforehand, John Thornley and I would get together to agree on what we wanted to do. John left rallying to me, his most significant input being to motor racing in America, where he knew he had to react to requests from BMC's importers that we should race our sports cars at Sebring fairly regularly. John Cooper would add his input, then we would go off to the Competitions Committee meeting, where I can't ever remember us not getting our way.

The process taught me a lot about running meetings, for John Thornley was very good. at it. And the meetings were decisive, everything was agreed and that was it for a year.

I've just dug out the minutes of the first meeting I attended, in August 1962, to find that although John Gott had left the team, he was still an 'Honorary member', though he didn't attend again. I reported that I'd tried to recruit Erik Carlsson, and failed, that we were thinking of competing in the Tour de France in 1963, and that we would continue to divert private-preparation requests to Daniel Richmond at Downton or to Don Moore.

I think Richmond, who was a close friend of Alec Issigonis, regarded us at Abingdon as rivals; certainly we tended to be wary of his involvement. Sometimes what he wanted to do regarding engines was in conflict with John Cooper's and my own needs, and we had to unscramble it all. I got on much better with Don Moore and wrote somewhere in reference to his cylinder head work, 'While other engine tuners make a song and dance about things, quiet flows the Don'.

Someone had obviously suggested using larger BMC models in saloon car racing, which I shot down by reminding them of the good publicity that followed 'David & Goliath' acts; there was even a proposal that we should enter a team of Morris 1100s in the 1963 Safari, a scheme that was mercifully abandoned.

By my second Competitions Committee meeting in October 1963 the Cooper S had started winning regularly, but even by this time I'd begun to worry about the competition. Once we saw the Lotus-Cortina earlier in the year, we knew that it was only a matter of time before Ford could make it reliable, then they would start to beat us. The fact that Ford had poached Pat Moss certainly made them serious rivals (when they were running Zodiacs and Anglias we didn't worry too much).

But for a time nobody believed me, just as they didn't believe me later when I started warning them about the Porsche 911's potential. That car's success on historic events now comes as no surprise to anyone who saw it fail to reach its full potential the first time round. (Seems strange now to think that in those days the Japanese were not a force at all. Some of their engineers would occasionally appear on rallies – with cameras – and, to confuse them on one event, we carefully poured baked beans into a petrol tank, having put a special container there for them. I was disappointed that no Japanese manufacturer ever launched a car with Heinz fuel injection.)

Complacency? Not at Abingdon, for sure, but on the other hand by this time there was a worrying atmosphere at Longbridge that 'we can do no wrong'. In any case, how could BMC's chairman Sir George Harriman spend much time on us when he had much bigger problems to face – with his dealers, the economic situation and, not least, the unions? Competitions got caught up in the latter because our pay structure and conditions were treated the same as the rest of the Abingdon factory. We were not alone in having occasional difficulties: all the British-based companies in rallying tried to find ways of not having to pay ludicrous overtime rates for Bank Holidays spent on motorsport. But they failed.

From the 1963 minutes I notice that I pointed out that 'Ford's ground organisation, from being a shambles at the time of the '63 Monte, has improved, and is still improving . . .' I also pointed out that 'Although they won the Austin-Healey class on the Alpine, Reliants motor very, very slowly, and are likely to dissolve into a cloud of fibre-glass dust at any moment.' The cruelty of youth.

I was clearly worried about the Mini's *and* the Healey's future: 'Even the Austin-Healey 3000, with 200bhp, is not theoretically capable of winning International events. That it has done so is a tribute to superlative driving . . .' Donald Morley knew how to harvest trophies as well as grain. He also once did a bit of giant-killing (usually a Mini prerogative) with the 3000 – after the 1962 Alpine Rally we came back via Mont Ventoux and put a late entry into a hill-climb there. Impossibly, he put the 3000 among the Ferrari GTOs. (Nothing to do with motorsport, but Mont Ventoux wine, made in the village at the bottom of the glorious hill, has a certain charm. Just thought I'd mention it in passing.)

John Cooper was pushing the Committee hard for what became the 970S and 1275S Mini Coopers, for the engine was important to his Formula 3 cars' future, *and* that of his racing Minis (that would happen in 1964). John Thornley and I wanted to see a new overhead-camshaft

16-valve engine developed for the Mini; this was promised but never materialised.

Other cars, such as MGB-engined A40s and Midgets, were considered and we also agreed that a 3-litre version of the MGB (this would become the MGC, but years later, and with an engine that was far too heavy) also had promise, this being accompanied by a note that 'This could be done if there were a war on. And this is WAR . . .' That was John Thornley's apt line.

In the meantime, on the battlefield, Rauno had taken third place in the Monte and had won the French Alpine Rally, but we were still suffering too many mechanical breakdowns.

Then Paddy put up a mighty show in the Tour de France, which, in theory, was all wrong for the Mini Cooper S. Ten days long and with a 1-hour or even 2-hour circuit race on most days, it was as hard on a Mini as the toughest rally in the world. It was a classic 'David versus Goliath' act, for the 1071S was by far the smallest car entered in an event littered with Ferrari 250GTOs, Porsches, Jaguars and Alfa Romeos. Paddy would go pouring through corners quicker than larger and faster cars, be passed on the straights that followed, and do it all again on the next corner. The press and public loved it – and so did Paddy. Amazingly, that was basically the same Mini that Paddy would use in the next Monte – at the time the cycle was build a new car for a rally, then use it as a recce car, then totally rebuild it for another rally.

It is difficult, almost impossible, today to appreciate the impact the Mini made when it was launched in the 1960s. The press coverage on its announcement was far greater than for any car launched in the last 20 years, not least because it was so different from anything else. The wind tunnel – the main reason why so many cars are now accused of looking the same – was not the god it is today.

Pop stars were seen in the Mini and Princess Margaret was photographed picking up the kids from school in one – even that didn't put buyers off. It was a time of the Beatles, the Rolling Stones, the Goons, Carnaby Street and mini skirts. Like, er, crazy man. Some people even had their pubic hair cut into heart shapes to reflect the loving times, although not in our village, mind you.

We got swept up in the giddiness and picked up any publicity we could. As an example, the Beatles flew into Paris, to mass hysteria, while we were there for the start of the Monte. Ringo Starr was delayed and came on a later plane to more publicity and I collected him from Le Bourget airport in one of the rally cars. The Beatles and the Mini? A perfect link.

In this atmosphere you will appreciate just how important Paddy's 1964 Monte win was to all of us, especially as we thought that the odds were stacked against us with the clever way the Ford Falcons had been homologated, plus the relatively mild weather and even the roads themselves – 'Ford Falcon Autobahn' was painted on some of the French stages because they were so suited to big, fast cars.

All in all it wasn't an easy win. Ljungfeldt's Falcon was quicker on scratch, but the Mini made up for that on handicap; it was one of the few occasions when I approved of such schemes ...

When Alec Issigonis arrived to join in the celebrations, he was obviously impressed by the theatrical atmosphere that built up, and I don't think he ever stopped smiling. Yet the huge publicity that followed hadn't been pre-planned – we weren't *that* confident – and getting the car flown back to England for the London Palladium show on television was BMC's PR idea, not mine. How much paid advertising would we have had to buy to match that? A point I was careful to make to marketing and sales colleagues.

Before we left Monaco, Margaret and I went into the casino and put all our money on a combination of Paddy's rally number. We won, bought a roulette wheel to bring home and I spent much of the following year with matchsticks perfecting a winning system. A year later I went back into the casino and proved that my system really was perfect ... but only if you used matchsticks.

After Paddy's Monte victory I went over to Belfast with him for a dealer show and while there got to know Eric McMullen and his wife – they were old friends of Paddy – and Margaret and I spent the next Christmas with them. Their Irish hospitality was outstanding and I went to bed so tired and emotional on 25 December that I didn't actually wake up again until 27 December. Belfast still owes me a day for that Christmas ... During the stay I spent quite a lot of time on my knees but this was not entirely due to the warmth of the Irish welcome. I was measuring their architecturally splendid bungalow so that I could copy the floor plan, and soon after we bought a building plot and had a house built at East Hanney. It was Margaret's idea to call it 'Penny Farthing' because, as she said at the time, that was about all we would have left when we had paid for it. As a result, we now have possibly the only 1960s penny farthing bicycle in the world, because Paul Easter's father built us a replica to go with the new house. Except for the garden hose instead of rubber around the front-wheel, it looks totally authentic and good enough, I reckon, to fool *Antiques Roadshow* experts.

The 1275S Mini Cooper came on stream early in 1964 and we had soon built enough of them to feel relaxed about getting Group 2 homologation, claiming that we had built more than 1,000 cars.

With the 970S Mini Cooper, however, it was a different story. Introduced in March 1964, and homologated in time for Pauline Mayman to drive one in the Alpine Rally in June, it was, in fact, very rare at the time. During the year there was one particular showroom demonstrator that sales chief Lester Suffield arranged to be shipped regularly around Europe to convince the world that they were widely available.

In July 1964 John Thornley pointed out in a memo to Longbridge 'the unpleasant and dangerous situation which existed in the motor sporting world because of the non-production of the 970 Cooper S'. Suffield's response was that 50 cars a week were to be built during the summer. In the end almost exactly 1,000 970Ss were eventually made, but not until 1965 . . .

But . . . er . . . how can I put this, right across the sport at that time, between the various factory teams there was an agreed level of how far to stretch the rules. Ford hadn't built enough Lotus-Cortinas when they got homologation, Triumph didn't have many aluminium cylinder heads for its Spitfires; we knew that, they knew that we knew, but it never went any further. It wasn't so much cheating as creativity really, and involved such things as making sure photographs of camshafts were taken from the right angle so that key features were highlighted (or hidden). And an awful lot of special bits were listed for African markets, but whether any manufacturer ever sold any cars there to fit them on is another matter.

On homologation, I think the finest compliment I was ever paid was by René Cotton, Citroen's much-respected team manager. He came up to me at one service point with a new Mini Cooper homologation form in his hand, grinned, and said, 'Le nouveau testament!' I felt very humble.

Stop for a minute. All this talk of the Mini ignores what a great car the Austin-Healey 3000 had become. We added triple Weber carbs to the engine for 1962 (Doug Hamblin spent some time at Weber's Bologna factory in Italy, learning all about their technicalities), and the aluminium cylinder head arrived at about the same time. The Healey just kept on getting better. The Morleys, in particular, called it a 'big hairy monster' but loved to drive one, while, more accurately perhaps, Peter Riley christened it a 'point and squirt' machine because you struggled round the corners, pointed it then squirted it up the straights. The Morleys set fastest scratch times in handicap-riddled Tulips on four consecutive occasions, and won the Alpine Rally twice, in 1961 and 1962. The longest minutes of my life came at a service point on the 1963 Alpine waiting . . . and waiting . . . for the Morley 3000 to arrive on its way to the Everest of rallying: a hat trick. It never came. The axle broke and grown men cried. I know, I was one of them.

By 1965 we knew that rule changes were going to outlaw the 3000 at the end of the season (and that the 1275S would be able to match it on loose-surfaced stages) but I was proud of what Doug Watts and his team achieved. I could never fault the co-operation from any of them, yet after the ordered existence they had had under Marcus, I know I must have been more difficult to work with. Bill Price was such an ideal 'Number Two' that he almost manoeuvred himself into the position of being indispensable in that job. (I later had much the same experience with Bill Barnett at Ford.) Price's book *The BMC/BL Competitions Department* is meticulous and accurate – just like Bill.

As well as the Morleys' efforts on the Alpine, the phenomenal Aaltonen/Ambrose Healey 3000 victory in the last of the 'proper' Spa-Sofia-Liège Marathons has to have a special place in Healey history. You had to be there to appreciate just how fast, how hard, and how damaging this particular event actually was – and I was never surprised that the Yugoslavian authorities later banned it from their roads. It was an indication of the Liège's importance that Bulgarian and Serbo-Croat were among the ten languages in an official-looking document I drew up to help get our cars and crews through customs posts. (A motorsport book is no place for political comment perhaps, but no one who was involved in Lièges can do anything but grieve over what has happened in Yugoslavia since then.)

From Tuesday in Belgium, to Saturday back in Belgium, there were no halts at all except one hour for 'dinner' in Sofia, the capital of Bulgaria. To quote from my service plan: 'The Liège this year is not a rally; it is a thinly disguised road race, and many service points will virtually be pit stops if the crews are not to lose time ...'

Not only was Rauno a great driver but his co-equipier, Tony Ambrose, was also fast himself. If ever there was a rally made for the Healey, it was the Liège, for by this time the car really was a tank – and tanks were what were needed for that event. Although we entered seven cars for the 1964 event – three Healeys, three MGBs and a 1275S Mini Cooper – it was the Healeys that were likely to win.

Petrol supply in Yugoslavia and Bulgaria was always going to be a problem so we had 100-gallon bags to tow on trailers behind service cars. Den Green and I towed one to what felt like the ends of the earth and were 200 metres from a crossroads when the cars shot across and on their way without spotting us! Fortunately they managed to get through.

There was no time for refinement, which explains why my service notes to the drivers included: 'If you break down up to Pec [in Yugoslavia] please use your initiative to get yourselves (and, if possible, the car) back to civilisation ...' To give you an idea of the service 'umbrella', we took along seven service cars, two of them with the fuel trailers, and managed to fit in 30 service points. I saw the cars only five times along the way before chasing them back along German autobahns to the finish.

In spite of all the service support, though, only two of our cars finished – Rauno's Healey, which won, and John Wadsworth's Mini 1275S. The latter was a miracle for no Mini had ever done it before and it was thanks to one of the mechanics, Pete Bartram, who'd slipped a set of front couplings in his kit 'just in case'. He was with me when we happened to come along within minutes of Wadsworth's Mini stopping with ... a broken coupling. Timo's Healey simply ran out of tyres when he had six punctures on one section. (No one could shred Mr Dunlop's best products quite like Timo – a front set on a Mini over an 11-mile Alpine Rally stage was perhaps his most extreme performance. Mind you, he was quickest on the test.) Paddy's car seized its gearbox in Bulgaria. In the end Rauno lost 57 minutes on an impossible schedule – which was 28 *minutes* better than anyone else.

We were also preparing MGBs, Midgets and Sprites for racing at this time. I must admit that sports car racing wasn't my first love and I asked Peter Browning (the Austin-Healey Club secretary who was also a qualified timekeeper) to do much of the organisation. In retrospect it was extremely good training for Peter, who would eventually take over from me in 1967. MG enthusiasts are so keen that they'll stone me however tactfully I put this but . . . the simple fact is that MGs, whether Midgets or Bs, were never potential winners on rallies and therefore had to take second place to Minis and Healeys. But, to stop the stoning, let me stress that they were great road cars. I'll never forget the day that Roy Brocklehurst (one of Syd Enever's designers) brought a prototype MGB GT round to our house, and Margaret and I found that a carrycot would fit comfortably in the back; we later bought one and loved it. A great car.

Syd Enever was much involved with the racing MGs, and personally looked after the smart Dick Jacobs Midgets. We treated these as arms-length works machines and, even though they were sometimes quicker than our in-house Midgets, we never got prickly about it, not least because Dick was so well liked. It helped too that Andrew Hedges, one of Dick's drivers, was hugely popular at Abingdon and could lift a team with his ebullient personality. I've seen a transporter rock as people in it laughed at a particular story Andrew told. (No I'm sorry, I can't tell it here because the book may be read by delicate people, like Formula 1 team owners.) I don't think that Syd Enever ever attended a major rally but he was always ready with advice, sometimes lateral (often the best sort), if we hit a development problem.

Because some long-distance races, like the Targa Florio and Sebring, involved similar planning to rallies, I at least took an interest in those events; I didn't need much convincing about the importance of Sebring to the American market, while after the snow and cold of Monte Carlo the chance to fly to Florida a few weeks later was always very seductive.

Except that we might fluke a class win, we knew that we couldn't win the 12-hour race at Sebring but we still took it seriously. Peter Millard of BMC Canada (not the BMC's USA importers) provided the core of the team personnel and we took one or two UK mechanics as anchormen. Peter and his wife Phyllis were great company and I know everyone involved enjoyed those races.

One year a mechanic from Canada, an Italian, got a bit excited at a pit stop. He took a wheel off an MGB and, in a frenzy, hurled it at the pit. It didn't actually hit anybody – how, I'll never know – but someone standing in the pit caught the wheel and angrily hurled it straight back. The Italian did the only logical thing. He re-fitted it and the car rejoined the race.

On another occasion a thunderstorm caused flooding on the track and our MGBs were the fastest cars out there for some time, faster than all the Ferraris. The action pictures were so dramatic that the BMC's American agency later ran an advert with the headline 'Sometimes it rains when you go shopping'.

There was always a 3-hour race the day before the 12-hour for which we often had Mini Coopers or an Austin-Healey Sprite team working in conjunction with us. At one 3-hour race I was surprised to find our pits a magnet for beautiful women. I knew it wasn't because of me and I felt fairly sure it wasn't the attraction of the British drivers. It was then that I realised that the driver the Americans had found for us was much better known than I'd realised. It was Steve McQueen, the film star, who fitted into our team well and was quite quick.

Perhaps most revealing was the way Stirling Moss arrived for practice in a Sprite, did a few quick laps, checked the time of the race, then left. Graham Hill did a few laps, had something changed, did a few more, had something else changed, repeated the process, *then* got down to a competitive time.

We had Pedro Rodriguez driving in another 3-hour race. When he came in to refuel, brother Ricardo in the pits called to him, so Pedro smartly *reversed* . . . over the fuel churn . . . Never dull, Sebring.

In planning for the race we used to organise test sessions at Silverstone at the end of each year, taking along whatever cars happened to be around at Abingdon at the time – MGBs, 3000s, Minis and Sprites, up to ten or so of them. We'd take along a bunch of potential Sebring drivers and give them a few laps in each car. 'There you are,' we used to say, 'get in and show us what you can do.' One year Ken Tyrrell rang to say that he had a young driver to check out, and would I mind including him in the test. We put him into a Le Mans MGB, and he was quickest, we put him in a Healey that he'd never sampled before, and he was by far the quickest, and he was a second quicker than anyone else in the Formula 3 car we had there. That was the first time I met Jackie Stewart.

Some of the drivers we invited were critical of the rather hit-and-miss session – the more precious ones felt that they needed more time to tailor the cars to their wishes (this didn't seem to bother Jackie). Perhaps they didn't realise that the sub-plot to the days was that we were also trying to see who would be able to cope with the odd things that can happen in a 12-hour race.

Geoff Healey used to attend the Silverstone sessions with his own cars from Warwick, and one year I noticed that every time a driver came into the pits, Geoff would open the bonnet, make a note and emerge with his moustache bristling. I found out afterwards that he'd fixed a second rev-counter with a tell-tale out of sight so that he knew who was over-revving, and who was not!

Talking of over-revving, I was a passenger in an MGB round Snetterton with a Finn who shall remain nameless (well, I've mentioned Makinen enough already) when Don Moore hung out a sign to him reading 'Use 9000'!

It did no harm if people got on well together for the Sebring trip. After the races we were always taken deep-sea fishing off West Palm Beach and we'd often come back via Bermuda or New York; I went to see the controversial comedian Lenny Bruce in a New York night club one year, caught the last 5 minutes of his first show, then the police arrested him and he never appeared for the second house.

Although we were always busy, we still found time to get involved in publicity stunts. On the 1964 RAC Rally, Lansing Bagnall sent a fork-lift truck to a service point close to their factory at Basingstoke. The Minis came rushing in, the fork lift hoisted them high in the air, and Doug Watts could look under them without ricking his back . . . and the press had a picture.

That, of course, was fun and games, for we all needed a bit of light relief after a very gruelling season. After Paddy's Monte win, Timo had won the Tulip Rally in a Mini and Rauno had taken the Liege in the 3000, but . . . there had been several retirements. And the opposition looked like getting tougher.

For 1965 I reckoned that we deserved more luck. In the next Monte, we got it.

Chapter 7

BMC – at its peak

BY THE AUTUMN of 1964 I was getting seriously worried about BMC's future competitiveness. In view of what the Mini Cooper S and the Austin-Healey 3000 went on to achieve in 1965, that may sound crazy, but I was serious. It was obvious that Ford's Lotus-Cortinas could beat us on tarmac rallies and in racing. As John Thornley's back-up material to a Competition Committee (written by me but signed by him) noted: 'The Lotus-Cortina is way out in front . . . therefore, a good showing in Saloon Car Racing is no longer possible, and outright wins in scratch rallies can only be achieved with a degree of luck . . .'

As it turned out, the works Minis would go on to win dozens of major rallies in the next couple of years, which made it look as if I'd been crying wolf, and made it more difficult for my concerns to be considered in the future.

In fact we were under fire from all sides, for Triumph had produced a fast little Spitfire race car, which worried John Thornley. About Sebring he wrote, 'The Sprite-Midget must attempt to beat the Spitfires . . .' and at Le Mans '. . . the Spitfire must be contained, therefore we should run one Sprite with the 1300 engine.'

Happily, funding was never a problem. Our total budget for 1964/65 was £203,000, of which the Donald Healey race programme took £25,000. At that time Paddy Hopkirk was our best-paid driver, at £5,000 a year, Rauno Aaltonen was on £4,000 and Timo £3,000 (so no flats or yachts in Monte Carlo there). No co-driver earned more than £400 per rally. Not huge amounts but healthy enough in those innocent days. The sums didn't necessarily represent our views of their skills, by the way – they were just the way the negotiations crumbled. No agents were involved – they hadn't been invented. (What *is* the collective noun I wonder – an irritation of agents perhaps?)

The Competitions Committee occasionally found time to consider minor but sometimes politically sensitive items, like my request to convert Austin Westminster saloons into estate cars for service use. This was refused because George Harriman was not in favour of the use of conversions by outside firms. Instead, I got a prototype Vanden Plas Princess R estate car. It must have been an impressive machine because on one Liège a policeman caught sight of us stuck in a traffic jam in Belgrade, thought it was a diplomatic car and swept us to the front – I drove through the city sandwiched between Nasser and Makarios on their way to a conference.

For 1965, by the way, the arrival of Hydrolastic suspension on the production Minis meant that we were obliged to try it for our works cars. At first we regarded Hydrolastic as a great wonder invention because the Longbridge engineers told us it was, although we hadn't tested any prototypes. Our initial reaction was to try to make it work on rallies, but back-to-back testing showed that it wasn't as good as the 'dry' cars had been. For racing purposes John Cooper and Ralph Broad (at Broadspeed) soon found ways to stop the fluid transferring from one end of the car to the other (nothing quite so crude as bunging up the connections, but you know what I mean), but as the official rally team we were reluctant to try anything like that.

Most of the well-used 'leaping' shots of Minis were taken near Rhayader where we spent days with Rauno in particular testing Hydrolastic cars near Strata Florida. We even took MG1100s along, hoping – forlornly – to turn them into rally winners. Eventually we resorted to carrying blocks of wood to jam in place to keep the cars mobile if the units failed. Tales mellow over the years (as indeed they should) but it is only marginally accurate to claim that British oak gave the best handling.

In the end we reverted to rubber on many events and, to their credit, there was no flak from the sales department about this. Historians have shown that some cars ran with 'wet', then 'dry', then 'wet' suspension again if, that is, you believed the registration numbers that were fixed to the cars. (Numbers were often switched to match customs documents; we inadvertently did one rally with an Austin badge on the front and a Morris badge on the rear of one Mini.)

1965 started well with a phenomenal victory by Timo Makinen in a Mini Cooper in the Monte Carlo rally. Paul Easter, who sat beside him (lucky devil), having taken over the seat from Don Barrow, later analysed his times and realised that Timo had not just won, he had absolutely murdered everyone else in the event. (Paul had actually begun in motorsport as a driver but told me recently that this was the event that made him realise his own limits.)

I contend that it was possibly the rally drive of the century. Only 35 cars even made it to Monte Carlo through blizzards. The weather was awful and before long Timo, ploughing through virgin snow, was arriving at the controls to find everyone sheltering in their cars, or in nearby cafés.

I phoned Bill Price from my base in Monte Carlo and asked him to take the transporter from Gap to Castellane to collect tyres with 'chisels' – vicious studs like triangular chisels sticking out of the treads. When he got back and went for a meal at 6pm, it was raining. By 10pm there was 4 inches of snow and they were nearly knee-deep by the time the rally cars arrived.

Timo's stage times on arrival in Monte totalled 112min 11sec. Bianchi was lying second with 2 road penalties and 120min 34sec of stage times and Bohringer was third in a Porsche with 4 road penalties and a stage total of 127min 40sec. Paddy Hopkirk was actually second fastest on the stages, on 117min 51sec, but he'd dropped 34 minutes on the road so was well down. As an indication of Timo's speed, only 10 cars got within *5 minutes* of him on the first two stages!

Our ice-notes expertise was irrelevant – all the route was under heavy, drifting snow. Despite having number 52, Timo was running first 'on the road' most of the time; this can often be a handicap but in fact he was the *only* driver to be unpenalised on the road sections.

Throughout the last night, during the Mountain Circuit, I kept trying to slow Timo down but, as Paul Easter will confirm, that was never easy; perhaps rightly, many rally drivers believe you are less at risk of going off if you are pushing on and concentrating. Anyway, he was fastest on all but one of the six stages, and pulled out another 4min 28sec on the Porsche. Neyret's Citroen, which had been lying fifth, dropped five places; perhaps that was one reason why we were to be given a hard time on the 1966 Monte.

Partly because of such success, Abingdon had a high profile and we – Bill Price, Doug Watts and I – were being inundated with requests for technical information, to build replica cars for sale, and to supply parts for private owners' cars.

The drivers and I were also doing quite a few forums for motor clubs. We had toy cap-guns and when I asked a questioner to stand (perhaps because he'd asked something provocative), it was a cue for the panel to fire at him. That always got a laugh but I wouldn't risk it today.

At one of the forums, a man came up and politely said that I should give his son a try because he was quick. I made the usual non-committal soothing noises . . . and didn't meet Roger Clark's father again until I joined Ford.

Perhaps because of my own motor club background I've always felt that motor clubs and private owners are vital to our sport and I tried to help as much as possible. But it was starting to get in the way of our prime task of winning major events, so after talking it over with John Thornley, we decided to set up the Special Tuning department. I certainly didn't invent the idea, but I thoroughly approved of it. First of all there was a small operation in a corner of the MG Service Department, but Basil Wales then took over in 1965 with a brief to expand.

Once established, it not only took the pressure off the 'Comps' department, but it also started making money for BMC. If nothing else, it made my pleas for high spending on motorsport easier to justify.

By the end of the year, I guess, you could say that the Mini was close to its peak. Even half-way through the year BMC was able to run an ad claiming 65 successes in 1965, and significant ones at that. Through a bit of judicious juggling of entries and cars, we found enough events for Rauno Aaltonen to become European Rally Champion. To do this we had to go behind what was then the Iron Curtain for a few events and this led to an incident that, looking back, I believe maybe illustrated that the writing was on the BMC wall.

I went to Longbridge (the 'Kremlin') to see the export sales chief to tell him that to score championship points we had to go to either Czechoslovakia, Poland or Hungary, where BMC didn't sell Minis – had he any preference? It was a constructive meeting and near the end, having decided where to go, I mentioned that we would perhaps use Austin 1800s, the Land Crab, on one or two events. His immediate reaction was to ask if I could get Alec Issigonis to re-position the handbrake, which at the time needed a strong man on steroids to operate. As it happened, I could see Alec over the way in his own office, so I pointed at him and said, 'Why don't you ask him?' The reply was that Alec wouldn't listen to sales people! It's all very well having a talented designer, a genius, but you still have to pay heed to your customers. The beginning of the end?

Alec was always helpful to motorsport, perhaps because of his own background in it, and I sometimes sat in his office as he summoned various people on his squawk box and told them of things to do to help us. It was only afterwards that I found they were some of his senior engineers. His number two on the Mini, Jack Daniels, was a key person in keeping things on the rails and always helpful to Competitions.

Alec was a hugely 'theatrical' man and had an innate sense of PR and promotion. I dined with him on several occasions when journalists asked him how he'd had the idea for the Mini – Alec would then sketch on the back of the menu to illustrate the process ('it was like this, dear boy') and a majority of the journalists would then ask for the drawing to be autographed. But he didn't please everyone and I remember that Abingdon needed stress counselling when Alec produced a prototype green front-wheel-drive Midget based on a Mini. I think they burned effigies of him that week.

Anyway, Rauno then went on to win the RAC Rally in a Mini – another event with blizzards – with Timo's Healey close behind. As always, studded tyres were banned on the RAC but everything else was allowed, so when the Healey desperately needed grip in Yorkshire I even sent mechanics into York, Ripon and Thirsk to buy up dog leads and choke chains to see if we could improvise something with them.

The 'Finnish War' between Timo and Rauno was certainly producing results at this time and I, for one, did nothing to discourage it – having drivers trying to beat each other in the same team can lift everyone's performance. Truly great drivers have to be self-focused and juggling some of the egos (including mine I suppose) was challenging at times, but Abingdon did what it could to create a happy 'team' atmosphere. The task for a team manager is to keep any rivalry *constructive* not *destructive*. Fortunately I never had the prattish inter-team behaviour you sometimes see in Formula 1 nowadays.

We developed very strong bonds with Castrol, not only for supplying lubricants, but because of the way they helped us gain publicity for our efforts. In some cases, too, they part-financed driver fees for certain programmes. As an example of Castrol's marketing support, from January to June in one year they spent £62,000 on ads in national newspapers, £5,992 in magazines and £36,710 on 30-second spots on all ITV networks at peak times – all to promote a Monte win. That made them heavy hitters and good people to work with.

I also enjoyed our dealings with Dunlop and in particular their rally king, David Hiam. We gave Dunlop a hard time because feeding up to 100bhp through tiny front tyres was almost Mission Impossible. That, plus our use of racing tyres on tarmac rallies, and our constant nagging for better studded-tyre performance in the winter, must have driven David to despair. However, he was not fazed because he was a real enthusiast who was totally straight in his dealings and a mean driver in his own right, as I knew from navigating him to a couple of wins on British events in his Mini (16 BOJ).

Even though we weren't paying them a fortune, we never seemed to have any trouble holding on to the world's best drivers; although other team managers were approaching Paddy, Rauno and Timo, they were very loyal. A real compliment came at the end of the year when Rauno said he would only sign a new contract if I guaranteed that I would be at Abingdon for the following season. At one point, when BMC's chairman, Sir George Harriman, heard that Ford had tried to poach Paddy, he was so irritated that he promised to discuss the matter with Ford's chairman, Sir Patrick Hennessy, to 'try to secure that these approaches should be on ethical and business lines . . .'

Ethical motorsport! That seems like a contradiction in terms today.

As I mentioned earlier, other drivers like Tony Fall (who worked at Appleyards of Bradford at the time and was recommended to me by Marcus Chambers) came along at exactly the wrong time. If Timo, Rauno, Paddy and the Morleys hadn't already been with us, there would have been more opportunities for them. I tried to encourage newcomers with one-off deals, support for oddball events, and by steering them towards a class win that we fancied. Sir Peter Moon appeared in Minis from time to time – a genial character who was to provide much innocent pleasure over 30 years later when his wife started altering his suits and freely distributing his wine around their village.

Drivers of course are only human (are you going to tell Nigel Mansell or shall I?) and could sometimes be gently fooled. If a driver was getting neurotic about a particular item on his car, Doug Watts would sometimes slide under it, bang about with a few spanners, come out looking triumphant, and shout something like, 'I found the problem. Everything's fine now.' The drivers would be happy and would dash off even faster than before – not knowing that Doug had done nothing but rattle the spanners. Great psychologist was Doug.

I found later at Ford that their Walter Hayes had written that 'BMC's Competition Manager is authorised to spend whatever he thinks necessary'. Not quite, Walter. But there was enough to carry out a full programme although we had to keep changing our attack to try to satisfy everyone. Both our American and Australian importers wanted us to send drivers to their major events, we were urged to tackle the Safari in 1800s (but wisely, in my opinion, turned that down), and there were even suggestions that we should enter special Mini Mokes or Austin Gypsys for the French Rallye des Cimes. (I once drove a Moke from New York to Bridgehampton when we were racing MGs there. There should be medals for courageous feats like that.)

At the BMC Competitions Committee meeting in August 1965, John Thornley and I had to mildly thump the table about the specification of the 1275S Mini Cooper. Up to that time we'd been frustrated by sales' insistence that 'the road car should be flexible enough for the District Nurse to drive it' (lucky District Nurse), which meant that we never got quite the camshaft or gear ratios we wanted, or the car deserved.

For 1966, however, when we realised that the Mini Cooper S would have to become a Group 1 car – that is largely standard, even to the seats – we pulled out every possible stop. Although BMC genuinely built more than the necessary 5,000 cars during 1965, enough to make the Mini Cooper S genuinely 'Group 1 legal' (Ford were miles away from their target for the Lotus-Cortina, but got Group 1 homologation anyway), we made sure that one or two extra features went into the new homologation forms at the same time.

I then wrote to Alec Issigonis before the Monte, heading my memo 'Highly Confidential – read, then burn' to get his attention. I listed 12 items that we intended to use on the Group 1 cars. Seven were already in production, others were covered by the homologation, while only one, the latest drive-shaft couplings, had not yet been incorporated or covered. I pleaded with Alec to make them series production items immediately, and was confident that I could deal with the other items under homologation allowances.

For 1966 I wanted to be sure that every car had twin fuel tanks, an oil cooler and $4\frac{1}{2}$-inch wheel rims. That was easy enough, and Alec Issigonis also approved the inboard metal drive-shaft couplings that we had been using as 'export options' for some time, but I didn't get far with a request for $1\frac{1}{2}$-inch SUs, a camshaft change, a 4.1:1 final drive, Downton exhaust manifold and special seats! I blame that District Nurse.

All this, of course, was vital to us, as the 1966 Monte was to run to a strict 'showroom formula', which we knew would be ruthlessly policed and scrutinised. Because we were going for a straight hat-trick of wins for the Monte in 1966, we would be the centre of attention (I nearly wrote 'under the spotlight' which, in view of what happened, was not far out) and have to be on the ball as never before.

Nothing could be done about the seats in production so we had to fit slip-over covers for the Monte to give the crew some sort of support – Timo was so disgusted with his seat that for his long run-in from Lisbon to the special stages he unbolted it, and had a large, flat, padded plywood throne build up instead, where he could recline.

To keep us focused, I had minuted at the previous Competitions Committee meeting that 'We renew our annual plea that no one should give an undertaking to loan a car to Press, policemen, or other fellow travellers, who have little or no chance of winning, and yet would tend to clog our organisation on the ground . . .' I further pointed out that 'even the clergyman gimmick was losing its impact'. This was a reference to Rupert Jones, a genial parson who occasionally drove for us. When he took a fellow clergyman on one rally, we gave them a black Mini . . . with a white roof . . . with a sticker saying 'Heaven' at a time when it was the fashion to display ones saying 'Bognor Regis', etc. Forgive me, Lord, for I knew not what I did.

Did that plea work? Yes, because for 1966 we only loaned a Group 2 machine to Raymond Baxter of the BBC, not only an important broadcaster but an excellent driver. Raymond, an ex-RAF fighter pilot and a real gentleman, was also very astute.

As an example, practising for one Monte, we were experimenting with Triplex heated screens that used a gold film embedded in the glass. The regular drivers couldn't understand why they were always slower in one particular practice car than the others until Raymond spotted that it was the one using the gold-film screen that reduced visibility. So next time you peer safely through a windscreen with fine wires rather than gold film heating it, give just a passing nod to Raymond. Give him a more vigorous nod when you think of rallycross too, because he helped 'invent' it. After most outdoor events had been cancelled because of bad weather, in February 1963 the BRSCC and the London

Motor Club arranged a display at Brands Hatch by 16 Monte Carlo rally drivers. Raymond was there for the BBC, and the TV transmission, electrified by Makinen in a 3000, was well received. Thus was rallycross born. (I thought it very unkind of someone to say recently that the MENSA rallycross group had had to cancel its annual general meeting ... because someone else was using the phone box.)

I guess there really isn't anything new to be said about the 1966 Monte – the event where Timo, Rauno and Paddy finished first, second and third on the road, only to be disqualified on a trumped-up technicality. The operation of the headlamps, the organisers said, was illegal, and they wouldn't be persuaded otherwise. The fact that Citroen, which was awarded the victory, was running white headlamps, illegal according to French and Monegasque law, must have escaped them ...

We should have seen what was coming – in fact some of us *did* see it. The organisers imposed a 'Group 1' requirement, hoping that our car, and the Lotus-Cortina, couldn't qualify. On their recces there was a feeling among the drivers that they were marked men, and certainly Wilson McComb (BMC's Competition Press Officer) discovered this the moment he walked into Monaco. They were told the same story: 'You cannot win this year, it is all decided. This year a French car will win, a Citroen, it is arranged ...'

This was a year that having good 'ice notes' alerting drivers to snow and ice on the stages paid off in quick times although they may have contributed to our scrutineering problems later. I was doing ice notes for some of the stages with Donald Morley and at Mont Ventoux – a truly classic hill-climb – we found that the bends on the upper reaches were snow-covered. But when we realised that it was only powdery snow, we waited until rival ice note crews had gone, then, just before the roads were closed, we took the floor mats out of our Austin A110 service car and used them to sweep the snow from the key corners. Partly as a result, the Minis were a lot quicker than our rivals expected, not just because they were the only ones on racing tyres, but because they had the confidence to go powering into corners, knowing that there would be no snow round them.

Road sweeping. And I bet you thought team management was glamorous. But the degree of effort indicates just how focused we were on winning. At one time we actually got recce crews to leave garden thermometers outside at night on stages so that we could log what the temperature had dropped to over several nights to help us decide tyre choices. Details count.

At this time, to make 'ice-noting' easier, I tried to impose common pace notes on all our crews so that we could locate particular corners in them quickly, but that didn't always work out. Perhaps just as well, because on one Alpine Rally an instruction that said 'medium left and how' (meaning that it was quite tricky) was misread by another co-driver as 'medium left and house'. The crew were still looking for the house as they went off on the tricky medium bend.

Those were the days before motorsport became truly international; certainly there was more national pride then. I suspect that there was great irritation in France (and Monaco was very French, if you see what I mean) that these little red boxes with white roofs were coming over from Britain and winning 'their' event, and remember the outcome of the Monte Carlo rally was far more important in publicity terms in the 1960s than it is today. Market research carried out only 10 years ago showed even then that the general public only really knew or cared about three motoring events – Le Mans, the Indianapolis 500, and the Monte Carlo Rally. (Digression: little red boxes . . . but with white roofs. I had read when planning central heating for Penny Farthing that white reflected heat best and thought that would help the crews on hot events.)

Even before the event we – and that included Henry Taylor of Ford, too – were sufficiently worried about the implications of a Group 1 event, and about the nuances of the latest regulations, that we had flown to Paris to check up on things, so we must have picked up the vibes at an early stage.

But – and maybe I'm being naive – until it actually happened I was never really convinced that someone was out to get us. I assumed that everyone was prepared to be friendly at first because they thought that Group 1 Minis couldn't possibly be fast enough to win the event. It was only when they saw the stage times that things got difficult.

The organisers, and our major opponents, I feel, were genuinely astonished by the pace of the Minis where the stages were not covered with ice and snow. Citroen – well, maybe logic suggested that the Minis could always beat them – but surely not the works Lotus-Cortinas? If Group 2 Minis couldn't live with Group 2 Lotus-Cortinas on the race track (there was no contest, by that time), how could Group 1 cars be any different on a Monte?

I genuinely think that the organisers believed rumours that we had secretly been swopping cars along the way, so that the cars we rallied were not those we presented at post-event scrutineering! Ridiculous – it might have been done once or twice by rival teams in the past (I even heard of drivers being swopped over on the Spa-Sofia-Liège Marathon, incidentally), but I wouldn't have been clever enough to work out how, or where, to do it. See the damage the road sweeping probably did?

The post-event scrutineering, strip-down and argument went on for around eight hours in all, so that the organisers could find something, anything, as grounds to disqualify us. In *Autocar*'s rally report I was quoted as saying, 'Yes, I've been to bed, but I couldn't get to sleep. I kept dreaming they were stripping the cars right down to the filaments in the turn-indicator bulbs.'

In the end they chose the operation of the lights – the Minis were using single-filament quartz-halogen bulbs, which only worked on main beam, so when they dipped those lights went out, and only the driving lamps remained – which, according to the Monegasques, was against Appendix J regulations.

The fact that we then offered the respected independent French driver Alain Bertaut the chance to try our 'winning' car up the nearby La Turbie hill-climb, to prove that it was no faster than standard (and even borrowed a new Mini Cooper S from a local showroom for comparison, *which was quicker*) didn't make any difference. Even though we went through every possible protest procedure, and had a bi-lingual barrister to help us, we never got anywhere.

In marketing terms, the disqualification worked wonders for us. In a way the Lighting Fiasco only underlined the Mini's successes in 1964 and 1965, and made us all the more determined to come back and do it again in 1967! Incidentally, everyone at BMC was always behind us, and no one, from Harriman downwards, ever accused us of cheating. No one suggested that we had over-stepped the mark, wasted BMC's money, or acted in an underhand way – which we hadn't.

The sales department, I know, sat back and basked in all the attention this brought to the Mini, although BMC's Sales Director, Lester Suffield, said something like, 'The team is getting a bit over-excited about this, but when the boys calm down it'll all be forgotten in a few days . . .' The fact is that it has never been forgotten. I was introduced to my table guests when speaking at a conference while this book was heading for the press and before we'd finished the soup someone asked if I was at BMC 'when all that lighting business happened'.

The team picked itself up and the Minis scored eight more outright victories in 1966. Organisers were happy to see us because the Monte publicity had lifted the interest in rallying. Only once did we enter troubled waters again – on the Acropolis, which we didn't win. Paddy Hopkirk's 1275S was fastest of all on the rocky stages, and was originally posted as the winner. Then, just 4 minutes before the 'protest period' was over, his victory was queried on the grounds that he had been serviced inside a control area. Against all the evidence and logic (the particular control area was badly marked, and any number of competitors, though not the Fords, were also affected) the protest was upheld, Paddy was docked enough penalty points to drop him to third place, and Bengt Soderstrom's Lotus-Cortina was handed victory.

A year later, after I'd moved on, Peter Browning must have taken particular pleasure in guiding Paddy's Mini Cooper S to victory in the next Acropolis . . .

By the mid-1960s, running the Minis and the MGBs had become such a well-developed process that I had time to think about other things. For instance, I wrote a long note to John Thornley suggesting 25 ways of getting more publicity for the cars and our team (a lot of the suggestions still apply today); I even got involved in some medical research whereby our drivers were wired up before a rally and had their heartbeats monitored during the event to see how much stress was involved. And we contacted the RAF – they seemed totally underwhelmed by the two years gallant National Service I'd given them earlier – to see if their ground-to-air communications could help improve the clarity of our pace notes. No joy: they felt they could learn from rallying instead. (Intriguing to observe that many of the pace note symbols developed then in endless discussions with people like Tony Ambrose and Henry Liddon are still in use today.)

Almost subconsciously, by mid-1966 I had started to realise that I might not want to be BMC's Competitions Manager for much longer, and I had developed a distinct leaning towards publicity and public relations; maybe years spent in theatres were coming out once again. The problem was, as I once told the *Oxford Mail*, that my job was 'The most glamorous dead end job in the world'.

Maybe it was selfish, although I didn't see it that way at the time, but in a way I think I was looking ahead to a time when the Mini wouldn't be a winner any more, and the fact that BMC didn't seem to have a successor coming along to take its place.

Because BMC had merged with Jaguar-Daimler by this time, there was talk of light-alloy-engined MGCs, and Daimler or Coventry-Climax V8 engines being fitted to MGCs, but this came to nothing, and in any case the MGC would not be homologated until 1968. Instead we were asked to put more emphasis on the Austin 1800, which was never going to be more than a good 'class' car. If that.

All the nagging that John Thornley and I had done about the Ford (and later the Porsche) threat was ignored and BMC was not prepared, it seemed, to invest in a 'rally special' such as the Escort would become.

For 1967, in any case, Abingdon was having to cut back on its rallying, for BMH (the new amalgam of BMC and Jaguar) was fighting a sales recession. At the annual Competitions Committee meeting, we suffered a 20 per cent budget cut, which meant that we had to cut down on entries, and to abandon rallying in Eastern Europe where there was little marketing potential to build on any successes.

Publicity-worthy events like the Safari and the Canadian Shell 4000 were also ignored because of cost (although in the end Rauno Aaltonen won himself a free Safari entry, so we changed our mind there). Le Mans was considered out of the question because of the huge performance differential between the Midgets and the 7-litre Fords, although we decided to take cars to the Targa Florio. I had the thrill of being driven round the course by Paul Hawkins; it was the year Carroll Shelby was there with Cobras, which after the event seemed to be spread evenly round the course – as retirements.

But our programme became a bit scissors-and-paste and as I'd completed five high-pressure years in the same job, I was beginning to greet each new season and each new event as routine, and familiar, and I was ripe for a change. Perhaps for the first time in my life I began to wonder where my career ought to be going. I was 33 and I knew – or thought I knew – that I didn't want to be in the same job by the time I was 40.

In 1966, by the way, I'd also prepared to become a father, for my eldest daughter Nicola would be born in December. All the old clichés about family responsibilities come to mind; I wanted to spend less time away from home. During 1966 BMC had entered works cars for 25 races and rallies. All but five had been overseas, and I had attended almost every one. And you didn't even get Air Miles in those days ...

Because of the publicity that BMC's motorsport team had attracted, and certainly because of all the interviews I had given, I suspect that I started to get big-headed about working with the media. Brian Turner (no relation, so no nepotism) was about to retire, so I knew that the publicity manager's job at Longbridge would soon be on the market and I thought that would make a suitable move.

But my friend Raymond Baxter got the job instead, actually as Director of Motoring Publicity, working from London. I was not bitter about that but I was still determined to make a change. I was ready to walk away from what other people still saw as one of the most glamorous jobs in motorsport, and was ready to say I'd climbed my last Alp.

Mind you, I knew that it wouldn't be easy to leave the great bunch at MG. A small example of the Abingdon spirit: one of the mechanics, Robin Vokins, had been asked to do a last-minute check of a few bends on a Monte stage. When he arrived to find the road closed to cars, he *ran* up the hill shedding clothes as he heated up with the exercise. I think the French called it English eccentricity. I'd call it a will to win.

This was the first time I'd ever thought of leaving BMC, and I'd had no approaches from other companies. Perhaps I was seen as a fixture? However, at one Motor Show Ford's Walter Hayes grabbed me and introduced me to Stan Gillen, Ford UK's Chairman, saying, 'This is the bloke who gives us all the trouble in rallies with the Minis ...'

Later, Walter suggested that he would like to talk to me about a future with Ford. Nothing concrete was discussed at that point but the implied offer was enough for Margaret and me to go and look at Essex. We didn't like it very much, not compared with the delights of Berkshire anyway (yes, I know Abingdon is now in Oxfordshire but I can't help it if politicians keep redrawing boundaries), so the discussions came to a halt. I have to say that I also felt it would be 'unsporting' to leave Abingdon to move straight to our biggest rival. Naive? Didn't seem so at the time. Maybe they were just more gentlemanly days.

Castrol then made an approach. Would I, they wanted to know, be interested in joining them as Deputy Publicity Manager, with a view to taking over later as Manager?

After some weeks of talking – during which Lester Suffield phoned to ask what equity I had in my house and to explore if finance was an issue – and of course discussing it with John Thornley, I accepted. It was all very amicable, and because I was proposing to move to friends, rather than rivals, there was never any unease.

As far as I know, Peter Browning, who was officially only the secretary of the Austin-Healey Club, but who was my right-hand man where racing events were concerned, was the only person seriously considered as my replacement. Although Bill Price might have felt disappointed to be passed over at the time, I'm sure he soon realised that he had different strengths to offer. It wasn't until I shared the stage with Marcus Chambers and Peter Browning at a forum at the National Motor Museum in 1999 that I fully appreciated what horrors were to face Peter under the Donald Stokes regime. I hadn't realised that my exit timing had been quite so good!

BMC made the announcement to the press that I was leaving in January 1967 and one of the first letters I got was from Raymond Baxter to say, 'You will know how disappointed I was when Lester Suffield phoned me the news of your decision on Monday evening . . . Who knows? You may be back yet!'

After that Peter and I worked together for a very short time. Our first task was to get into the delights of working out the service and tyre plan for the 1967 Monte.

Even after the dramas of 1966, the Monte Carlo Rally organisers had still not learned to keep it simple and for 1967 had a category with a 12 per cent time advantage provided drivers used only eight pre-chosen and branded tyres on each leg. As the Minis were known to be particularly hard on tyres (especially when there wasn't much snow), whereas cars with larger wheels fared better, this looked like another poorly disguised attempt to stop them from winning.

Half an hour after the Monte regulations arrived in Finland, Makinen was on the phone to ask if we could break a Dunlop contract and use Pirelli banded tyres, which had special covers in which the bands of the treads could actually be changed. Lateral thinking it's called today, but it indicates how determined the drivers were for the Mini to win in 1967.

I'm as proud of BMC's 1967 Monte victory as of any other event we won. I must be, because it's the only one for which I have preserved the pre-event 'Bible', the movement schedule and service plan.

We actually started thinking about the event in September, began testing various tyre combinations in October, entered five cars in November, and started recce-ing in December. Incidentally, even though the organisers were proposing to limit tyre usage, Dunlop actually provided 420 covers of seven different types! In the initial plan, it actually started out as 572 tyres of nine types.

Before the convoy was ready to leave Abingdon in January 1967, 38 people and 18 vehicles were involved, of which seven were recce Minis, some of which had broken down, and were dotted all round the French Alps!

I tried to stop the tension getting too much as the event approached, so my team instructions included such items as:

'If T. Fall stays at the George Hotel, Dorchester, on his way to Dover, will he please refrain from smothering his steaks in HP sauce – we have had complaints from the chef.'

'Service crews must remember that the rally does not really start until Monte; save any late-night revelry until the Mountain Circuit is over'.

'Don't weight your rally car down with junk. All service crews will eventually go to Monte, so swimming togs and surplus sweeties can safely be given to them.'

Those, however, were only three out of 36 points, of which this was perhaps more helpful:

'According to medical evidence, it takes time for your eyes to re-adjust after being in bright light. At controls where there are photographers and TV cameras etc, it may help to wear sunglasses. It's worth looking a birkinshaw at a control if you are quicker on a subsequent test.'

We also thought we had covered everything:

'The armchair passenger' seat weighs 41lbs. A standard Mini seat with a cover (as used last year) weighs only 18lbs. Five of these will be taken to Monte in the van to be fitted when you arrive.'

Incidentally, I was obviously under pressure from the accountants because of currency regulations in those days:

'There has been some difficulty in getting currency for such a large party. Therefore, in case there are investigations later, mechanics must note that expense accounts will be under particular scrutiny, especially regarding hotels, petrol, etc'

It was one of the events where we gambled, and won. Five cars started, all five finished, with three in the top ten. Although Vic Elford's Porsche 911 led for much of the way, he lost ground on the

Mountain Circuit when it started to snow, and in the end Rauno Aaltonen's 1275S eventually won by just 13 seconds.

Rauno instead of Timo? Well, it was his turn and in any case as Timo and Paul came round a blind corner a rock fell in front of them. Timo avoided it but it then bounced back from the wall and hit the car.

Three times (or really four) in four years. Truly, the Full Monte. Alec Issigonis flew down to join in the fun, and this time round we needed a bigger plane than ever to rush the cars back to London – a CL44 Carvair instead of a Bristol Freighter. It was the perfect way for me to sign off.

Just before I moved out at the end of March 1967, as an indulgence BMC let me go to see Rauno competing in the Safari in a 1275S – which was a real do-or-die effort if ever I saw one; there were Safari pot-holes in Kenya big enough to swallow a Mini.

The event nearly brought my career to a more permanent close because of a crash during servicing. I was in the front passenger seat of an A55 with two local helpers. The one in the back asked if I'd put my seat belt on because it was a full harness and was cluttering his footwell. I'm glad I did because only a few miles later the vehicle we were following swerved, the dust blinded our driver and we barrel-rolled along Kenya; the driver was actually thrown out past me. We were all a bit shaken and way out in the wilds but, in one of those magical moments that Africa seems to throw up, we saw a sign reading 'hospital'. We staggered to it and, to treat a cut, I had my head shaved with a Blue Gillette blade by hurricane lamp (this was during the time that the Mau Mau were active) and then, as it was a small hospital, we spent the night at one end of the maternity ward.

I suspect that the strange ointment they put on my wound was a local concoction using wild animal blood because ever since then, whenever there is a prolonged dry spell, I feel a restless urge to migrate across Salisbury Plain.

I left Abingdon in March 1967 and put my new Castrol hat on. I was quite convinced that I had got motorsport out of my system. What is that Biblical quotation – '. . . when I became a man, I put away childish things'.

I thought that's what I was doing at the time.

Chapter 8

Castrol – an interlude

CASTROL WERE CLOSE partners of the works team at Abingdon and I had several friends there so I was interested when I got an approach to work for the company.

They were very diplomatic. They were major suppliers to BMC and because of this they were careful to do the right thing when I was negotiating with them. Quite sensibly they didn't want to upset the mighty British Motor Corporation, which was a heck of a lot more important to Castrol than I was. They waited until the end of the 1966 motorsport season before we agreed that I would join them as Deputy Publicity Manager, with the promise that I would be moving up in a few months time. The salary was to be £3,000 a year – a significant increase for me, but 'running costs' would be higher than at Abingdon, not least because I'd have to return to the *Motoring News* days of commuting into London.

Although things turned out rather differently, I looked on this at the time as a long-term career move into mainstream business life; I would have absolutely no responsibility for motorsport matters so, although I saw the motorsport people, Jimmy Hill and Ray and Jimmy Simpson, regularly at Castrol House, I had no influence on what they were doing.

To move to Castrol and a 'conventional' business life was a culture shock and the shock started before I even got there because I got a letter saying I was to go on a computer course. Although I wasn't totally convinced about computers – only a minority in those days believed that they would ever become as all-pervasive as they have – the letter didn't shock me, but the thick computer magazine with it certainly did because I couldn't understand a word beyond page 2. As a result I arrived on the course petrified that Castrol's new recruit was going to be revealed as a total ass. Happily for me, I found everyone else in the same state.

Not everyone left the course converted to the computer cause but full marks to Castrol who were ahead of their competition in looking towards computers for stock control, invoicing, planning tanker routes – all the things taken for granted today.

When, finally, I reported to Castrol House I got another shock, this time a more pleasant one. I was given the address of Dorland Advertising, Castrol's agents, and told to go and spend six months with them 'to learn the advertising business'. I got there to find that the executive handling the Castrol account, which was a big one in the world of advertising, was David Roscoe, a motor racing enthusiast (who went on to great things with Rolls-Royce and later Vickers). I am certain that David needed me foisted on him like he needed a hole in the crankcase, but he was cheerfully laid back about it and was an enormous help to me; I had a totally absorbing few months with him and his colleague David Sparks. I did no actual work but spent the time in various departments looking at copywriting, design, pack testing, market research, media buying and, perhaps most important of all, something of how the relationship works between advertising agents and clients.

My spell at *Motoring News* was the perfect introduction to journalism, and those six months with Dorland were an equally effective indoctrination into advertising.

After this elderly Youth Training Scheme, I moved into Castrol House, now as Publicity Manager, and had to stand on my own at the time when we were about to launch Castrol GTX, a major new product. This gave me a steep but exciting learning curve to climb and it was a heady day when I presented the publicity plans for the new oil to the field force. Concerns about drink driving were coming into the news and I remember that an ad about low consumption with the new oil, headed 'Stop your car drinking while you drive', got the most applause.

Before I arrived I don't think I'd realised what a responsibility it would be to launch GTX oil, by Castrol's standards a new 'wonder product', well ahead of anything they had previously produced. Fortunately, David Roscoe and Bill Fulton (Castrol Marketing) were both safe pairs of hands and supportive, so my obvious inexperience was hidden from the outside world. Bill had come in from the soap powder world and brought a breath of fresh and modern air into Castrol; he made some of the more traditional sales people mutter when, for instance, he suggested, quite sensibly, that sending a lorry halfway up a remote hill in Cornwall once a year to deliver just one gallon of oil was not really an economic use of resources.

That was the time when there were agonised debates about whether oil should be sold in, horror of horrors, places like Woolworths and supermarkets. Nowadays, when you can buy everything from coal to contraceptives at filling stations, you wonder what all the fuss was about. Trading in the 1960s was a touch more compartmentalised than it is today.

My areas of responsibility included a distribution department of close to 40 people based at Cowley near Uxbridge, led by the indefatigable Fred Dixon and geared to support the sales and marketing people with literature and special offers. These included lubrication charts for virtually every make; cars were simpler than today and more people did their own servicing.

Cowley also sent out 300,000 or so Castrol Achievements Books every year and to my joy I found that some time earlier they had sent out 'novelty letters'. One with two pins stuck to it carried the message 'For two pins you should do this or that', while another with a razor blade taped to it urged 'Don't cut it too fine to change your anti-freeze'.

We sent a monthly bulletin to the field force and I couldn't resist sending up those letters whenever Fred Dixon came across some oddball item from some long forgotten mail shot – at one point he unearthed yards and yards of lighter wick, presumably from a campaign saying 'Does life get on your wick?' It taught me an important lesson, that humour can be a useful business tool because taking the mickey out of ourselves broke down any 'them and us' between publicity and sales, and between the field force and head office. It helped too that I'd spent time out in the field with sales and service people during my spell at Dorlands.

Fred Dixon's department was responsible for an innovation of mine that made me less than popular with them. This was the movement around the country of a wooden starting ramp for any rallies supported by Castrol. It was one of, if not the, very first and we were groping over design and therefore erred on the side of safety in its construction. I won't say it was big but, well, if the Government had accepted our offer to donate it to them, it might have formed the basis of a Channel bridge and saved all those chaps with buckets and spades digging the Tunnel. As it was, it probably kept the home fires burning for someone for a very long time.

Domestically, moving to Castrol meant yet another house move and by this time friends were complaining that we were filling up their address books. Margaret and I found a plot of land at Shiplake, near to Henley-on-Thames and (most important) close to a railway station. Using the same architect we built another 'Penny Farthing', an evolution of the 'Mk 1' near Abingdon.

We lived in a caravan on the site while the house was being built. But living in a caravan, on a building plot, wasn't considered quite the thing in the Henley-on-Thames area and we detected a mild sniff of disapproval among the neighbours. Solution? David Roscoe arranged for me to borrow a factory Rolls-Royce; we parked that outside the caravan for a weekend and had no more problems. After motorsport, this was the period of some stability as I became the archetypal commuter with the same corner seat, on the same train, every morning.

My BMC background still paid off at times. When Castrol were pitching against Shell for lubrication bay business with BMC dealers, I was asked to give the slide presentation to them, and naturally the introduction highlighted the BMC-Castrol link over the rally successes.

At this time Castrol was increasingly worried by the growth of Duckhams, then an independent oil company. We saw regular market research figures that showed Castrol with a healthy lead in oil sales; there was a figure for 'others', which usually ran at around 7 per cent. Then it was discovered that most of this 7 per cent was Duckhams. The reason was simple: if you ran a notorious oil-burner like the Mini on Duckhams, you got twice as many miles to the pint as with other oils.

The field force was telling us this, as were people in motorsport, but the boffins at the research centre in Bracknell took longer to get the message. To try to speed things up, I arranged a test using Minis and 1800s in which we compared Duckhams and Castrol consumption. Our test route went via the M4 to Maidenhead and Henley and the drivers were from Castrol's advertising, competition and marketing departments – they volunteered willingly because all those without their noses in test tubes were worried about the Duckhams threat. We used one of our Agricultural Show display units as a base; fortunately this had a kitchen, which kept up a constant supply of sausage sandwiches.

The test was totally unscientific but the figures were so startlingly in favour of Duckhams that I like to think the project acted as a useful prod.

Although GTX was going to do wonderful things for our image (but at a premium price), we knew that we had to hit back against Duckhams. I argued for the use of motorsport, maintaining that a member of a motor club was likely to be seen as an 'expert' by his friends and that we should target the clubs because word of mouth would help sell the product.

Fortunately, Roger Willis was at Castrol at the time; anyone who knew him will still wax lyrical about what a genial, loveable character he was – a great enthusiast and a great Castrol man. Between us we thought up a free service for motor club editors, of a couple of features every month for their magazines, and we had Castrol stickers done with motor club names overprinted. We tried to get Castrol stickers everywhere. That infamous organisation, Ecurie Cod Fillet, happened to have a members' get-together around this time, and when the exotic dancer they had hired revealed her 'all' it provoked ribald comments from the audience because her 'all' was covered by, you've guessed, a

Castrol sticker. John Hopwood, the driving force behind Cod Fillet, reminds me that the lady in question had her sister with her, as well as a minder – a big lad with tattoos and a leather coat but who, to his credit, drove a Bristol 401 (if he can remember things like that, it really is time John got out more).

During this period we also built up Castrol roadshows based on earlier ones at BMC where contracted race and rally drivers attended events round the country, sitting in on forums, and taking questions from a well-fuelled audience.

Although they were under a Public Relations budget, I was consulted over the subjects suitable for the annual Castrol films that motor clubs found useful. With so much motorsport on TV nowadays (at times even *too* much, I venture to suggest) it's difficult to appreciate that Castrol and Shell motorsport films were once so important. The BRSCC even held a Midnight Matinee of them in London – I remember how thrilled I was to be allowed to stay up so late (mind you, I was 34 at the time).

Not least, we launched a nationwide motor clubs quiz series: the Castrol-Guards Quiz (Guards being a popular-price cigarette at the time). It was based on TV's University Challenge and clubs were invited to enter teams to answer questions like 'Who won the RAC Rally in 1965?'

For the first series we were amazed to get entries from something like 420 clubs and Roger Willis and I spent a day sticking pins on a map of the UK to locate them all. We then divided up the country into regions, and invited well-known characters to be our regional chairmen. Because the series went on throughout the winter, eventually producing Regional Champions and finally a National Champion, it generated a useful amount of publicity. It also helped clubs to keep going when motorsport was banned because of an energy crisis.

Somehow, though, serious motorsport and I were not to be separated for long. Early in 1968 the first of the modern intercontinental rallies, the London-Sydney Marathon, was launched and I was approached by Jack Sears to join the organising committee.

The plot was very simple. Cars (of any type – Keith Schellenberg even entered a 1930 8-litre Bentley) first had to tackle a seven-day run to Bombay, without any official rest halts. Then, after a two-week break that included a nine-day sea voyage to Fremantle, in Australia, they had to complete a four-day dash across Australia to the finish at Warwick Farm race track, near Sydney.

Following the 'I'm Backing Britain' hysteria that had gripped the country at that time, and the gloom that followed currency devaluation in November 1967, this was a typical Empire-linking drum-beating exercise by the *Daily Express*, but it soon developed into a very serious event indeed. Although most of 1968 remained to get it organised, there was a lot of rushing round to do before the first car could leave Crystal Palace on 24 November.

Ford entered five Lotus-Cortinas, BMC prepared three 1800s, there were two Hillman Hunters from the Rootes Group, a couple of works-prepared Citroens, John Sprinzel in a self-prepared MG Midget, a team of Ford Australia Falcons, plus more than 80 private owners.

Fortunately, there was a very strong organising team, which included Jack Kemsley (of RAC Rally fame), Jocelyn Stevens, Jack Sears and Tommy Sopwith.

Even so, there was an element of string-and-sealing-wax about the control arrangements in the field. I ended up flying out, with a clock, some banners, control boards and a list of entries, first to Istanbul and then on to Kabul in Afghanistan; getting from one city to the other, even by air, wasn't easy.

Although those were the days before civil war hit Afghanistan, my visit to Kabul was frightening enough, purely because of the number of local people pressing around the control table on the massive parade ground before the cars arrived. Later, marshalling at the end of the Lataban Pass with a blanket over my head to keep off the sun and with only a camel for company, I felt, and probably looked, like Florence of Arabia.

From Afghanistan I had to fly down to Bombay. While the cars and drivers were on board the SS *Chusan* on an interminable sea trip to Australia, I went ahead to do a couple of TV programmes for BBC's *Wheelbase*. One was on a homestead in the Kalgoorlie area and I remember the owner casually mentioning that his nearest neighbour was '110 miles in that direction'.

I then moved on to the Flinders Ranges, to run another control, eventually getting to Sydney on 17 December to catch up on the sensations of the last two days, which included Roger Clark's Lotus-Cortina cooking its engine when well ahead, and Andrew Cowan's Hillman Hunter taking the lead, literally in the last 12 hours.

By that time, after more than three weeks away, I just wanted to get home. So did Jack Kemsley, but the only way that our travel agents could fly us back in a hurry was via New Zealand and North America. It was a joy to sit for hour after hour on aircraft, listening to Jack's wonderful reminiscences of rallies past – he had been involved in motorsport, in major international rallies, since the 1930s.

Around this time I did several other features for *Wheelbase*, and I always admired the work the producer, Brian Robins, did. He was a realist and sensed that if rallying was to reach a broad, as opposed to a purely enthusiast, audience the TV coverage had to feature more than just a car coming along a special stage ... then another ... then (yawn) another. As a result, the rally programmes he produced were part motorsport, part travelogue. But much as I enjoyed the work I never hankered after moving in to it full time – not that I was offered anything anyway.

There was, in any case, some concern within Castrol that the TV work I was doing might interfere with my duties in running a very substantial publicity budget. But Laurie Sultan (Castrol's hugely experienced PR man) pointed out to the Chairman that because my links with Castrol were well-known, any media exposure I got must be a good thing. The Chairman, Angus Barr, withdrew his objection.

My trip round the world on the London-Sydney Marathon re-kindled my love for motorsport so when I started getting calls from Walter Hayes at Ford early in 1969, asking me if I knew where my destiny *really* lay, I was more receptive to yet another move.

I don't think I short-changed my friends at Castrol, but after two years I knew that being involved in oil, and nothing other than oil, for the rest of my working life would be too boring. Viscosity indices and winter ratings were of all-consuming interest to many of my colleagues, but to my dismay I found that they really mattered very little to me. I suspect that the mysteries of oil went over most other people's heads too. When we organised motor club forums we used to put out questionnaires to discover what enthusiasts thought about various things, including oil, and when we asked 'What does the phrase 20-50 mean', to sound out if people knew about viscosity, more than one club member put 'The years during which a woman is at her best ...'

Walter Hayes, who missed little, must have sensed my boredom because he asked me to meet him at Ford's London office. Would I like to take over Ford's Competition Department?

Chapter 9

Ford Motorsport – marathons and RS1600s

WHEN GRAHAM ROBSON wrote *The Works Escorts*, he asked Walter Hayes about my move to Ford. Walter said, 'It was obvious how much he was enjoying officiating on the London-Sydney Marathon, so after the Burmah takeover I rang him again, asked him if he knew where his destiny lay'.

By this time, you'll realise, I had a great admiration for Walter Hayes: he had a magnificent way of getting things done and reaching his objectives and I was flattered by his approach. Our only formal meeting was at Ford's London HQ – a beautiful town house not far from the Ritz Hotel – where I was suitably impressed, even though it was 1 April! When it came to salary and I expressed mild disappointment over the figure proposed, Walter produced a pen, slashed through the sum in the appointment letter, and substituted another; I only realised later what havoc this elegant gesture probably caused when he revealed the impromptu amendment to the industrial relations people at Ford.

Until I talked to Walter I couldn't really see where I could fit in at Boreham because Henry Taylor was well set as Competitions Manager. However, Walter let me into his plans for Ford's Advanced Vehicle Operations (AVO); Henry, he told me, was to move to AVO, to work for Ray Horrocks, which left a gap at Boreham. He, Walter, was not planning an internal promotion – which explained the approach to me.

Simply, I was to take over a department at Boreham that I already knew not only by repute but because of Castrol's motorsport sponsorship of the team.

Because Castrol relied so much on Ford's patronage for their production car business, the Chief Executive, Eric Hughes, was very kind about my move (perhaps he was glad to get rid of me), there was no friction and it was agreed that I would move to Boreham in June 1969.

Margaret and I bought a cottage in the country near Marks Tey, then eventually found a house near Danbury where we lived for the next 20 years until after I retired from Ford. Our second daughter, Sarah, was born while we were at Danbury, and as it is in Essex she has asked me to make it quite clear that she has *never* at any time owned a white handbag.

As at BMC, the prospects were exciting, for I would be moving to manage a formidable team and there was every chance of things getting even better in the future.

To quote Walter's appointment letter, I would be '. . . in charge of all the company's [ie Ford of Britain's] direct racing and rallying with the single exception of Formula One, which is regarded as an International activity and is, therefore, my concern'.

There was no more formal brief, as such. If anything, it was to 'go out and win' in selected events that would bring the most publicity – Monte Carlo, Safari and RAC, for example. We had no clear commitment to a rallying World Championship, which got little publicity at that time.

The big advantage of a flexible approach like that was that we could react quickly to a one-off opportunity for good *local* publicity. This also worked better in advertising terms; it's all very well finishing second or third in a World Championship event, with great honour, but the brutal fact is that second is still the first loser.

I soon realised that things at Ford were going to be different from BMC because the first person I met when I arrived at Boreham was Brian Brackenbury, who told me he was the financial controller for the department. Financial controller? We didn't see many of those at Abingdon, although that may help explain why Ford is still around today, while BMC is long gone. The accountants had every justification for keeping a close check, for Ford was spending more on motorsport than BMC had ever done. By the late 1960s the budget was nearing £300,000 a year and this was before major spending on the Cosworth DFV F1 engine kicked in.

Ford's reporting structure was also different from that at BMC. There I had reported to the head of a manufacturing plant, but at Ford motorsport came under Public Affairs; our financial controller at Boreham reported to Harry Golden (Walter's finance man) who, thank goodness, was definitely on our side and a genius at juggling funds when necessary.

There was a historical precedent for this. Walter had always been the inspiration behind Ford's motorsport activities; towards the end of my spell at Ford the department was finally moved under Marketing, which by then made more sense as the use made of motorsport by manufacturers had changed over the years. The switch made things easier 'politically' too. Under Public Affairs motorsport was a huge percentage of their budget, whereas under Marketing it looked a relatively tiny operation.

However, despite a greater emphasis on financial control, in day-to-day terms I felt totally free because Boreham was stuck out on its own, east of Chelmsford, up to half an hour's drive from HQ at Warley, and not even Walter made many attempts to come out to see what I was doing; he left me alone to make almost every decision.

And Boreham had all the right vibrations. It had been built as a USAF airfield; the West Essex Car Club had used it for driving tests in 1949 and its opening speed event was held in 1950; Peter Ashcroft still recalls starting a 500cc race there in the 1950s, with a thrusting young man called Bernard Ecclestone right behind him. That left a lasting impression on Peter I think.

Some years later I was talking to John Surtees (still the only man to have become a motorcycle and car World Champion) and when I mentioned Boreham he proceeded to describe the layout of the track in accurate detail. It turned out that he did one of his first motorcycle races there back in 1951.

No sooner had I walked into Boreham than I realised mine was not necessarily a popular appointment. I was not, by any means, flavour of the month, because I had come – even if only after an interval – from the deadly rival organisation, BMC. Also, in every organisation there are people who think they should have been considered for the job, instead of it being offered to an outsider.

If ever there was an individual who might have sulked, it was Rally Manager Bill Barnett, who had brought order to the team when it was still at Lincoln Cars, in Brentford, and who had already proved to be an ideal 'Number Two' to Henry Taylor. I must say, though, that I always got unwavering and invaluable support from Bill. He was, in many ways, a completely unsung hero – in military terms he was almost the perfect adjutant. Like Bill Price at BMC, he was a superb details man, a workaholic, and clearly in love with his job, and the team.

However, Bill Meade and I got off to a bad start. Bill was not only the team's Rally Engineer at the time but had also been one of the real inspirations behind the birth of the Escort Twin Cam. In the early days we had one or two vigorous disagreements before a pecking order was established. Many years later Bill told a journalist that he soon knew when to stop arguing with me – when I took off my glasses, rubbed my eyes wearily, and started pursing my lips. A twitch in time perhaps?

Our opening spat was over the choice of drivers. Before I arrived, the two Bills – Meade and Barnett – had a great deal of influence over who would drive the cars, but I made it very clear that I was going to do that. Neither of them, I know, liked my idea of importing talent like Timo Makinen and Rauno Aaltonen from outside, and Bill Meade still recalls getting apoplectic when my idea of Tony Fall partnering footballer Jimmy Greaves in the World Cup rally was first mentioned. (Mind you, he has admitted since that their excellent sixth place justified the pairing.)

One thing Bill and I firmly agreed on was that Jim Clark was a much better rally driver than Graham Hill! Graham had driven for me in a Mini Cooper on the 1966 RAC Rally and, failing to really get to grips with the car, had hated every minute of it. Jim, on the other hand, having started his motorsport career rallying a Sunbeam Talbot, revelled in the event and set competitive times until he crashed his Lotus-Cortina. Years later people at Boreham would reminisce about what a great bloke Jim was and how well he'd fitted into the team on that occasion.

There was no 'chief mechanic' as such but most of the workshop recognised Norman Masters as the senior man. Then, of course, there was Mick Jones, a great extrovert character and not only an accomplished mechanic and car builder but also a great 'front man' for our operations; he must surely be the only rally mechanic to have had a complete TV programme (on *Wheelbase*) made about him. When I was at BMC and arranging a fry-up at a service point, Mr Jones crept up, speared a steak with a screwdriver and ran off, so I already knew that he showed enterprise, if not culinary discernment.

Two BMC people came to Boreham at my invitation, 'Ginger' Devlin, who had been the engineer/team manager of the John Cooper racing team of Mini Coopers, and Robin Vokins, one of the well-known team of BMC mechanics. Robin settled so well that he stayed on for the rest of his career, going on to run the workshop at Boreham in the 1980s and 1990s, although 'Ginger' soon tired of being what he called a 'cross-country tinker' and went off to Devon.

As in my first year or so at BMC, I made several driver changes at Boreham. Ove Andersson, who had never had a lucky time with Escorts, left the team at the end of 1969. At the time I didn't think he had enough 'tiger' (Denis Jenkinson's apt word to describe what a driver needs to take charge of an event and make it his); I thought he was too nice a person to have the killer instinct. He then went on to win the Monte Carlo Rally and the Safari for other teams, which shows what a fine judge I was!

I gave Rosemary Smith a trial, and Jean François Piot with a young co-driver called Jean Todt (who went on to great things at Peugeot in the 1980s and Ferrari in the 1990s) came in to drive an Escort for Ford France who were always keen motorsport enthusiasts. Other Ford national sales companies were spurred by their example to use the sport as a PR and marketing tool, which helped later when we needed support for various new cars.

Hannu Mikkola had already been discovered by Bill Barnett and was quickly on board, although it took time to get Timo Makinen in the team (his first event was the Monte in 1970), but I thought it was vital to get one of the world's fastest drivers on our side, rather than competing against us.

Fat and successful books have already been published about Ford Motorsport's activities in those years, so I certainly don't intend to give a blow-by-blow account of who won what or who crashed where. Let's just say that everybody – drivers, Boreham staff, mechanics and supporters – seemed to enjoy themselves and that the Escort's record is still remembered with some affection to this day. Even while I was writing this book, I was delighted to attend the works Escort's 'retirement party' in November 1998. How many other occasions would have attracted seven World Rally Champions and all the rival rally team directors? *All* with an earlier Escort connection, either as driver or co-driver!

Less than a year after I arrived at Ford the 16-valve Escort RS1600 was launched with the new Cosworth BDA engine. Not everyone realises that in 1969 there was no concrete plan to mate that engine to the Escort; the first car fitted with the BDA was actually a Cortina. In early 1969 Bob Howe had discussions with Walter Hayes and Keith Duckworth about installing the BDA into the Twin Cam so that the Lotus engine could be dumped. Keith went to Warley with a Cortina into which he had installed the first BDA and left it for a couple of weeks trial. It ran on 2-star petrol, was remarkably flexible and made the Cortina a much more pleasant car to drive. It came at about the same time as Bob Howe had started to search for a suitable site for AVO, having been told that under no circumstances was the Twin Cam replacement to be engineered or built by mainstream.

I didn't really know much about Cosworth at that time, or about its founding genius, Keith Duckworth. However, in one of life's more interesting experiences, almost as soon as I got to Ford rallying enthusiast Graham Robson called me from his home in Warwickshire, suggesting that there was someone I really ought to know, and that was how Keith and I met, over the Robson dinner table. This was the evening when he began to do a selling job on me, on the BDA engine, how Ford was being half-hearted about it, and didn't I think it ought to be used in the Escort?

I don't think Graham set out to be an agent in all this, but there's no doubt that this was a very important evening for me. Before then, I'd heard of Keith, and laughed at all the tall stories that surrounded him. If you ask an ordinary man a question, he will answer you, maybe in two sentences, but if you asked Keith he would think first, then reply, at length, and expect you to follow his towering intellect as the discourse developed. Later in life, after I came to know Keith a lot better, I realised that I must never call him for a 'short' phone conversation, because with him there was no such thing. At one time I thought of instituting a 'Boreham Cosworth Cup', to be awarded to the person who had the longest phone call with Keith. My record was one of 53 minutes! Where would Ford have been without his genius in the 1960s, '70s and '80s?

Not long after I arrived at Boreham I faced the major challenge of the *Daily Mirror* (London-Mexico City) World Cup rally of 1970. Because this was a one-off, there was nothing for it in our budget and we didn't really know how much it would cost. In 1968 Ford's London-Sydney had gone seriously over budget (before my time, I hasten to add – I did enough budget over-running of my own without needing to take credit for other people's), so anything we did in 1970 was under scrutiny. In the end I was allowed £40,000, and gave the go-ahead.

Immediately after the 1969 RAC Rally I held a meeting with all the engineers, drivers and co-drivers to work out some strategy for the event: how many cars we could support, what sort they should be and how many people should be in a crew. It was all a bit fluid.

Since the German-built Taunus had just won the Safari, some of the drivers believed we should choose big, comfortable cars like that with three-man crews, while others favoured Escorts. One of the few things we all agreed on was that because of the doubtful petrol quality in South America, we shouldn't take cars with Twin-Cam engines because that had cost victory in the London-Sydney Marathon. As test projects I sent Roger Clark to tackle the Alpine Rally in a V6-engined Escort and an east-European event in a Mark IV Zodiac (he never really forgave me for that).

Roger became a key factor in our success so it was sad that his car crashed out of the World Cup when he wasn't even driving; it was his advice about the high mountains of South America that was crucial. When I sent Roger out on his recce I told him that the Scandinavians were supporting a Taunus approach, three up, and asked for his opinions. In particular, I wanted to know how he was going to cope with Primes (special stages) that were more than 500 miles long, and sectors of more than 50 hours between time controls, without rest *and* at altitude. Did the drivers need oxygen, for instance?

Now I'd better admit that an oft-quoted tale of Roger's high-altitude experiment was fictitious, but as his widow, Goo, suggested I mention it during a tribute at his funeral service (in fact I chickened out once I was in the pulpit) I know she won't mind if I repeat it here:

'Roger,' I am alleged to have said, 'we need to know the effects of lack of oxygen at height in the Andes. Find a local girl, at 14,000 feet, make love and report back ...'

Roger (equally allegedly) sent back a cable reading, 'Unable to find a girl at 14,000 feet but don't recommend oxygen because no problems when I did it 14 times at 1,000 feet.'

In fact, the phone call (and this was for real) that I got from Roger was absolutely vital to our London to Mexico success. 'It's high and it's horrible, for sure,' he told me. 'It's going to be tough, worse than the

Liège, and longer, but still just a rally. Let's treat it as a tougher, longer Liège and go two-up in Escorts.'

That was the big decision. I talked to Bill Meade about preparing a super-tough Escort and to Peter Ashcroft about developing a simple engine, and collectively (more of a Boreham decision than a driver decision) we went that way. If we had listened to the Scandinavians and taken Taunuses (Cologne taxis, as they were nicknamed) I don't think we would have won.

Mind you, it wasn't all smooth going. After just seven days and the run round Europe from London to Sofia, Monza and on to Lisbon, our so-called Escort wonder cars were beginning to break up. They were quite a bit heavier than standard with 28-gallon fuel tanks in the boot, and in that first week we found that all the axles had started to break up, with the tubes actually splitting away from the casing in the centre.

Bill Meade had flagged his concern over axles well before the event and Len Bailey (Ford's resident racing/rally car design contractor) had agreed to have some made with tubing to aircraft specification. Something went awry, however, because we ended up with standard cold drawn tubing which was 50 per cent *softer* than the standard Ford material we'd used in testing. All of which proved the truth of the old adage that you should never use untested parts in a race or rally, not one covering 16,000 miles anyway.

Without the two-week gap, while the cars were shipped to Rio de Janeiro, all the Escorts would have been out of the rally, but Bill Meade and Roger Clark flew home, Len Bailey was consulted and we came up with a crude but effective bolt-on Duralumin brace which locked the axle casing and tubes into a straight line.

Roger tested another Escort fitted with the brace at Bagshot and couldn't break anything, then we flew mechanics out to Brazil with braces, U-bolts and fixings for all the cars. These didn't look elegant, but they worked and they lasted all the way to Mexico. It was a miraculous cure, solely due to the 'can-do' approach of Len and Bill – but we had come close to complete disaster. Later we sold a lot of them as Motorsport Parts.

Apart from Roger, the other person who was pivotal to what we achieved in South America was Benito Lores, a Ford dealer in Lima in Peru. He was a genial bloke, multi-lingual and already running various motorsport programmes out there; Benito proved to be an ideal organiser and 'fixer' in what was a strange environment for all of us. I remember going to bed one night high in the Andes and thinking that I was hallucinating when I woke up and saw walls and pictures moving about, and wardrobe doors opening. Next morning a local dismissed it all by telling me that there had been an earthquake, but only a minor one, nothing to worry about.

It was through Benito Lores that we arranged for spares to be dumped at Ford dealers all over the South American continent; I reckon there are still some bullet-proof windscreens out there, in packing cases, ready for use. It was through Benito, too, that I was persuaded to send Tony Fall on the Rally of the Incas in 1969. He won with Gunnar Palm using a World Cup practice car, which not only taught us a lot about the terrain but was good for our relations with Ford Peru.

The story of the London to Mexico Rally itself, I guess, is well known. The specially developed Escorts were ideal for the event, Hannu Mikkola and Gunnar Palm won it, with other works cars finishing third, fifth, sixth and eighth; only two of our seven cars retired, both having been hit by non-competing cars on road sections. In almost every way, I think, it was a seminal point, which finally put the Escort on the motorsport map.

A great example of team work followed towards the end of the rally. Timo Makinen, knowing he could no longer win the event, came up to me with only 4,000 miles still to go (only!) and suggested that extra spares and even welding kit should be stuffed into his Escort, so that he could 'shadow' Hannu all the way to Mexico City.

The winning car's colour scheme? Well, whenever we couldn't find a paying sponsor for an event, I'd offer a car to a magazine or newspaper provided that we got some publicity in exchange (it also hid the fact that we'd failed to find financial support). Hannu's car was linked to the *Daily Telegraph Magazine* and one of their in-house designers came up with the livery we sported; the basic striping decals, without the words, were then used on the Mexico production cars that followed.

An ideal result? Well, yes, but although Ford's Managing Director, Bill Batty, flew out to Mexico City to greet the winners and Ford made a film called 'Five for the Fiesta', I got back to find a crisis over costs waiting on my desk! In the nine months leading up to the event, it seems, we had spent £127,666 – some £87,666 (or 220 per cent) over budget – and the questions being asked were, 'How did I account for this? And where was the money to come from?'

I could account for it easily enough but while I thought that £4,500 insurance for Jimmy Greaves, £10,000 for a special charter aircraft to get the cars back to the UK for magazine tests, and £9,900 for 900 new Minilite wheels was all justified, there were those who gulped at the sums.

You only had to look at the amount of paperwork we generated to see where all the time and money slipped away. The co-drivers actually worked up detailed routes (not pace notes, but accurate navigational notes) for the entire 16,000-mile route, and there were so many pages that these had to be issued in sections. Travel plans alone occupied as much space as an entire 'Bible' for a conventional event, and we had to make allowances for Time Zone differences, weird medical jabs, the carrying of oxygen cylinders, and for mechanics to be flown, not driven, from point to point.

During one recce Henry Liddon phoned from the wilds of South America to say that he couldn't find a hire car. 'Buy something then,' I suggested. 'I'm glad you said that because I already have,' he replied! Unflappable and very resourceful was Henry.

If nothing else, the post mortem showed me how carefully Ford monitored its spending, and how it always wanted to get top value. At that time, and later, I also realised that as far as the finance people were concerned, the worst crime I could commit was to go back and ask for more money. The point about budgeting, and financial plans, was that we were all meant to live within them. Financially, Ford didn't like surprises, yet the problem with motorsport was that it was always such a volatile environment.

But I recall this as a 'tut tut' rather than a 'this is terrible' session with the accountants (it might have been a lot more painful if we hadn't won), but we still had to make serious cuts in the programme for the rest of the year, along with cancelling our entry in the 1971 Monte Carlo Rally.

As it was, the World Cup generated massive coverage. In fact a memo from one of the Ford finance men noted that, 'We appreciate that some people could hold that this over-run situation is a little hard on Ford of Britain because they are standing the whole cost of the World Cup Rally, although the benefits have been just as great in places as far away as South Africa and Australia.'

Ford Belgium put together a huge portfolio of press clippings that helped our case and it was remarkable how much media coverage Jimmy Greaves got. When we first announced that he was to drive a car in the rally, it was denounced as a gimmick, but I sensed that it would work when Jimmy came out to Boreham to meet the team. He drove me away from a crowd of photographers then pulled in after the second corner and said, 'Look, if you think I'm making a prat of myself let me know and we'll call it off.' I knew then that with such a non-prima-donna approach he would be no gimmick.

On the event, he entered into the spirit as well as everyone, and I know he enjoyed himself. When the London-Mexico Retrospective was held in 1995 (the event that Hannu and Gunnar also won), he and Tony Fall wanted to repeat the trick, but his TV commitments got in the way.

As an aside, it was about this time that I first got involved with the Springfield Boys' Club, whose identification appeared on many of our rally cars over the years; I went along to one of their meetings with Jimmy, where he was definitely welcomed as a superstar. It was Anthony Marsh, commentator and enthusiast, who had got the motorsport link going in the 1960s for this club for under-privileged kids. It was based near Mill Hill where Graham Hill lived at that time and he became the original President. Jackie Stewart took over later.

Even though we had to cope with all manner of budget cuts at this time, we still persevered with rallycross (for too long, I now reckon – saying 'no' is one of the most difficult things to do if you are an enthusiast), and especially with campaigning the brutish four-wheel-drive Capris. Roger and Stan Clark, who had to drive them, could always find the traction to be first off the line, but their handling was awful; I'm not sure if Roger, or Mick Jones, made the rudest remarks about them. Before we built the cars, Ferguson told us that there would be no more transmission drag than with a rear-drive car, yet I can clearly remember teams of mechanics sweating to push the cars on to the transporters.

By August 1970 I must have been forgiven for overspending, because I was then promoted to Director, Motor Sports. I mentioned Wesley Tee, owner of *Motoring News* and *Motor Sport*, in an earlier chapter – it was an indication of his influence that my Ford title was changed from 'Motor Sport' to 'Motor Sports' with an important 's' because he felt that there might be confusion! No one wanted to upset *Motor Sport* in those days. Anyway, the new title added to what I was already doing: an advisory and planning function for all the European sales companies, along with responsibility for all Formula 1 and other racing programmes in Europe.

That's what the job description said but I couldn't really see Walter Hayes relinquishing his links with Cosworth, Jackie Stewart, Ken Tyrrell and Colin Chapman. And he didn't, but it was no matter because we always seemed to be on the same wavelength and he had a finely tuned ear for any adverse vibes that could affect what we were planning.

Nevertheless, adding Formula 1 to my responsibilities meant that I went to quite a few Grand Prix races, including the South African where I first met Jody Scheckter, then a local Formula Ford talent. I remember that when we met he called me 'Sir' – I've always liked that in a driver. Mind you, he only did it once. We later helped him when he came to the UK by finding him garage space at Boreham – perhaps the only time we favoured one Formula Ford driver over the rest, and it was only the loan of a lock-up.

Another GP I remember is the German at the Nurburgring where Ford of Germany hired a helicopter in which I flew above Jackie Stewart and François Cevert for a couple of laps as they led in their Tyrrells. Not a flight to forget.

At the time, I tried to formalise an agreement with Keith Duckworth that if a DFV engine won a Formula 1 race, it was to be called a 'Ford'; if it blew up, a 'Cosworth'. He wouldn't wear it. People can be very unreasonable.

After the World Cup Rally there was maybe an element of 'Turner can do no wrong', at least for a few months, which meant that my forlorn attempt to develop the GT70 sports car was tolerated for a time. This mid-engined machine was born out of our failure to win the 1970 Monte, the first I had tackled for Ford.

Maybe I had got a bit blasé because at BMC, after all, the Minis had finished first on four consecutive occasions, but when Boreham came to build the fastest Twin Cams of which we were capable for 1970, we got blown away. It wasn't that the Escorts weren't powerful enough – they were certainly that – but they couldn't get the power down through the rear wheels on slippery stages. On the BEA Trident flying us back from Nice to London, Roger Clark and I sat miserably wondering what could be done.

Roger, who had finished fifth behind three Porsche 911s and an Alpine-Renault, all with engine-over-driving-wheels layouts, said, 'Well, I couldn't have driven any faster.' Knowing how hard Boreham had worked, I could only reply, 'Well, we couldn't have made them any faster.'

At which point the traditional sketching on the back of an envelope began. Before we touched down at Heathrow we had sketched up a new idea: a two-seater sports car with its engine behind the cabin, which at least should have the same grip and potential as the Porsches.

Once back at Boreham I talked to Walter. We somehow found a bit of money to build a car (we only spent £5,000 in the first year and that included making the first prototype), we got Len Bailey involved, and he produced a design we called the GT70 (well, this was 1970). *After* we had built the car, Walter wrote a typically elegant paper to Stan Gillen pointing out why we needed such a car, what it could do for Ford's image in general, and that we needed to build 500 to gain homologation. One of his most telling points was:

'The conventional configuration of the Escort places it at a handicap against mid-engined cars, or cars with the engine over the driving wheels. The only events which the Escort can now win are those where sports cars are banned, or where the going is very rough, such as the World Cup Rally. A major prestige event such as the Monte Carlo Rally is beyond our reach. We think the GT70 can win the Monte'.

To keep the project secret, and to keep it out of the way of the World Cup programme, Len had the steel chassis made at Morris Gomm's workshop (Morris was a genius with metal), and we had the prototype assembled upstairs above a small fibreglass specialist's workshop in Brighton. The biggest initial problem we had was getting it down from there – we had to take a window out and use ladders, I remember.

Now, although the GT70 was inspired by what Roger Clark thought he needed to win the Monte, and Len Bailey tried to give it to him, the fact is that Roger never liked the car once it was running, although the handling became a lot better when a BDA engine replaced the original cast-iron V6.

In terms of styling, I thought the front of the car was terrific, but it lost something towards the rear. When I invited Colin Chapman down to Boreham to see it, he was polite, but wary of the aerodynamics of the car. So, although we finished the first car by October 1970, only nine months after Roger and I chatted on the Trident back from Nice, there was still a lot to do.

Early in 1971, for sure, we had a master plan for the GT70: to build 500 cars to be legal for motorsport. The obvious place to do that would be at Advanced Vehicle Operations (AVO) in batches, and not on any flow-line system. At this time all the estimates showed that it could have been quite profitable for Ford, but only if priced above £2,500 with a BDA engine fitted. Since the Escort RS1600 currently sold at £1,495, that was never going to be easy. (The figure sounded high. We didn't realise that, years later, the Escort Cosworth – a roughly equivalent car of its day to the RS1600 – would be over *16 times* that amount.)

By the end of 1970 the GT70 project engineer at AVO, Mike Cadby, had written a 15-page report, identifying over 100 points which needed attention – 20 in the body shell alone and 13 in the chassis. Although all manner of Ford production-line parts were in the car, like a Zodiac Mk IV radiator, an Anglia 105E heater, and we even had thoughts of using a modified version of the front-wheel-drive Taunus's transaxle for the transmission assembly, we were a long, long way from production and I was getting distinctly uneasy about its prospects. This was the first time I realised what a clash there would often be between Motorsport, who wanted things done yesterday, and mainstream engineers who, quite correctly, needed to follow 'the system'.

Even mainstream stylists got edgy that this thing had suddenly appeared from an outside designer and were spurred into doing a mock-up of their own, which looked gorgeous; maybe the GT70 would have had a better chance if it had looked like that from the start. Although perhaps not, because the design was not really feasible – there was no room to package a radiator for instance. Details, details.

GT70 prototypes entered French events in 1971 but never finished, although François Mazet was leading a Tour de France with one until he went out on the Col du Minier. It took most of the year for another four cars to be built at Boreham where, frankly, we might have been better advised to sort out the RS1600's transmission problems. Everything might, only might, still have worked out if Ford had not then had an enormously costly pay strike, and Motorsport suffered sharp budget cuts.

Once Boreham got back on to some sort of even keel, the will to make the GT70 succeed had waned; if it had been an immediate winner, in prototype form, I'm sure that would not have happened. Before long the project was quietly abandoned, and we had to soldier on with the Escorts for the whole of the 1970s. But maybe that was a blessing in disguise because 1972 saw Safari *and* RAC Rally wins with the Escort.

Away from rallying, with the Ford Cosworth DFV engine becoming widely available by 1970, some teams wanted to use it in sports cars for long-distance events. Ford, and in particular Keith Duckworth of Cosworth, were against this. Keith was adamant that his beloved DFV was not a sports car engine – 'If they'd wanted a sports car engine, I'd have designed one' being a typical response.

It was partly because of this that a dreary three-year saga of a Weslake V12 3-litre racing engine began. Because of my newly granted motor racing responsibilities, I got involved in it, although a triangular correspondence between Walter Hayes, John Wyer (of the Gulf-sponsored JWA team) and Weslake & Co also continued, unabated, for three years.

Harry Weslake started out on this project, with high hopes, in 1970, with support from Walter Hayes. The plan was that Weslake should develop a reliable, high-output unit for sports car racing, and that John Wyer's Mirage should get first pick at the unit. This engine was inspired by an earlier Weslake unit, the V12 used in Dan Gurney's Eagle F1 car.

Walter wrote to John Wyer in January 1971 that, 'Although it is not general knowledge, and will not become general knowledge, it is a fact that we have a new Ford 3-litre engine, which is being developed under contract by Harry Weslake . . .' He went on to suggest that development would shortly be complete, that JWA could have exclusive rights to its use and that Len Bailey would be loaned to JWA as 'Chief Development Engineer'.

Even though JWA didn't need this engine until 1972 (they were campaigning the works Porsche 917s in 1971), delays then began to build up, along with development problems. A series of rather prickly financial deals had to be done (Ford guaranteed to repurchase the engines from JWA/Gulf if they didn't deliver their promised performance), and although Weslake always claimed that their V12 was more effective than a Cosworth DFV they could never prove it in a car.

Even in 1972 Weslake's test-bed figures claimed 455bhp at 10,500rpm, compared with a typical DFV's 430bhp at 9,500rpm (although the Cosworth produced *much* more torque all the way to its peak). But when Cosworth was already building up to 50 DFVs every year, Weslake managed only to build six V12s in three years and these were unreliable.

Even so, Harry dabbled with converting the V12 into an F1 engine (he would later claim that he had recorded 491bhp at 10,500rpm), and he loaned an engine for abortive tests in a Brabham single-seater in mid-1972. That was a fiasco, JWA/Gulf encountered further electrical misfiring problems, and I got thoroughly alarmed.

In September 1972 I wrote to Harry Weslake, pointing out that '. . . quite clearly the V12 project seems to be getting into a tangle. The unfavourable publicity which has recently appeared in the motoring press did none of us any good . . . frankly unless John Wyer and ourselves reach an amicable agreement fairly soon, I feel that our own interest in the project is going to wane.'

This had no effect, the problems persisted, and in January 1973 I wrote another letter commenting that, 'I feel it is imperative that you should concentrate wholeheartedly on the John Wyer Sports Car project. I think it would be a big mistake to go off at a tangent by getting involved in Formula 1 before the unit has proved itself in long-distance racing.'

But there was still little progress. In the end I sent Peter Ashcroft and John Griffiths down from Boreham to Rye, to get a 'horse's mouth' opinion, and Peter got straight to the nub of the problem in a letter he wrote to John Wyer: 'There is definitely an attitude of non co-operation [from Weslake], which I have pointed out. If the engine is to survive this attitude must stop.'

He was even more blunt in writing to Harry Weslake himself: 'There was still this get-stuffed attitude in their mind and this I felt to be quite strong. In the interest of all concerned, this is a silly attitude that has got to stop . . .'

You'll begin to understand why I was always impressed by Peter's earthy approach to motorsport – it lined up fairly closely with my own.

Frankly, Peter did not believe Weslake's own dynamometer figures because independent Gulf test bed figures, recorded in the USA, quoted a very disappointing 410bhp. Things then went from bad to worse, and it was almost with relief that when our budgets had to be cut following the Energy Crisis of 1973/74, we had to drop the engine completely.

Although Weslake claimed to have spent £100,000 of their own money on the project, it was no more reliable than their earlier, Gurney-Eagle V12 had been. They offered to sell us everything – engines, designs and pattern equipment – for £40,000 but we turned them down.

As a total contrast to sports car racing, I tried to encourage 'grass roots' growth in our motorsport, notably with the evolution of the Ford Sport Club. Barrie Gill had been a prime mover in this. He was at Boreham when I arrived and provided many creative ideas before moving over to Ford of Britain Marketing. Years later, Tony Mason was to supply a similar fizz for Boreham.

We also did several question-and-answer forums at Ford dealers for enthusiasts – at one I remember Barry Sheene being asked why he hadn't rolled into a ball when he came off his bike during a race in Florida. He replied that if he had he would have ended up in Bermuda.

Other initiatives to help the grass roots included the expansion of the Motorsport Parts department (which Charlie Mead would run successfully until the 1990s) and the introduction of the parallel one-model Mexico series, one in circuit racing and one in rallying.

If I had a philosophy at that time, it was that I wanted to spread motorsport in Ford cars, Escorts mainly, as widely as possible. This was one reason why we started regular bulletins to Ford owners involved in motorsport; we tried to be totally honest and tell them what had broken on the works cars, and how to prevent the problems on theirs. The Escort was basically a very simple car, available in several different specifications, and I wanted to make sure that everyone out there could take part, somehow, in the Escort of his or her choice.

It was at about this time, though, that I began to cut back on our involvement in British motor racing, where the Escort had had a good run. That meant saying goodbye to Alan Mann, and to Ralph Broad, who were both probably as relieved as I was.

I don't think Alan and I ever really understood each other. I was full of admiration for the results he got, and for the immaculate way he presented his cars, but somehow we never got on with each other. We never ever had an argument but there wasn't any business chemistry, and we drifted apart.

I knew Ralph a lot better because he had been racing Minis when I was at BMC and had embarrassed John Cooper's works cars at times. He was an inventive engineer, quite a character, very volatile and very entertaining but perhaps I didn't give his team enough to do or maybe I just didn't enjoy motor racing as much as rallying. Perhaps he couldn't cope quite as well with the slightly more formalised world of Ford as he could with the free-and-easy atmosphere at BMC. Anyway, as with Alan Mann, we just lost touch.

At the end of 1971 we were all glad to shake off the dust of that season and to look ahead to better things. At last, I hoped, we had sorted out the problem of breaking Escort half-shafts (at this time I commented that if I died suddenly and was subjected to a post-mortem, 'half-shafts' would be branded on my heart), and we had finally dropped Twin Cams in favour of RS1600s with the BDA, so engine problems should now be a thing of the past.

Personally I hoped it would also be the end of budget cuts and that we could build a coherent programme for 1972, and carry on improving the Escort.

Once again we failed to win the Monte, but then we picked up a victory in the 1972 Hong Kong Rally (our Far Eastern dealers were delighted about that), and I got a healthy budget to tackle the Safari. This was one of those events that had been niggling at me for years. At BMC we'd sent Rauno Aaltonen to tackle the event in a Mini Cooper S in 1967, which was rather a waste of resources, and our big Ford effort in 1971 had failed because the Twin Cams were simply not fast enough.

I wouldn't have minded so much if Ford Germany, with almost no experience of rallies, hadn't supplied a Taunus 20MTS to Robin Hillyar and Jock Aird in 1969 and they had won the event outright! For 1972, therefore, Boreham prepared a team of RS1600s, faster (with 205bhp) and stronger than ever before.

That was an event I managed from the air, in a private plane, jammed in with Mick Jones, where we could keep in radio contact with the cars on the ground. One of my most memorable moments was taking off from an airfield in the bush. We'd been caught out because darkness had fallen fast, as it does in Kenya, and the pilot had to send a local down the grass strip in his car to check that there were no wild animals wandering about. He turned at the other end, flashed his lights to give us the OK ... and we took off. We must have been mad.

Later we quite literally spent the night flying round and round the tip of Mount Kenya, which was sticking out through the cloud, in order to act as a communications 'satellite' for the cars below. There was a rally going on beneath us but we couldn't see it. Eerie – but unforgettable. Looking back, I see that I completed 31 flights, and spent 46 hours in the air, and since I'm not wild about small planes I reckon I deserved some sort of medal for that. It was no comfort for my nerves to be assured that 'we have a 100 per cent safety record ... we've never left anyone up there yet'.

Anyway, Hannu Mikkola and Gunnar Palm won the event (finally laying to rest the idea that you simply had to be a local to win) with Vic 'Junior' Preston third and Robin Hillyar fourth.

It's difficult now to realise the impact this victory had on the Kenyans. Before 1972 I'm convinced that most of the drivers out there thought that Europeans were simply not versatile or tough enough to win in Africa. There was even talk of a 'Safari fever' that stopped overseas drivers coping with the conditions.

Along with the World Cup victory of 1970, this Safari completed a remarkable double for Hannu and Gunnar and I was extremely proud for them. Those were the days when the Safari was seen as *the* most difficult rally in the world (in many ways, probably, it still is, but much of the mystique has gone), and Ford's win made headlines.

I was also proud to see that those famous cars were retained by the factory as display cars for many years. Hannu's World Cup car (FEV 1H) is still at Ford – I last saw it at the Escort 'retirement' party in 1998 – while the 1972 Safari-winning machine is now owned by Malcolm Wilson.

However, in the interests of strict historical accuracy, I have to record the fact that a different vehicle altogether made the most impact at Boreham. An exchange had been arranged whereby a Formula Ford was sent to America, and a Bill Stroppe-prepared

Bronco was shipped over in exchange. Jaws dropped when this monster arrived. As it was taken off the transporter and fired up, universities over a wide area reported unusual readings on their earthquake monitoring equipment.

It was huge – so huge that when Rod Chapman took it down to the cross-country Rallye des Cimes in France, it wouldn't go through some of the gates and he had to withdraw! Rod then took it on the Hill Rally in Wales where it retired because its enormous balloon tyres kept puncturing on the Welsh slate. (I never found out what the Americans did with the single-seater we sent them – perhaps they fed it to another Bronco for lunch.)

But the Bronco wasn't the only excitement for me at least, because my life was to change yet again. I was off to Advanced Vehicle Operations.

Chapter 10

AVO – a business in miniature

WALTER HAYES WAS the founding enthusiast for the setting-up of Advanced Vehicle Operations (AVO) in 1969/70. Way back in 1965, even before the Cosworth DFV F1 engine had got off the ground, he had started campaigning for 'an entirely new performance organisation . . .' and stated that: '. . . the answer, therefore, is to set up a small, self-contained Company organisation to run and control this part of our business.' At the time the suggestion was that the organisation should operate hand-in-glove with Lotus, but this was abandoned.

What was fascinating about Walter's proposal, made five years before AVO actually came into being, was that it suggested most of the things that later became central to the AVO concept: a factory-within-a-factory, a dedicated 'Performance Dealer Network' and the Performance Parts division. However, as he pointed out, 'It would also require a major acceptance by the Car Division that it is willing to have an independent car division operating within the Company.'

He recognised that some of the traditional fences between departments would have to come down and the timber used to build bridges instead; the territorial warfare seen between government departments (and ministers) is often just as bloody in companies between divisions (and managers).

Four years later Walter had refined his proposals, got almost everyone on his side, and in October 1969 made the final proposal to Henry Ford II, where he asked for a budget of $790,000 (£329,000 at 1969 values) to prepare the factory.

Bob Howe started to set up the AVO facility from his position within Product Planning. Ray Horrocks was appointed as manager, then, when they had the basic plan laid down, they got Rod Mansfield in to head up the Engineering section. Many of the successful performance Fords over the years owe a lot to Rod who himself later raced in the Mexico one-make series.

In setting up AVO, the idea was that if mainstream factories couldn't build low-volume, specialised cars (which, at the time, was thought to be true, although it was disproved from 1975), a factory-within-a-factory should be set up to do them. Further, it was reasoned, specialised cars would only sell if they had a unique and obvious purpose and if they could be marketed through specialised dealers.

Inevitably there were shake-down problems between AVO and Motorsport. In fact soon after I got to Boreham I wrote to Walter Hayes, 'It is clear from reports filtering through to me that there is a growing attitude that Competitions is a wholly owned subsidiary of AVO. If this in fact is so, let me know so that I can act accordingly, and read no further! AVO face a formidable task in running their own affairs without getting too involved in ours . . .'

That misunderstanding was cleared up within 24 hours and until I actually moved in to the manager's chair at AVO it never had any control over Boreham. Motorsport, on the other hand, always had plenty to say on what AVO should be doing because (rather like John Cooper pushing BMC for hotter and hotter Minis) we were certainly aching for new Escorts, the simple-to-run Escort Mexico being a case in point.

By 1972 I'd heard that Ray Horrocks would soon be moving on and, at the time, he was rumoured to be lined up to run the Transit van plant at Southampton. That, by the way, was perhaps one reason why he chose to leave the company, to join the axle-makers, Eaton. There was no clash of minds, or boardroom revolts, but after managing an exciting plant like AVO I suspect that Ray could not face the boredom of overseeing the building of thousands of vans every week.

I was surprised to be invited to run the AVO operation because I thought that there must have been many better-qualified people than me to do so; in fact I'm quite sure there were, but clearly Walter thought otherwise, and although it qualified as a Manufacturing operation and wasn't formally within his bailiwick, he obviously had a say in key appointments because he had effectively invented the operation.

Many things in my life seem to have happened by fortunate chance, and as far as I was concerned this was yet another lucky opportunity that I certainly wasn't going to turn down. It was a major step for me and I was thrilled to bits. I seemed to be having a quick job change, perhaps, but that was not unusual – people were moved around regularly from position to position in Ford, often from country to country. I once interviewed a 30-year-old who thought his career was at crisis point because he'd not had a job change for 18 months!

My new position at AVO was slightly complicated because I retained all my motorsport responsibilities but had to run AVO as well. Bizarrely, I had two titles: 'Director, Motor Sports activities in Europe' and 'Manager, Advanced Vehicle Operations'. With my 'motorsport' hat on I was to report to John Waddell in Public Affairs, and with my AVO hat on I had to report to Bill Batty, who was Managing Director, Ford of Britain. In effect I had two heads – and at times it felt like it.

But there was more. I've always believed that people can be impressed by titles (they can also be a low-cost way of motivating employees) and I felt that something simple was needed when working with the outside world, so after discussions it was decreed that I could use the title of 'Director, Motor Sports and Advanced Vehicles' – quote, 'when neither of your internal designations is suitable'!

Nowadays of course I suppose someone in that situation could turn to the Psychiatric Hotline. As you may know, if you are schizophrenic and you ring this line, a little voice tells you which number to press; if you are co-dependent, you have to ask someone else to press 2 and if, like me with all those titles, you have multiple personalities, you have to press 3, 4, 5 and 6 . . .

Anyway, much more important than what I was called (and I've been called plenty in my time) was the fact that for the first time Motorsport and AVO were directly linked. Once I was committed to moving down the road to South Ockendon, Peter Ashcroft was my logical successor at Boreham, not to direct strategy but to manage the team. Peter ran Boreham for the next 18 years, and eventually took over from me as Director when I retired at the end of 1990.

I suspect that Bill Barnett (Boreham's Rally Manager) was unhappy to be passed over at this point, but I had to play things as I saw them and Bill, I thought, was ideally placed where he was; his talents as Rally Manager were indispensable and I wanted to preserve that. I wanted to maintain continuity and not go in for wholesale changes.

Peter Ashcroft reported direct to me at AVO where, by switching 'mental hats', I could influence the plant to produce what was best for all of us. Now, more than ever, I hoped that AVO's products could be tailored directly to Boreham's needs.

I was so busy at Aveley that I didn't have much time to devote to the works rally team – so it was a pleasure to see it go from strength to strength under Peter's day-to-day control.

Apart from Hannu's Safari victory, two particular successes stand out in that 1972 season – one was that Roger Clark finally won the RAC Rally (which he'd deserved to do on more than one previous occasion), and the other was that he totally dominated the RAC British Rally Championship.

To this day I wince to think that I gave Judith Jackson a TV interview on an earlier RAC Rally, in mid-rally at Machynlleth, in which I suggested that all the best rally drivers were Scandinavian. I don't recall actually *saying* that Roger wasn't good enough to beat them, but later he let me know that he'd always taken it that way. Maybe what I said helped to wind him up (Roger was a self-confessed lazy sportsman at the time) because he not only proved a lot to himself by winning that Championship (and there would be more, in later years), but it was also a perfect response, an 'up yours', to me too!

Roger and I got on much better after that; in fact we really became good friends and had some great times on club forums together. I considered it a very real honour when his widow, Goo, asked me to give the final oration at his funeral in 1998.

It wasn't until he'd gone that I realised how much I was going to miss Roger's dry sense of humour. I remember him once being asked why he preferred rallying to racing. Answer: 'Who wants to drive round and round with a petrol tank strapped to your arse?' And when asked for advice on what to do if you just know you're going to have an accident on a rally, Roger said, 'If all is lost, and you're going off, then declutch and keep the throttle pressed to the floor. Then when the ambulance men come to take the body away, they'll look at the 9,500 on the rev counter and say, with admiration, "By God he was trying . . ."'

Roger's high profile in Britain helped, of course, when we sought sponsorship. This was the period when we gained support from Colibri (the cigarette-lighter makers) for an RAC Rally. Timo won the rally that year and we then set up the 'Colibri Rally Man of the Month' award. This meant that we had a monthly meeting with key motorsport journalists, which was useful in itself, but the main reason for the award was that I had an office full of Colibri lighter desk sets, and I had to move them somehow! But don't knock it: sponsorship in kind, if properly structured, is always useful. Later, for instance, Bjorn Waldegard won the RAC in an Escort sponsored by British Airways. Guess how that sponsorship eventually came to us? Correct. In airline tickets, not in hard cash. Drivers, teams or motor clubs seeking sponsorship today are wise not to neglect material support, whether in free printing or whatever, because it's often easier for companies to help this way than with cash.

Clambering off yet another hobby horse and getting back to AVO, which is what this chapter is supposed to be about, I was impressed by the neat organisation I found there, although I was able to streamline it slightly because now that AVO and Motorsport were linked there was less need for formal liaison people.

Dick Boxall, a no-nonsense ex-Halewood manufacturing man, looked after production, ably backed up by Harry Nelson, and Bob Howe was running engineering and product planning, with Rod Mansfield as his chief engineer. Mike Moreton was in charge of Advanced Product Planning and Timing and Mike Kranefuss was running the German end of the operation.

Dick Boxall was a long-serving Ford employee and a marvellous anchor man, a father-figure for me at AVO. He might have been close to retirement even then, but he had a huge amount of energy (one soon learned not to challenge him at press-ups) and we couldn't have managed without him.

Dick was a hard man to please, obsessed with getting high quality out of the AVO plant so, mirroring mainstream, we had a quality audit of a car picked at random off the line every day; we gave marks for all aspects of the car. Dick was red hot on paint quality and we were respraying a high percentage of cars for what I felt were fairly minor faults; I persuaded him to ease up on this for a spell and we monitored the warranty claims on the cars built then. Claims were lower. Why? Because if buyers spot even a trace of over-spray anywhere it encourages them to assume the worst – perhaps their car has had a bump – and they then go actively looking for faults.

To his credit Dick took the point. I only saw him discomforted once and that was when I said that I'd had a call that Bill Hayden, Vice President of Manufacturing, was due to pay us a visit. Dick visibly shook at the news and it was then that I realised what a fearsome reputation Bill had. Many years later Jaguar felt the edge of his tongue when he was put in charge; in fact I was booed when I simply mentioned his name when speaking at a motor industry dinner in Birmingham soon after he'd compared the factory to one in Russia, but the subsequent turnround in Jaguar's fortunes owed a lot to his forthright approach.

Bob Howe later became 'Mr RS200', not only selling all the cars, but looking after the difficult legislation programme. After AVO had closed, Rod Mansfield eventually set up and managed Special Vehicle Engineering (SVE), which helped Motorsport so much with the design of the Sierra RS Cosworth and, later, the Escort RS Cosworth; even later he was Aston Martin's engineering director, and for a short time he then became Managing Director of Lotus during its links with Artioli and Bugatti. Mike Kranefuss eventually took over as Director, Motorsport, Europe, later moving to Detroit to tackle the same sort of job over there, while Mike Moreton was the product planner, wheeler-dealer and fixer who did great things for us with many cars.

I couldn't have asked for a more resourceful team and I was relieved to have them because controlling something like AVO was new to me. Here I was, responsible for a staff of 251 people (with another 35 in Cologne), running an operation that had already expanded to 110,000sq ft, which could produce over 3,000 cars a year on a single-shift basis.

Every aspect of mainstream was mirrored at AVO – production, engineering, sales, marketing, parts, service, finance and industrial relations – which made us self-contained. This was AVO's strength, because it kept us out of mainstream's hair. But it was also a weakness. When demand turned down, as it did in 1973/74, the structure was simply too unwieldy to survive.

Looking back, did it really make sense to truck painted body shells from Halewood all the way to Essex, add mechanical parts that could surely have been fitted in, somehow, at Halewood, then feed them into an existing dealer sales organisation? Perhaps it did when Halewood and Saarlouis were bursting at the seams (it had earlier been calculated by the bean-counters that every Twin Cam built at Halewood 'cost' 1.25 standard Escorts). But when demand for mainstream products fell, guess what, the factories found that they could cope with the production of oddballs after all. As an illustration of how rigid 'the system' was, we couldn't even find a way of re-introducing unused seats and wheels, taken off cars at AVO, back on to the Halewood production line.

The plant had been officially opened by Graham Hill on 2 November 1970, and was originally making 60-70 Escort RS1600s and Mexicos every week. When Lee Iacocca studied the AVO progress report, and reported to Henry Ford II, who was making a visit to Aveley in October 1971, he noted that the 1972 Motorsport budget was projected at $1.5 million, while the projected AVO profit before tax could be $1.3 million – which would make this almost a self-financing set-up. The facts, however, did not match up to the forecasts and by almost any reckoning we were only barely profitable. Before I arrived, production had been pushed up some more, and the carousel track could make up to 23 cars a day. But Sales were not able to shift every car we were capable of making, so a key need in 1972/73 was to add another model to the line-up.

We considered many alternative products to build, not all of them sporting. One way we found to pay the rent for a while was to assemble thousands of limited-edition Escort 1300Es – not RS models by any means, but just the sort of cars AVO was capable of handling to keep complexity out of mainstream.

I wish now that I'd pushed one particular idea I had a lot harder: the Marshal. What was it? A design study by Len Bailey for a Range Rover type of vehicle with Granada running gear. It was code-named Marshal because the spec included a clip-on awning to the tailgate for use when marshalling on events, or, I suppose, selling things at car boot sales today. Tooling would obviously have been a major issue but it never got that far. Frankly, I didn't realise that similar vehicles would become such essential fashion statements when battling to get to . . . well to schools and supermarkets mainly.

The GT70 might have been made at AVO, although I reckon we would only have made the absolute minimum to get it homologated, and we looked at Mexico estate cars (this caused the *Sunday Times* to suggest we were Ford's 'boutique'), a Frua-designed Escort coupé with a pretty all-new body, 3-litre V6-engined Cortinas and, yes, even the possibility of building a version of the DeTomaso Pantera. I believed (still do in fact) that the original Pantera was one of the truly classic car styles, and during the period when Ford were involved with DeTomaso I put forward a proposal to build a handful of cars a month in Essex. Visiting the DeTomaso factory in Italy and having to halt meetings while workers marched through rattling tin cans as a gesture during wage negotiations at least made a Latin change from British labour relations.

We had allocated bays and the Panteras were going to be hand-built on axle stands but with 'Essex' 3-litre V6 engines instead of the big American V8. Sacrilege? It didn't seem so at the time and the V6 prototype we built went fairly well. It all looked very seductive and we convinced everyone in top management except Harold 'Red' Poling, the European finance Vice President who would go on to be the head of Ford worldwide. 'Hang on,' Red commented, 'I know what's going to happen. When Lee Iacocca and Henry Ford come over for reviews of important things affecting mainstream production, a disproportionate amount of time will be spent on the Pantera.' He was perhaps right of course, although it would have added glamour to the Rallye Sport franchise and I regretted not being able to have one as a company car. Come to think of it, the Pantera project was not our first flirtation with Italy because Bill Bourke, the Australian-born then Chairman of Ford of Europe, had earlier suggested that we try to use Vignale as a Continental AVO to create a special Escort for Italy. An interesting idea, but it proved impractical.

What in fact became our second car line was the Escort RS2000, so called because it was to be sold only through RS dealers and had a 2-litre engine (at one point 'Puma' was considered as a name – what goes around). The management team at AVO came to the conclusion that the RS1600 was already too expensive (and we weren't selling many anyway) not least because warranty costs were horrendous mainly due to the time needed to set valve clearances. There was a big gap between that and the Mexico. We needed to bridge that gap. More critically, we needed an Escort RS product that we could readily sell to Ford dealers in Germany, who had no interest in the Mexico, which was too slow, or the RS1600, which hadn't the right sort of long-legged performance Ford's customers wanted for autobahns.

Mike Moreton and I spent a long time casting round and decided that we had to reach out to another market, a more affluent one than motorsport – young executives, marketing men, those who wanted performance but not big cars, that sort of person. We actually wrote in the design brief 'the sort of car a doctor, dentist or newspaper executive might buy'.

The result was the RS2000, a car with RS1600 performance but without its complications, and we hit the target market with one customer at least because soon after launch I drove through London's Fleet Street to see Jocelyn Stevens (then a key executive at the *Daily Express*) getting out of an RS2000.

A lot of the development on the car, particularly the handling work, was done by Gerry Birrell. I'd got to know him as a racing driver, initially in the Ford Germany Capri RS2600s, and by this time he was living near me in Essex. He'd already worked up to driving F2 cars, and many people thought he would make it into Grand Prix racing.

We trusted his mechanical judgement, he was a very methodical tester and, considering that he was a racer, a real racer, he was thoughtful and analytical in a road car. He certainly couldn't be swayed from his own opinions. The first time we put him in a prototype RS2000 he did three laps at Boreham, pulled up, opened the window, smiled innocently and asked, 'Is it too early in the morning to be rude?' He then was! As a result the rear suspension was redesigned and all springs and damper settings revised. It then had outstanding handling for its class. (Tom Walkinshaw played much the same role later with the Mk2 RS2000.)

A lot of the credit for the RS2000's refinement, and its easy-to-drive road manners, was due to Gerry. Even the German dealers, who were real sticklers for quality, were impressed. We were all shaken when Gerry died in a single-seater crash.

Incidentally, as we wanted to launch the RS2000 in Germany we brought a group of dealers over to see the factory at South Ockendon because at that time they had serious reservations about British build quality. I thought it would help if I addressed them in German, but as I don't speak it I wrote something out in English, had it spoken into a tape recorder in German by Lothar Pinske in Ford Motorsport in Cologne, then wrote phonetic gibberish on to paper which, when said, came out as German. My 10-minute speech worked. The only trouble was that people then started asking me questions . . . in German.

Looking back I think the only significant product issue we had with the RS2000 was engine noise with a big 2-litre unit in a small shell; the silliest cock-up we made was to order far too many years' supply of the dramatic body stripes.

One of our more interesting projects, which actually made it into production – very limited production – was the Capri RS3100, a car needed for motorsport homologation so that Ford Germany could go racing in 1974, using a bigger and more powerful engine than the old RS2600 had ever had. The BMW versus Ford Capri race battles were taken very seriously, although personally I always thought that BMW were on to a hiding to nothing because the Capri could only benefit by association with BMW irrespective of the result.

The RS3100 was announced just before the end of the original Mk I Capri's run and as (bad) luck would have it, this was launched in the same month that the Middle East War and subsequent Energy Crisis erupted, almost guaranteeing that it would be hard to sell. In fact Bill Bourke called me on the morning of the public announcement, tongue firmly in cheek, to congratulate me on my impeccable timing in launching Ford's fastest and thirstiest car on the same day as a fuel crisis.

In theory 1,000 cars were to be built at Halewood in the winter of 1973/74 (just before the Capri Mk I production run ended), and in theory they should all have had larger, 3.1-litre engines, but memory tells me that only about 240 cars were made, and that some of them had bog-standard 3-litre engines. The over-size engine wheeze had been used before – we had homologated the Escort RS1600 and the Mexico at 1601cc to take advantage of class divisions – but we had to squeeze every advantage out of a formula. We knew we had to do so with the RS3100 to help Mike Kranefuss in Germany because Jochen Neerpasch, who had set up Ford of Germany's Capri race programme before moving to BMW, had homologated their 'Batmobile' with aerofoils and aluminium panels.

Capri RS3100s hung around at Halewood and in the showrooms for ages, which might explain why we eventually used some as management lease cars. Somehow we got homologation and Cosworth's amazing 24-valve 3.4-litre version of the Essex engine, which we were then able to fit for racing, produced well over 400bhp and turned them into winners. The engine was also good enough to win British single-seater Formula 5000 races with people like David Purley at the wheel.

When the Energy Crisis struck (it made such an impact that it deserves its capitals) AVO had not been established long and there was still a healthy scepticism about its future and its financial standing. I know that Ford's finance people, especially those who were not motoring enthusiasts, were never convinced and could always prove (to their own satisfaction, at least) that the business was a loss-maker.

Even though the Escort RS2000 was beginning to sell well (later, as it filtered down the second-hand and third-hand markets, it became one of the most successful clubman's competition cars of all time), demand for our sort of cars slumped almost at once, and we finally killed any ideas of making things like turbocharged or V8 Granadas and Capris. Instead we turned to thoughts of making Granada Ghia Coupés (building right-hand-drive versions for the British market – that shows how desperate we were) but the problem was that every other Ford production plant was doing exactly the same thing: hunting for things to build. Work on the Mk 2 Escort RS models was well advanced by then and we'd assumed that we would build them at AVO but we were soon told that they would all have to be built at the Saarlouis factory in Germany instead.

By the autumn of 1974 I knew a crunch was coming and we completed several 'paper' exercises to see where we could save money. One proposal enacted at the same time was to close down Ford of Germany's Motorsport department (the Capri RS3100's race programme had come to an end anyway), although I made sure that Michael Kranefuss was retained, and kept busy.

Walter Hayes, thank goodness, agreed with my thinking, and even went so far as to rehearse the alternative effect (with Bob Lutz, who was President, Ford of Europe at the time), of closing Boreham instead.

'If we decide to stay in motorsport,' Walter wrote in a note to Lutz, 'there is only one way to make reductions, and that is by cutting into the fixed costs. And there is no other way to do that except to close one of the two Competition Centres: either Cologne or Boreham. Shutting either of the two Centres will cause a lot of agony. . . A study of the facts, however, leaves no doubt that Cologne is where we should close down . . .'

The telling fact was made that although the Motorsport department of Ford of Germany had only five more staff than Ford of Britain (27 compared with 22), in 1974 its budget was more than twice as high as that of Britain.

None of this was pleasant, but it paled into relative insignificance when the decision was made to close down the assembly line at Aveley when the last Mk I RS Escorts had been built. The decision had finally been made that the new Mk 2 RS models would be built in Germany, and all we would have left would be development staff. I got the instruction to shed all but 35 of the AVO workforce.

That was the worst time of my business life. Calling people in to my office and discussing redundancy with them was shattering. John Kerr was AVO's Industrial Relations man at the time and he worked his socks off to do the best for those leaving, while at the same time keeping in mind the organisation we needed to retain. Most of the people who, in dreadful business-speak, I had to 'let go', understood the problem, so I didn't encounter any personal bitterness but, ye gods, those were traumatic weeks.

Bill Bourke must have known how difficult all this was, for on 19 December he took the trouble to write to me at home: 'We have been going through a fairly destructive couple of months . . . I wanted to thank you personally for the way that you have handled this very difficult business of transforming AVO. I know that it has not been easy for you, because nobody likes to undo an organisation . . .'

He could say that again.

Yet there was still much to do. I retained my Boreham Motorsport responsibilities while, at AVO, development work on Mk 2 RS Escorts was still to be completed. This included the slant-back-nosed RS2000, styled for us by Jack Telnack (which later sold over 25,000), a 1.6 Mexico for Ford of Britain, plus a handful of RS1800s built in the Aveley plant for motorsport homologation. We even had a 'Blue Letter' signed by Henry Ford – which meant final approval – to produce an RS2800 Capri; in fact this was not built because of the general business climate at the time but the idea lived on to become one of the first Special Vehicle Engineering cars.

Although the AVO concept didn't survive the various energy and financial problems affecting the industry then (it might all have been different if we'd had facilities to build special bodies), a great deal of good came out of the idea and I think that the company learned a lot of lessons.

As even the core of 35 AVO people were absorbed into mainstream, I wasn't quite sure where I was going to end up until, as one of my colleagues later pointed out, quoting from Arthur Conan Doyle, 'With one bound, you were free ...' I was about to move once again.

Chapter 11

Public Affairs
at Ford

THE PHONE CALL from Walter Hayes came at home, one Sunday evening: 'John Waddell, Ford of Britain's Public Affairs chief, is going to join Ford Canada, and we'd like you to take over from him at Warley.'

There was no warning; in fact I hadn't got a clue that anything was brewing, possibly because I'd been too busy with AVO's problems to be plugged in to the mainstream grapevine.

Anyway, this was to be a total break from motorsport because although my Public Affairs responsibilities included putting our Motorsport story over to the media, I had absolutely no influence on what Peter Ashcroft and Boreham did. There were comments that I would never be able to let go of the sport, but I can only say that I did. Peter Ashcroft will confirm that. It was Peter, not me, who ran the rally team in the late 1970s and early 1980s – I merely watched from the sidelines. By that time Bill Barnett, then Tony Mason, had left Boreham and Charles Reynolds had become Peter's right-hand-man. I first got to know Charles when I invited him to get involved with the Ford Sport Club and later with various quizzes we ran. He was a totally honest and highly effective operator – Ford's record in rallying at the time proves the point.

Moving over to the Public Affairs department in November 1975 was relatively easy for me because I already knew most of the staff. However, just as on my first day at Boreham, I knew my arrival was not necessarily welcome. They were all going to miss John Waddell, who was a superb PR professional as well as a very rounded character, and I was going to need a lot of help; in fact at John's send-off party the staff produced a batch of dummy press clippings that included a 'Private Eye' cover with me shouting 'help' on it. How perceptive. And true.

That was the bad news. The good news was that I would still be reporting to Walter Hayes and I was comfortable with that. (When Walter went to the States later, John Waddell returned from Canada as Vice President of Public Affairs for Europe and I then had a dotted line to him.)

At this time Ford's Public Affairs reputation was riding high; Walter Hayes (and, until I arrived, John Waddell) had so much flair and such wonderful contacts with the media that it was almost as if they could do no wrong; it would have been arrogant on my part to think that I could make any improvement. Perhaps one of the few significant changes I made was to push PR 'downwards' and get the dealers more involved in their own local programmes.

Walter was the great thinker, the great philosopher. Throughout the years I worked with him he refused to get bogged down in detail – there were occasions when I would walk into his office to find him with his feet on the desk, pipe in mouth, just thinking. Some of the get-up-and-go Americans were puzzled by this approach but it was when he was at his best, at his most creative. I seriously feel that today there are too few people in business who have time, or force themselves to find time, to *think*.

I always envied another of his skills. I would walk into his office, tell him about a particular problem and he would call in his secretary, Brenda Woodford, and dictate an incisive note that struck absolutely to the heart of the problem – and invariably solved it. A peerless skill.

His diplomatic skills were sometimes needed when the 'press clips' were circulated. Someone in Public Affairs came in early every morning and clipped key items from the day's newspapers; photocopies were then circulated to key executives. All hell would sometimes break out over some relatively trivial item – trivial when tucked away on page 7 of a minor newspaper, but much more visible on the front sheet of the clips. I became convinced that if we'd put a hoax press cutting in that General Motors were thinking of building a three-wheeler, we'd have had feasibility studies under way by lunchtime.

As with Abingdon and Boreham, I was lucky enough to inherit an excellent team in Public Affairs, including John Waddell's splendid secretary, Olive Ambridge. (Incidentally, for the uninitiated who think public affairs are what Government ministers have, in this context I'm talking about the department that acts as a communication 'bridge' between a company and its audiences – the media, politicians, public, etc.) The work of the department included launching new products to the media; fielding endless phone calls; doing employee communications via a house newspaper; running a large photographic department; writing speeches; and providing educational material for children. Oh yes . . . and occasionally persuading sales or marketing colleagues that Fleet Street was unlikely to run page 1 stories just because sales had shot up by all of 0.3 per cent. Sales and marketing people can have weird priorities at times.

Public Affairs ran a 70-strong fleet of cars to loan to journalists for road tests – a big enough fleet for me to lend a car to Damon Hill for a few weeks at one point to help him. I was awed to find that the fleet actually included not one but two GT40s. If my memory serves me correctly (and it usually does where money is concerned) they were in the books at under £10,000. For the pair! Even more bizarrely, the fleet carried three March F1 cars when we were trying to help them get under way.

The team was headed by Sid Wheelhouse and Reg Wheatley. Sid had been at Ford, man and boy, for all his working life, and was extremely well-liked and respected; his ability to handle journalists was matchless. Sid had every right, I'm sure, to feel aggrieved that he had not got the job I was taking (at the end of my tenure I was delighted to see that he finally got the position) but he never gave less than 100 per cent.

Reg was a quieter, more laconic, operator, equally reliable, a jazz enthusiast, and another utterly safe pair of hands where Ford's image was concerned. PR isn't always about trumpeting triumphs – as a fine example of the *defensive* role PR can play, Reg took a call one Friday lunchtime from a researcher on TV's *That's Life* to say that a Capri was to be named 'Lemon of the Week' that Sunday. Reg handled the call so well that not only did a rival manufacturer have the dubious honour instead, but by the end of a long telephone conversation the researcher had almost decided to buy a Capri herself.

It was just as well that I had such great support because there was one part of the PR job that scared me to death at first – not dealing with Fleet Street motoring correspondents, but with the hard-boiled heavy-hitters among the industrial correspondents; that was a world I neither knew nor (at first) understood. But I did know one thing: that one insensitive comment could easily escalate into a headline that, bizarrely, could cause a strike in the volatile industrial relations scene at that time. Sid and Reg, in particular, handled most of these queries, and kept me out of a lot of hot water over the years.

Having an office at Warley (near Brentwood), which was company HQ, was a new Ford experience for me because until then I had been in outposts, either in Motorsport, or at the Aveley factory. Now I was to be where the company's heart was beating and where other directors were developing policy.

My office was sandwiched between those of the top finance man, Stan Thomson, and the sales chief, Ernie Thompson. To reach them was all of a 10-yard walk. Ernie was often an island of reasoned calm when everyone else was flapping about something. A great man. For some peculiar reason that I never really understood, Ford sales every month started slowly then built up to hit target nearer the end – Ernie was the one who held things steady when panic set in half way through a month when a target seemed out of reach. I'm not convinced it necessarily helped that daily SMMT figures showed sales in Britain by model for the previous day and for the month to date. The figures often produced nail-biting anguish and left me convinced that it's sometimes possible to have too much information.

As a multinational and a major employer, and one often in the media because of industrial relations problems, Ford took public affairs very seriously indeed (as should all companies really – too many tack it on as a poor relation of marketing; the two are not the same). Although I had a dotted reporting line to Walter, my day-to-day boss was the Managing Director of Ford of Britain. I knew three of them during my Ford period and they couldn't have been more different.

The first, Bill Batty, had come up from the shop floor and I saw both sides of the man within one 24-hour spell. I was scheduled to talk to dealers on an AVO matter and when I arrived at our London office at 8.20 for the rehearsal – scheduled for 8.30 – I found it well under way; Bill had arrived early so had started things early and firmly put me in my place for my 'late' arrival. The same evening I was due to speak at a major dinner and was reduced to a nervous wreck by spotting Bill among the audience. The next morning he phoned to congratulate me on my speech! A mercurial character and an industry legend.

By the time I moved to Public Affairs in 1975, Terry Beckett had become Chairman and Managing Director; he was very much a thinker and planner who had come up through product planning, marketing and sales. He was one of nature's quiet men, organised, soft-spoken and courteous. He was an accomplished and persuasive talker and some thought that he would have made an ideal university professor, although that was far below his potential in life.

From 1980 Terry – Sir Terence, no less – moved up to take the top job in the Confederation of British Industry and Sam Toy took his place. Sam was the typical salesman, flamboyant, expansive, always optimistic, volatile and exuberant. I learned a lot about the motor trade from Sam. In fact, until I met him I actually thought that *Glass's Guide* was a magazine for the shortsighted; mind you, with some of the crazy discounting that went on, perhaps I wasn't so far wrong.

We never had any trouble in promoting Sam to the media – he relished talking to journalists. There were times when I wondered where some of his opinions were coming from – until I realised that his chauffeur took *The Sun*, and Sam would flick through it on his way in to the office.

The Saturday on which Sam's promotion to Chairman and Managing Director seemed likely to be announced, I arranged to collect him at Heathrow off a plane from Detroit because I needed to get some quotes for our employee newspaper, and I knew that he was off on holiday the next day. My two young daughters were with me and they sat in the back, with Sam in the front, and his chauffeur following behind. I handed Sam a pad and asked if he'd mind jotting down answers to my questions. He said it would make him car sick so one of my daughters had to write things down instead. To my question 'What hobbies have you had?', his answer 'Breeding dachshunds' appeared as 'Breeding Datsuns'. I don't think Nissan would have approved somehow.

Tired as he was after an overnight flight, and with a lot to think about, Sam suddenly told me to stop so that he could show the girls the great views of London from Shooters Hill. Typical of the personal touches that made Sam so loved.

He tried to do too much at times and, like many of us, he sometimes got caught up in the tensions between Ford of Europe and Ford of Britain – both housed in the same building. Ford of Germany envied Britain because they were on the doorstep; we envied them because they didn't get running interference.

There seemed at times to be a constant power struggle between Britain and Ford of Europe and we even saw it in a mild way over Public Affairs. One senior colleague commented that 'Britain has less authority than Ford France' and I don't think my British sales colleagues were ever given enough credit for their huge sales figures; often Britain was the *only* European Ford company making any money.

It didn't help that Bob Lutz could sometimes be patronising about Britain; he was a lot less popular inside the company at times than his press coverage suggested.

On a happier note, one of the joys of that time was being a trustee of the Ford Charitable Trust. We'd meet, with one or two outside trustees to keep us in touch with the real world, four or five times a year to give to various causes, and we moved the meetings around the country so that we could visit projects we'd helped.

I remember one occasion when we visited a home for severely handicapped children that the Trust had supported. Over coffee, Sam asked what the school was aiming to do next and was told that they hoped to buy a minibus to take the kids out in. When Sam asked how they would fund it, the headmaster said that the Variety Club were helping and that they would raise the rest through various fund-raising activities; he said they had around £3,000 to go. Sam looked at the other trustees, raised an eyebrow, got nods, then turned to the headmaster and said, 'You've got your £3,000.' At which point the deputy head threw her arms round me and burst into tears ...

That was typical of Sam. He was a great character, and I never really understood why he didn't get the knighthood that several of his predecessors had been awarded – he earned it. Maybe it was because he was too honest to always say the right things to Margaret Thatcher.

As a major employer, we used to hold meetings once a year with the Cabinet, then the Shadow Cabinet, then MPs with constituencies near our plants, to tell them about our financial performance and thoughts of the future. Terry Beckett had a favourite slide showing our roller-coaster profitability with the multitude of changes to car tax, VAT, etc, marked on it. Harold Wilson took one look, sucked on his pipe and said, 'There you are, Terry, highest profits under a Labour government.' And he was right!

Under Mrs T, Ministers would arrive late for our meetings muttering darkly, even in front of complete strangers, about 'that bloody woman'. I only met her a couple of times and only for as long as it took her to find someone more important to talk to. To this day I still have to use the corner of a blanket as a comforter if I wake up whimpering after dreaming of those meetings.

Mind you, in an attempt at fairness, I must report that whenever I met European colleagues, they seemed to envy us the Iron Lady – the weaker their own domestic leadership, the greater their envy seemed to be.

In the main, I have to say, endless meetings with MPs left me convinced that politicians are rather like baby nappies: they should be changed regularly. And for very much the same reason.

Around this time, and again as a major employer, Ford supported Youth Training Schemes. We had young people at Dagenham and Halewood building wooden go-karts, with a similar scheme run at Ford Swansea by the manager, Len Stuckey, who was very community minded. I still cherish a model cannon given to me by the trainees at Swansea as a 'thank you' for support.

Although the YTS project didn't report to Public Affairs, we were closely involved because of the media possibilities. This was not us seeking to promote ourselves as the Good Guys but the YTS people encouraging us to trumpet what we did so that other employers would be nudged into following suit.

To get publicity we invited the Bishop of Liverpool, David Sheppard, and Archbishop Warlock to visit the YTS unit at Halewood. They came together to show secular solidarity and posed with the wooden go-karts. Then, as we walked them down the assembly line, out popped two workers wearing mock robes and cardboard mitres – much merriment all round and typical of Merseyside irreverence. Quickly: why did they call one Halewood foreman 'Balloons'? Because his mantra was 'Don't let me down lads'. And if a senior manager with a fearsome reputation was nicknamed 'The Animal', why was *his* boss known as Dr Dolittle? Because he talked to the animals of course. (Do please try to keep up.)

As well as youth training, Public Affairs also helped the environment. A 'Save the village pond' scheme had been started in John Waddell's time and over the years the ripple of this spread to

European conservation awards. It is said that when the pond scheme was described to European PR managers, one looked puzzled and asked, 'But why are we trying to save the *pound*?'

Looking back more than 20 years, from a time when we now have relatively stable labour relations, it's difficult to credit the huge industrial problems Ford had in the late 1970s. Trade negotiations were often extremely difficult – which reminds me that Ford had yet another long strike to contend with in 1978, which resulted in every unionised department being closed down, including Motorsport at Boreham. Peter Ashcroft had to support several small 'dealer teams' to make sure his drivers could still compete in the RAC Rally and the result was that Hannu Mikkola won his first RAC Rally in a car that David Sutton prepared.

It was also the year in which Ford was faced with an empty stand at the Motor Show due to strike action. I think I can claim mild credit for suggesting that we might just as well put old cars on display instead. That didn't sell any new Fords, of course, but it garnered quite a lot of sympathy from the press and public. It also gave me a welcome laugh to overhear one elderly gentleman say to another as they peered at the removable back seat squab of a Ford Prefect, 'I've had more fun on one of those than youngsters today get with all their in-car entertainment'.

Main negotiations between our Industrial Relations people and trade union officials were carried out well away from the factories themselves, in a scruffy outpost of the Ford empire, a garage complex not far from Paddington called, with unintentional irony, Moscow Place. The choice of this unlikely venue was dictated by increasing difficulties with previously used London hotels becoming 'unavailable' (perhaps because they didn't relish pickets and TV cameras on the doorstep). In fact, after major reconstruction, the garage became a first-class conference centre with a more calming name: Bayswater House.

While these meetings were going on, a coach or two of pickets would often arrive. Everything would be amicable and quiet except, that is, when the TV lights were turned on, whereupon the pickets would put down their playing cards, get out banners, start waving them and chanting slogans. Radio reporters would sometimes even go on a coach and ask for 'a bit of background lads' and would then record their pieces to the sound of chanting. 'Here I am at the tense Ford wage negotiations' indeed. I was never sure whether such TV and radio people were reporting events or creating them.

Our wage negotiations got much more attention than those in other industries, probably because (as one TV reporter once admitted to me in an aside) Ford was a lot more 'sexy' as a news item than a company making cement, pipes or chemicals. Ford, in any case, tended to have its annual negotiations in the late autumn, at the start of the wage round, so eyes were on us as something of a barometer for the rest of the nation. (As they were for any price increases – there were agonised discussions over how big they dare be and how we could announce them to get least flak. I bet there are political PR people today who mistakenly think that the Friday night release, to get low coverage in the Saturday papers, is a new idea.)

Bob Ramsey, and later Paul Roots, were the two Industrial Relations Directors who had to stand the brunt of the wage negotiations. Sid Wheelhouse sat in on all of them; I only went to a few because, believe me, they could be mind-bogglingly boring and drawn out. Public Affairs did not take an active part but we had to know what was going on. The unions' viewpoint would be fed to the media as soon as they walked out of the door and Sid and Reg had to be ready with our own interpretation of things. I suppose they'd be called 'spin doctors' today although they were infinitely more ethical than the political pests we now see in play.

Sometimes wage negotiations would be completed at Bayswater House by the end of a normal working day, but there would then be a recess for two or three hours before everyone convened again mid-evening. The talks might drag on again until 10 or 11 o'clock partly, I suspect, so that union delegates could tell factory meetings just how tough it had all been.

However, if we thought our labour problems were bad, others were in even worse shape. After *The Times* had been off the streets for a year, Bob Ramsey and I were asked to meet the Chairman and Managing Director to see if we could help them. Bob and I came away shaking our heads because their problems were beyond even our comprehension.

A fascination of this period was the major difference in attitudes that followed the 1979 General Election, when Margaret Thatcher became Prime Minister. No political lectures, I promise you, so please don't turn the page, but in our discussions with government we immediately noticed that it was now down to *us* to decide things, rather than have everything decided for us by legislation. For a time I felt we were really quite nonplussed by this. It was almost as if we were prisoners in a cage, the cage door was opened, and yet we still cowered in a corner, not sure what we should do. Business had to re-learn to think for itself.

This was the period when the Japanese motorcycle industry had swept all before it in Britain and when Japanese car companies were threatening to do the same. Considering the lesson of the bikes, the motor industry was still slow to wake up although I think Ford saw the threat before most. Bill Hayden, a truly formidable production man at Ford, went to Japan to see for himself, came back totally converted and, almost as a missionary, decided that we had to change our attitudes. When someone asked in a meeting, 'How do the Japanese do it', Bill was crisp: 'They work.' A new term 'AJ' (After Japan) was coined following his trip and from that time heads began to roll from previously over-manned areas.

Another result was that Bill made a video, which I helped to produce, in which TV's Martyn Lewis interviewed him. Bill went through what could, what might, happen if Ford did not react to the Japanese threat; the video ended with a bell tolling – a cliché, maybe, but it was a sobering message. We showed this to all the workforce as well as to many politicians. Sir Keith Joseph saw it and I heard that he went round muttering about the threat from Japan for days afterwards.

During that same time period there was major concern over the Japanese moving in to manufacture in Britain. We blew a bit hot and cold about whether we were for or against the idea. At one meeting with Ministers, a senior civil servant had a crystal-clear view: 'The UK has been whores for the USA for years – let's try Japan!'

On a lighter note, I managed to find enough in the PR budget to produce one or two videos for motorsport, including one called 'You Can Save Lives', made by leading film-maker Barrie Hinchliffe, which I was delighted to see win awards around the world.

I also found time to write a book about renovating cottages, and I'm sorry about this, but it's time for another dose of culture, because I had another poem published, over 20 years after the first (I must have had quite severe writer's block). This time it was in the *Sunday Times*:

All myopia
When girls I was courting
Weren't sporting
They'd breathe on my specs
Stop me dead in my trecs.
But I found a way to beat their defences –
Contact lenses

It later became the first poem in a book the *Sunday Times* published called, quite rightly, 'Worse verse'.

I got involved occasionally with Jackie Stewart on charity projects, which invariably involved an exchange of rude letters. The score was about even, although I think I did once (just once) get the better of him in a phone exchange. He rang and said, 'It's Jackie here, I'm in Detroit, I've just got in from Paris.' I said, 'It's Stuart here, I'm in Brentwood, I've just got in from Chelmsford.'

Formula 1 legend Graham Hill, who had been the official opener of the AVO assembly line back in November 1970, got involved with Ford in a series of promotional evenings with dealers. He was charismatic: I saw him make a speech at a mixed function in South Africa at Sunday lunchtime and roll people in the aisles with jokes I wouldn't use at an Ecurie Cod Fillet function today. The dealer evenings attracted big audiences and he suggested that we could use the events to raise money for the Lord's Taverners; as a result I became a Taverner myself and subsequently served on the Council for a couple of years. It was a privilege to be involved with an organisation that raises money to help handicapped youngsters and has fun at the same time. It gave me equal joy around this time to become an Associate Member of the British Racing Drivers Club, as well as to be one of those awarded a commemorative medal when Roger Clark won the Segrave Trophy for achievements in the rallying field.

I hope this isn't name-dropping too much (Prince Charles keeps telling me I shouldn't) but the last time I saw Graham Hill was at Buckingham Palace. In fact a few hundred others were there because it was a Taverners' function. Graham and I happened to leave together and I remember him stressing that manufacturers had to be careful not to make motorsport seem too easy with their various one-make challenges 'because it's bloody difficult to get to the top'. At the time he was concerned with the cost of running his Formula 1 programme but the remark forever influenced me in my attitude to junior teams and the like. I often think how proud Graham would be that Damon overcame the odds to reach the top.

I'd flown back from the South of France with Graham in his plane only a week before he was killed in an air crash approaching Elstree airfield, and like everyone else I was devastated. When we were having an ushers' briefing at his funeral, someone said that a member of the public was praying where family members were due to be seated; boxer Henry Cooper smacked one huge fist into another and said, 'Shall I go and have a word with him?' Graham would have liked that.

In business those were the happy days when Ford had a 30-per-cent-plus UK market share, with the Cortina on its own hitting more than 12 per cent, which meant that we could afford (and justify) going in for quite lavish new model launches to the media.

My Lord's Taverners connections helped with some of the personalities who 'sang for their supper' at our car launches – Eric Morecambe, John Cleese, Cleo Laine, Rowan Atkinson, Peter Cook and Dudley Moore for instance – not to mention the Grimethorpe Colliery Band. One or two colleagues were concerned whether a brass band would work in the close confines of the Craiglands Hotel in Ilkley; all I can say is that some of the overseas journalists stood on their chairs to cheer. There's nowt like a good bit of triple tonguing on the cornet, sithee.

Sometimes there would be a personal bonus. Once, after a press dinner at a vineyard near Bordeaux, when the journalists had boarded the coach back to the hotel, Sid Wheelhouse and I, together with the chateau owner, his wife and Peter Cook, had an hour's private jazz

Lack of skill at the wheel, demonstrated here with my father in an early Le Mans car, and while crewing for my mother on the Round Britain Duck Race, encouraged me to concentrate on the passenger's seat and rally navigation.

Left Some clown always puts two fingers up in a group photograph – in this case it was me (centre, third row back). Taken outside our living quarters, a little wooden hut, during National Service in Bodmin.

Below left First special influence was this 'Gaskin' with tubular chassis, Morgan front suspension and an auxiliary engine from a Catalina flying boat.

First car was a shortened 1937 Model C Ford seen on driving tests before and after it was re-bodied. The reduced weight improved the performance of the car but, sadly, not that of the driver.

With John Bedson in his Rover-based special after the all-night 1954 Measham Rally. Hypothermia came as standard.

Geoff Keys and I with his A40 Sports and a season's spoils. Badge-carrying was popular then – ours included BRSCC, BARC and Midland Auto Club. Sadly, the pattern for my pullover is no longer available.

This shot illustrates two things: 1) how many people it takes to scrutineer a Fiat on a Mobilgas Economy Run and 2) the importance of a navigator grabbing the only bit of shelter, leaving your driver – in this case Geoff Keys – to the elements.

With Ron Gouldbourn on a driving test in his TR2. Note the tuning – a coat to keep engine temperature up.

First RAC Rally was with 'Mac' Mackintosh in this Beetle. I was on my knees (appropriately in a praying position) when this was taken to keep the weight down.

With John Sprinzel, an Austin-Healey Sprite and total fatigue at the end of the Liège-Rome-Liège. To the left is the brilliant organiser, Maurice Garot.

1959 Monte with Ron Gouldbourn in a Standard 10. Strangely, my pudding basin helmet never really became the fashion.

Wolfgang Levy at Prescott on his way to another best-in-class time in the works Auto Union we used on the '59 RAC Rally.

With Erik Carlsson at the 1960 RAC Rally prize giving at the 'Talk of the Town'. Pat Moss flags off Erik Carlsson and myself on the Canadian Winter Rally.

On the way to a rally win with David Hiam. His talent as a driver was just one reason why he was such a great rally man with Dunlop.

Some may argue that an Austin-Healey 3000 should never be let out on snow and ice. Timo Makinen proved otherwise on the Monte with Christabel Carlisle.

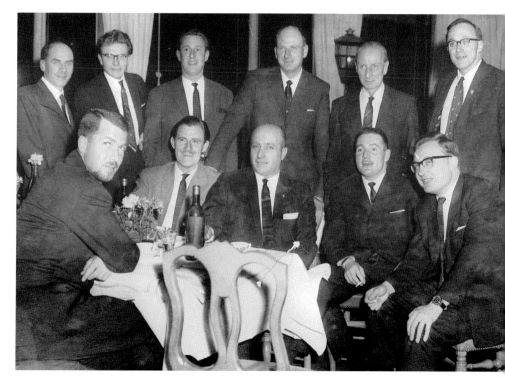

Top left BMC testing near Rhayader in Wales. The need to change couplings (often) led to the tipping-on-the-side routine.

Middle left Left to right: Bill Blydenstein, Christabel Carlisle (the eventual winner), John Whitmore, John Love and Peter Harper at the Easter Monday meeting at Goodwood in '62.

Bottom left The '64 Monte wasn't all in the mountains – Paddy Hopkirk on the circuit at the end.

Above Front row: Jo Bonnier, Graham Hill, Fangio, Paddy Hopkirk, ST. Back row: left to right, Donald Morley, Tony Ambrose, Patrick Vanson, Erle Morley, Alec Issigonis and Henry Liddon. Taken in Hotel de Paris, Monte Carlo in '64 after Paddy/Henry won outright and Donald/Erle took the GT category in an MGB.

Right Donald and Erle Morley in an Austin-Healey 3000 on the lower slopes of Mont Ventoux, a classic hill.

Above Too many people to caption but this shows the size of the BMC sorties to Sebring (this was 1963). Paddy 'Legs' Hopkirk is near the front, Geoff Healey far left, Donald Healey far right and John Thornley left of centre.

Below left Tyre selection was critical when we were only allowed 8 tyres on the '67 Monte. Here Timo Makinen helps me decide.

Below right This ad was based on a press release that Wilson McComb, BMC's comps. press officer, put out announcing that we'd already won 65 major trophies by half way through 1965.

The prototype MG Castrol sports car, presented at my last Sebring before I moved to Castrol, had certain stability problems.

It must be true that one's retentive powers are the first to go because I simply can't remember whether this was an Ecurie Cod Fillet re-union, or the time I spoke on global warming to Cheltenham Ladies College.

As usual, I'm too busy talking to watch the birdie at this GKN Motor Show lunch shot, but can you spot Colin Chapman, Max Mosley, Chris Amon, Ron Tauranac, Keith Duckworth, John Webb, Graham Hill, Ken Tyrrell, Jack Sears, Jackie Stewart, Phil Kerr, Harry Weslake and John Wyer?

A forum at Boreham to help private runners on the London to Mexico rally. Henry Liddon takes the class through the route while Jimmy Simpson of Castrol and Ford's Bill Meade wait to speak.

Although it sometimes seemed like it, not all the World Cup Rally was in the Andes. This shot of Rauno Aaltonen was taken on the San Remo special stage in Italy.

With Hannu Mikkola and Bill Batty, managing director of Ford of Britain, in Mexico after Hannu's win.

Among my souvenirs – a Michael Turner watercolour of Paddy Hopkirk on the Monte and a Dion Pears oil painting of Hannu Mikkola in the Andes on the World Cup Rally.

Hannu Mikkola and Gunnar Palm again, this time on their way to winning the '72 Safari – a first for Europeans.

We hoped that parking the GT70 alongside a GT40 would allow some of the latter's magic to rub off.

Mainstream body design for the GT70.

Ken Tyrrell brought an F1 car to AVO to put it on the rolling road.

Thanks to the meticulous housekeeping of Dick Boxall, the AVO production line always looked this clean.

Although the RS2600 Capri was mainly raced, Ford of Germany Motorsport also tried a rally version.

Down in the forest something stirred. Left to right: Anita Taylor, Roger Clark, Chris Sclater, George Hill, Mike Wood, ST, Tony Fall, Hannu Mikkola and Jim Porter while testing.

'Will you look at me while I'm talking to you.' With Ken Tyrrell and Colin Chapman.

Typical scene in the Boreham workshop. To the left is the Ford France Escort driven by Jean François Piot and Jim Porter.

Top *A drive in the Players No 6 celebrity car when they were clearly very short of celebrities. The only time an autocross car has ever been lapped I believe.*

Above *1953 Underwood Special with 1172 engine and Dellow(ish) chassis.*

Below *Bjorn Waldegard on his way to winning the '77 Acropolis in his RS1800.*

Above left *With Mike Kranefuss and Peter Ashcroft at Le Mans.*

Above right *First sight of the RS200 model at Ghia. Left to right: Filippo Sapino, Ken Kohrs, Ed Blanch, ST, Mike Moreton, Jim Capolongo.*

Below *RS200 alongside an RS1700T*

With Bob Howe and Jackie Stewart during RS200 testing at MIRA.

The first international outing for the RS200 was the 1986 Swedish Rally where Kalle Grundel and Benny Melander finished third.

Half an RS200 weighted to simulate a full size vehicle for steering column penetration measurement.

RS200 assembly by Reliant at Shenstone.

This was due to be part of a research programme in to which parts of a car get the most media coverage. The aim was to prepare a 'rate card' for sponsors.

'I swear to tell the truth about your engine power.' With Carlos Sainz in Corsica.

Above '88 Tour de Corse winner, Didier Auriol.

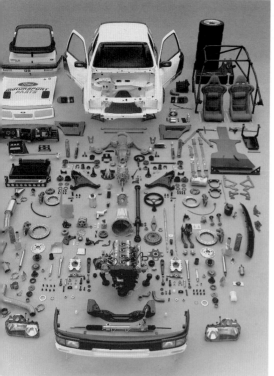

Left Intended to show private owners something of the range of Motorsport Parts for the Sierra.

Above right Why are they waiting? Because they are Sierra Cosworths stored at Dagenham before being converted into RS500s.

Right The Eggenberger-entered RS500s were World Touring Car Champions in 1987.

Above A one-off: the 'Escort Sierra' mule which eventually gave birth to the Escort RS Cosworth.

Below A Formula Ford French championship race – a fairly typical scene in the formula.

Above right Once this ad ran to celebrate a win on the Talavera Rally in Spain, I reckoned the Escort RS Cosworth was safe from cancellation.

Above far right The Autosport Award in 1990 made me feel very old because the last one I won (on the right) was over 30 years earlier.

Right Flying tonight. François Delecour on the Portuguese Rally in an Escort RS Cosworth.

First time out.

First.

The first glimpse of the new Escort RS Cosworth 4x4 was a very brief one for the drivers in Spain's Talavera rally.

All they saw was its distinctive rear-end as it hurtled past them and crossed the finish line in first place.

Perhaps even more alarming for these drivers was the revelation that the winner of this gruelling mountain race was a prototype. The fully developed model won't be

ready until 1992. Then we'll see what this fuel-injected, turbo-charged, 4 cylinder, 200bhp plus engine can really do.

You can get a better view than the rally drivers in Spain. Escort technology is on view at the Motorshow at the NEC in Birmingham until Sunday, September 30th. Not just the victorious RS Cosworth 4x4 prototype, but the whole of the new Escort family.

**The new Escort RS Cosworth 4x4.
Breaks the Law of Averages.**

Left Margaret plus our daughters Nicola and Sarah with 'Uncle Cliff' and Jill Summers.

Below With Marcus Chambers, Stirling Moss and Jean (Kimber) Cook at an MG Talk-In at the 70th birthday celebration for 'Old Number One'.

Above right A classic profile and understated elegance. The Dellow isn't bad either.

Below right With Des Large, President of The Society of the Irish Motor Industry, and Eddie Jordan at a dinner in Dublin.

Only the Escort could have attracted so many top rally people to a party to say farewell to it, and welcome to the Focus. Walter Hayes, father of it all, is by the nearside door.

Professor Sid Watkins fights hard but will soon be in as deep a trance as Jackie Stewart. Warning: hypnosis should not be treated lightly – do not attempt this trick at home.

concert by the Dudley Moore Trio. I wish I could have bottled that moment.

But however good the food, wine and entertainment, the cars still had to deliver and we had fraught times when the dismissive description of the Sierra as a 'jelly mould' took hold, and as we did when the Mk 3 Escort handling caused comment. To some extent we deserved headaches over the latter because, when we were running-in the press test cars, we all felt the ride was poor but we'd been so brainwashed by the engineers who insisted that it was wonderful that we thought it must have been us, and we didn't create as big a fuss ahead of the launch as we should have done.

I don't feel I have to apologise for the fairly lavish press launches – I say 'fairly' because other manufacturers were even more extravagant. Anyway, those were perhaps the dying days of motoring correspondents being of major significance in making or breaking a car; nowadays the 'doyens' of Fleet Street no longer have quite the same impact. This is perhaps partly because a fragmenting media world – and falling newspaper circulations – mean they reach fewer people. And it's partly because motorists – irritatingly – seem determined to decide their own priorities, whether dealer service or whatever, when buying. As a result, there have been several instances where motoring correspondents have gone into collective raptures about a car ... and the public have yawned and decided not to buy.

Because Ford needed to keep its dealers happy, new-model launches for them were often more theatrical, and even more inventive than our press ones; I got involved simply because I had to present our PR plans to the dealers. When the time came to show them the Sierra in 1982, Ford of Britain hired a massive, empty warehouse in Docklands and installed a complete movable gantry complete with seats so that when Sam Toy said 'Come with us on a Ford journey', the whole audience moved down the building. It all looked supremely high-tech, but when I went backstage I found the journey was created by burly blokes turning what looked like mangle wheels.

Arguably, car launches can go over the top but if you don't show your dealers that you are serious, and believe in a new car, how can you expect them to get behind it?

Incidentally, every year a minor part of my job was to prepare the submission for honours to go to the Government's Honours List committee, which perhaps proves that there is more to PR than feeding Fleet Street with stories.

One of the satisfying things that occurred during my period in the Public Affairs job was an involvement in a scheme to help disabled drivers. It all started when a motoring correspondent asked if we realised that disabled people found it very hard to learn to drive because driving schools didn't have properly equipped cars for them to learn on.

We feared that if we supplied special cars, less scrupulous schools would simply disconnect the controls and use them for normal business. So we looked into things further and realised that the Government's Motability scheme was there to help disabled drivers provided that they knew what special equipment fitted their individual needs. As a result we joined forces with the Banstead Mobility Centre – run by Morag Cornwell, a dynamo – to supply a mobile assessment unit to help check and advise disabled drivers so that they could get the right car and equipment on which they could then be taught. I have to say that I was influenced in pushing for the scheme by the fact that a very close friend has spina bifida, and I could see how such a scheme could benefit her. I'm delighted that the link between Ford and Banstead continues to this day.

Early in the 1980s I had a most bizarre invitation – one I certainly didn't expect. Sir Leonard Crossland, who had been one of the top bosses at Ford in the 1970s, had retired and become Deputy Chairman of Lotus. He called me and asked if I would be interested in moving to Lotus to become Managing Director. He presumably thought my AVO experience would be useful.

Sounds flattering perhaps, but even then, although Lotus was highly regarded by enthusiasts, as far as the financial community was concerned it had a controversial reputation. Furthermore, there would be the problem of working under Lotus's chairman and founder, Colin Chapman, who was a technical genius but also a maverick in so many ways and someone, I knew, who liked his own way.

Even so, it was intriguing and I guess I was flattered enough not to say no immediately. Colin Chapman called me, then we discussed the whole thing over a discreet dinner and eventually agreed that it was probably not a good idea. Somehow I didn't feel comfortable about making a leap of that sort and I got the feeling that Colin probably wanted someone who was more engineering-minded than I was. As an aside, I've never had much engineering knowledge, as photographs in this book of my early specials may indicate. Anyway, when I could call on the top people in the technical world, like Keith Duckworth or Brian Hart, chipping in my two pennyworth of nuts and bolts seemed like impudence.

By 1982 I was once again conscious of approaching that familiar seven-year point at which it seemed I began to get a bit twitchy. Seven years at Boreham/AVO, and now seven years in Public Affairs. I was 49, and although I'd not actively begun to look around for a change, I wondered whether Ford thought I was so comfortable in my current position that I should stay there for the rest of my career.

The Ford staff appraisal scheme was so detailed that most of us knew, for the next several years or so, what we might be asked to do so I felt that Ford had nothing urgently pencilled in for me. Promotion was likely to be difficult anyway in mainstream because I hadn't got a 'conventional' Ford background with time spent as a Zone Manager and so on.

I had never lost complete touch with motorsport because whenever Peter Ashcroft needed to make an important announcement, Public Affairs got involved, and we kept in touch as friends. As a result I knew that things were not going well at Boreham but I was still surprised by what happened next. Once again it was Walter Hayes who precipitated a change, but this time his phone call came from North America. He wanted advice . . .

Chapter 12

Return to Motorsport – new policies and the RS200

WHEN WALTER CALLED in January 1983, he had been in Detroit as Vice President of Public Affairs for Ford Motor Company Worldwide for nearly three years and retained responsibility for motorsport globally. He had nudged Ford back into the sport in the United States and did not want a mess in Europe to queer his pitch. He told me that he was picking up vibrations that all was not well with the RS1700T rally machine and the C100 sports cars. Would I talk to a few people and write him a note about it?

Motorsport was then being run by Karl Ludvigsen, an American who had been drafted in by Bob Lutz in 1980, with the job title of Vice President, Governmental Affairs and Motorsport, Ford of Europe. Karl, who had originally worked in the USA for many years, had become a distinguished motoring writer, after which he had a spell as Vice President of Corporate Relations with Fiat in North America. Along the way he wrote a number of excellent books, including one on Porsche, and it would be fair to say, I think, that he probably knew a lot more about sports car racing than rallying.

At this time I was still keeping well clear and minding my own business in Public Affairs, but occasionally people who had been in to see Karl (his office was not far from mine) would pop in to see me and I sensed an undercurrent of unhappiness.

Ford, after all, had not been actively involved in sports car racing since the GT40 days of the 1960s (apart from the ill-fated F3L) but they had been consistent world-beaters in rallying. Now it was already four years since the glory days of the 1979 World Rally Championship season, the new rally car was still not ready, and it looked as if it now might struggle against the new breed of four-wheel-drive cars that were coming along, led by the Audi Quattro.

At Boreham, in any case, there seemed to have been an unworldy atmosphere for some time as attempts had been made to make a rally car out of a 250bhp BDA-engined front-wheel-drive Fiesta, which simply couldn't get its power down. Having seen Minis become progressively more difficult to drive as engine sizes and power increased, I was convinced that the chances of making a front-wheel-drive car into a rally-winner were remote. Nowadays, you might point out, front-drive cars with well over 250bhp contest the World 'F2' category in rallies, but that was then and this is now ... and, all other things being equal, front-wheel drive will never beat rear.

Anyway, I made a few phone calls to people I knew to be discreet and to the question 'If it was up to you, what do you think Ford should be doing in motorsport in the future?', I got a crisply consistent response – the Escort RS1700T, and particularly the C100, had virtually zero support. Not only that, but the phrase 'four-wheel-drive' kept recurring, while special two-seaters like the Lancia Stratos were mentioned more than once.

I duly wrote to Walter on 17 January 1983 and pointed out that 'I must be cutting across many company procedures in writing to you ... but the situation is too serious for niceties. We should have one key objective in motorsport: winning. Anything which gets in the way of this should be stopped ...'

Among my other comments was that 'The C100 should be given a dignified burial. It takes one third of Motorsport's budget and even more of its nervous energy... We need a competitive Group A (ie 5,000-off) car. As Capri is nearing the end of its life, Sierra is the most suitable case for treatment ... We really need a competitive Group A Escort to back up Sierra ...

'We must accept that the new Audi will be a *formidable* competitor, and in 2WD form the RS1700T will struggle to beat it... Any car which, like the RS1700T, takes an eternity to come to life, makes me nervous ... I think as a safety net we should commission *in total secrecy and outside the company* the prototype for a run of 200 unique 4WD sports cars: if the RS1700T doesn't win then we should put a sports car into production at Lotus, Reliant or Tickford ...'

Then, in conclusion, I stated that '*If* we can introduce a new sense of purpose, with clear-cut objectives and the model programme outlined above, then Ford can, once again, be a major force in the sport. If we are not prepared to take such action, then we should stop. Anything is better than the present lingering death, which is making us a laughing stock.'

Within a month of receiving the paper, Walter had clearly talked to other top colleagues, because I got the message, 'We need you back at Motorsport. Now.'

I was comfortable where I was in Public Affairs so the approach was a shock – certainly not something I'd been angling for when writing the report. I've never been over-weeningly ambitious (I've certainly never aspired to a Rolls-Royce with a personal number plate – the height of naffness in my book, although I admit that the matching cashmere sweaters the owners always seem to wear do have a certain charm) and I thought I was beyond the point when I would ever get back into the sport. But it was almost like a First World War recruiting drive with an element of 'Your Company Needs You' about it.

Ed Blanch, Chairman of Ford of Europe, was in Austria at the time, but I got a call from him one Sunday asking me to take on Motorsport again, and two days later I started a series of meetings with Jim Capolongo, President of Ford of Europe.

I must have sensed that this would be an eventful period, because I actually kept a scribbled note of most of the significant events in the next few months. This is why I know that only two days later, and before I had actually said 'yes', Jim Capolongo called me again, this time to help him word the press release about the changes. It all started to look inevitable, but I could see the problems that existed, so almost as a delaying tactic I tried to negotiate a Vice President's title. But that didn't work – even back then there was a growing recognition that the company was top heavy on titles; as a sop I was, however, offered easy access to the company planes! More beneficial was the fact that I would become a member of the Product Strategy Group, which would be useful in getting new models approved. There was no question of me taking over Karl's job *in toto*; the 'Governmental Affairs' part of it was ushered back into the Public Affairs orbit where it should always have been.

Finally, I accepted the renewed challenge, as Director of European Motorsports, but on one condition: that I would have a completely free hand to reshape motorsport strategy. I got that assurance and, as a recognition that sorting things out would need powerful backing, it was decreed that I should report direct to the President of Ford of Europe rather than to a Vice President further down the food chain.

Incidentally, although I disagreed, fundamentally, with Karl's vision for what Ford should be doing in motorsport I got on well with him as an individual and he was always totally sincere in his beliefs. When he left Ford he set up his own London-based motor industry consultancy business, which thrives to this day.

A totally free hand? Yes, that's what was agreed. However, the honeymoon lasted only until the autumn of the same year, when Mike Kranefuss, by then operating from Detroit, was given the assignment of co-ordinating motorsport and related activities worldwide. In theory central co-ordination should offer benefits, although often with the loss of local flexibility, but I was not willing to see myself second-guessed from the other side of the Atlantic, so I wrote to Ed Blanch and Jim Capolongo saying, '. . . the change would break the spirit of the promises made to me when I was asked to take over Motorsport and would also be something of a vote of "no confidence", so if it is implemented I would like to be assigned to another job within the company . . .'

Quite properly, my ludicrously pompous huffing and puffing was ignored and I heard no more about things and although Mike progressively took more control of Formula 1 and other motor racing matters, mostly he left me alone; to this day we remain firm friends.

The good news, at least, was that Mike got to deal with Cosworth and the new turbocharged 1.5-litre Formula 1 engine programme that was just getting under way; I knew that this would be ticklish and I wasn't wild about getting involved.

Anyway, back in the bosom of the sport, I decided to keep my existing office on the sixth floor at Warley, quite literally in the 'Corridors of Power'. Crazy not to move to Boreham to be at the heart of things? Superficially yes, but I knew that I'd need a lot of support from other departments and the way to get that support was to be where the key people were.

Talking of key people, I met Henry Ford II for the first time during this period. I happened to be the only other person in the London office when he was there one day and had coffee with him. We got on to the subject of decision-making and he said he didn't want 'weather vane' colleagues – his description for people who told him what they thought he wanted to hear and adjusted their own views accordingly. He said he wanted honest opinions. That session left me quite thoughtful because I knew that I was going to be seeking a few honest opinions myself quite soon.

I quickly discovered that in the seven years I had been away from Motorsport, the way of developing new sporting Fords had changed a lot. RS models had all but disappeared (rear-drive Escorts had been superseded by front-wheel drive in 1980), and less specialised new cars like the Escort RS1600i had to make their way through the same 'filtering' system as all other mainstream types. One of my first tasks was to attend a progress meeting in the main boardroom about the RS1600i. The session dragged on for ever, partly because faltering steps were then being taken towards 'employee involvement'. This was the business 'in' thing at the time and everyone had to have their say; if the lady who brought in the coffee had had an opinion, I'm sure she would have been listened to . . . And, I suppose, why not?

While I'd been in Public Affairs I'd helped initiate one staff move that turned out to be crucial. Realising the difficulties Motorsport were having with the RS1700T, I'd suggested to Sam Toy that he should winkle Mike Moreton out of the Truck Marketing Strategy department, to move to Boreham to work on new products for Motorsport. In the next six years Mike, who'd done such great planning jobs at AVO, became invaluable as either the product planner or the project manager behind the RS200, the Sierra RS500

Cosworth and the Escort RS Cosworth. Some people have all the luck.

An urgent early task was to decide the future of the Escort RS1700T rally car and the C100 racing sports car. I thought I already knew enough about the prospects for the RS1700T, but I needed to take advice on the C100 so I went to Cosworth to talk to Keith Duckworth about the DFL engines (modified F1 units) that were to power it.

An aside here. The C100 had already progressed though several designers in three years, had had several homes (Gomm Metal Developments, De Cadenet Motor Racing, and Zakspeed among them), and had already used several different versions of the DFL. Although it showed promise, sometimes tested well, and made plenty of headlines, the C100 never came close to winning a World Championship race. For 1983 the plan was that the three 1982 cars were to be sold off, and one new car was to be constructed. Ford was proposing to spend £666,000 on racing this car; even after all this time, the 1983 machine was still only being described as a 'development' car, and was only to race four or five times.

For 1983 it was not only to have used a 3.9-litre DFL 'endurance' version of what had originally been a dedicated 3.0-litre Formula 1 engine, but a turbocharged version of that engine was also being developed. According to the forecasts, this engine, complete with a newfangled balancer shaft (to reduce the vibrations from which DFV-type engines suffered), could have produced 650-700bhp.

At Northampton, Keith Duckworth, ruthlessly logical as ever, was not hopeful, telling me that the chances of this engine surviving 24 hours at Le Mans were nil. My mind, accordingly, was made up for me: both the C100 *and* the Escort RS1700T projects would have to be cancelled. We had to get on with new projects as soon as possible.

As far as the C100 was concerned, I didn't have a qualm. Any company – even one as large as Ford – can only do so much in the sport, and I've always felt that sports car racing has the least direct marketing impact for a mass-producer, albeit fine for people like Porsche. In addition, sports cars seem doomed to remain fourth in importance, and a distant fourth, behind Formula 1, rally and touring cars. You can say only one thing about sports car racing – it's charming to have a category that sometimes gets such little support that crowd changes can often be announced to the drivers before a race.

I was genuinely sad that the RS1700T had to go. For more than two years Boreham had sweated on the development of this car, often without much help from other areas of Ford, except for SVE in the last few months. Motorsport was geared to run competition programmes, not produce production cars for sale, and this explains why the schedules had persistently slipped – at one time it was due to go rallying early in 1982, then before the end of 1982, and most recently in mid-1983.

Even then there was no chance of a full World Championship programme before 1984, and it wasn't Boreham's fault that the RS1700T had become a potentially great rear-wheel-drive car . . . at exactly the wrong time. John Wheeler and Peter Ashcroft had been lobbying for the chance to develop a four-wheel-drive version since early 1982, but had always been turned down.

On 14 March ('Beware the Ides of March' and all that) I attended a meeting of the Product Strategy Group and recommended that C100 and RS1700T should both be cancelled. To justify this I had briefing papers of less than one page covering each car and, as I recall, the discussion before the axe fell took less than 5 minutes. There was a tangible sense of relief that two troublesome projects had been killed off and the meeting smoothly moved on to the next item. As soon as I emerged I phoned Peter Ashcroft at Boreham, and work stopped that day.

Ford issued a press release stating that the two projects had been abandoned, and quoted me as saying that 'Having spent some time looking hard at our existing plans, I have become convinced that we are not moving in the best direction if we are going to resume our former position in international motorsport. This does not mean we are giving up . . . Make no mistake – we shall be back, although not with the cars we have under development at the moment . . .'

When the news broke there was much reaction in the press, some of it well-informed, and some of it quite unpleasant. I even got a letter addressed simply to 'The world's stupidest team manager'. I believe in free speech and I didn't mind the invective, I was just hurt that the Post Office knew who to deliver it to.

Autosport's editorial was balanced, noting that this would be a body blow for the new racing Group C category but that, 'On the rallying side, there will be few repercussions for the time being because the RS1700T's competition début was still some way off'. But a comment that: '. . . there must be questions about Peter Ashcroft's position as Competition Manager; the decision must be seen as a total vote of no confidence . . .' was rubbish. What they did not know was just how unhappy Peter (and his senior designer John Wheeler) had become about slow progress in the previous 12 months. It wasn't ability they lacked but support from way up the tree.

Motor thought that '. . . with last week's announcement, Ford have effectively abandoned five years' preparatory work – and wasted millions of pounds', which was the right sort of money, but too long an estimate of the time involved. The magazine also wrote that the

RS1700T 'was a Len Bailey design', which was both wrong and unfair to John Wheeler's efforts. The car was fast and promising, but had been overtaken by the four-wheel-drive revolution.

Writing an editorial, Ray Hutton of *Autocar* queried, 'What on earth is going on at Ford? Most people expected a change but few anticipated the wholesale slaughter of plans that last week heralded the appointment of Stuart Turner ... In one move, Turner cleared his new desk. It is hard to believe that Ford or Turner ... would cancel everything without an immediate replacement strategy. For a firm that has won Le Mans, countless Grands Prix and the RAC Rally eight times, the present situation is hard to understand. No doubt Stuart Turner knows what's going on ...'

Well, although I did know what was going on (to quote politician Harold Wilson, *I* was going on – at least I hoped I was) and already had a 'replacement strategy' in mind, there was no way that Ford could get back into motorsport immediately.

Almost as soon as the release had been drafted, I met with Ken Kohrs (recently appointed Vice President of Product Engineering) so that I could get a feel for what new mainstream models were on the way. Before the end of March I also found time to lunch with Frank Williams (whose F1 team was about to ditch Ford-Cosworth DFV engines in favour of turbocharged Hondas – and there was another reason, as you'll see below), and I took every opportunity to talk to 'grass roots' enthusiasts about what they thought Ford should now do.

Next, I wrote to the 15 national sales companies within Ford of Europe, up-dating them on the current situation, and enclosing a detailed questionnaire. This asked things like 'How important is Formula Ford?', 'Which branch of the sport gets most media coverage?', 'Which does most to help your *sales*?' and so on.

I got a 100 per cent response, all very supportive. Nine of the 15 companies put success in rallying as their top priority to help sales and six chose Formula 1 racing, with rallying always second. Sports car racing was only mentioned by two countries – Germany and Holland – neither making it their top priority.

One of the joys for me over the next few years was to meet the managing directors of all the national sales companies across Europe, including William Clay Ford Jr when he was running Ford Switzerland. (He later became Chairman of the entire company.)

I did whistle-stop tours – sometimes managing to visit three countries in a day – to meet the MDs and their marketing and PR people. As I was there only to discuss motorsport and not to kick them for any sales falldown, I think I saw the more relaxed side of them.

They all impressed on me that strong national programmes and personalities were important – Martin Schanche in rallycross for Ford Norway for instance – but they also all agreed that Ford efforts internationally were needed as an umbrella for it all.

Anyway, as a result of the 'round-robin' questionnaire, we established what was christened Ford's 'Ladder of Opportunity', which linked everything we might do in the next couple of years so that enthusiasts could stay with Ford as they progressed in the sport. This assumed that we could rely on driver loyalty – a naive assumption perhaps because (as is sometimes seen most brutally in Formula 1) loyalties and friendships don't always count for very much if someone comes along and whispers a better offer into a driver's ear.

With few competitive models on the stocks, we had to make as much noise as we could with what we'd got and this led to the many and varied 'Find a Driver' schemes run for us by John Taylor. He discovered that through psychological testing – via nothing more complicated than a 30-point questionnaire – it was possible to weed out no-hopers and headbangers before letting people loose in actual cars over short stages on mainly loose surfaces. We ran programmes in several countries over the years and, in more than one, found people with absolutely no previous experience who went on to win things. Many of the lady applicants came from show-jumping. If they went the wrong way round the various pylons we had laid out, some of them followed equestrian custom, touched their crash-hats to the judges and rode their cars out of the arena.

It was also with a view to making a lot of noise from an empty drum that we took another look at Formula Ford. I found that the good old Kent engine was about to be dropped from the category but felt that we didn't need the hassle of the change with all the other problems we faced. Therefore, once we'd established that engine supplies would still be available from Ford South Africa, we decided to leave the formula alone, which gave it stability for a few more years.

Later, Formula Ford went into new territories including France, where it had not featured for nearly 20 years. Jean Rondeau (who had raced Ford-engined cars at Le Mans) took ten Reynards, then built them himself using kits of critical parts shipped out by Reynard. I was amused to find only recently that Rick Gorne of Reynard could still remember the exact details of the deal quite vividly. It had the makings of a nightmare but in fact went quite smoothly.

One-make Championships and more emphasis on Formula Ford were important rungs of the 'Ladder', while at the top there were three major projects: a new Sierra-based Group A race car, a new Group B rally car and, possibly, a new Formula 1 engine.

I did not, for one moment, think that everything in the 'Ladder of Opportunity' could be achieved, but nothing ventured . . .

So much was going on at that time that the rest of this and the next chapter could get a mite confusing. So no change there, you may feel.

Anyway, to try to make sure that doesn't happen, I have put each new project into its own context.

B200 – THE RS200 PROJECT

Well before any definite work could go ahead, I had become convinced that Ford needed to start work on a special four-wheel-drive rally car to take over from where the Escort RS1700T had left off. Everyone I talked to had stated that they thought four-wheel-drive was essential; looking back it seems amazing now that there was any debate about the issue. But there was.

In an ideal world I would have commissioned a new project at once, had a prototype running before the end of the year, and got it homologated by the end of 1984, but this was never going to be a realistic target. With luck I thought we might be back in World Championship rallying by mid-1985.

It was with the Group B car in mind that in mid-April I went to Brabham, where I talked to Bernie Ecclestone and, more importantly, to his chief designer Gordon Murray (this was on the urging of Keith Duckworth). Later, Brian Hart and I went to Gordon's house and listened enthralled as he set out his ideas on how a special sports car should be engineered. It was a memorable evening and a master class in design.

Among many issues covered, Gordon was sure that the car should be mid-engined, that it should have a longitudinal, not a transversely mounted, engine, that the fuel should be located centrally and low down – and that high-tech materials like titanium should be avoided for what, after all, was meant to be a small-scale production car, and one that might need to be fettled at the side of the road on rallies.

Although I became convinced that he should personally design the car for us, and he tried to work out a way in which he could fit it in with his Brabham Formula 1 commitments, it wasn't feasible. In the end he called me in mid-May to say that while he was tempted, there simply wasn't time to do it.

I then went to Williams to see if Patrick Head (Frank Williams's technical chief) would be interested in doing the job but, very honestly, he turned me down. It wasn't until later that I found that he, and Williams, had already done a lot of work for Austin-Rover on the MG Metro 6R4; at that stage Williams had been keeping very quiet about that and, to their credit, they respected confidentiality and revealed nothing about the Metro.

Having talked to Gordon Murray and Patrick Head, I then drew up a designer's brief for the B200 (as it was then called) based on my discussions with them and anyone else I could think of. I knew – or thought I knew – that what Ford needed was a four-wheel-drive sports car, of which 200 would have to be made, and on that basis I was ready for it not to be based on an existing or projected Ford road car.

This brief started with an underlined paragraph: 'Key Objective: To produce an outright international rally winner. Nothing must be allowed to compromise this.'

Other objectives stressed the need to make it simple to service and operate, to be safe, to have good driver visibility ('NOT a lie-down racing position. Windscreen angle is critical for rallying . . .'), to use standard Ford parts wherever practical and, ideally, to use developed versions of the RS1700T's BDT turbocharged engines, for these had already been manufactured, tested, and were in store. Using those engines, we could claw back more than $1 million that had been written off in the Escort RS1700T's cancellation, which was bound to make me a little more popular with the number-crunchers.

I said that the designers should first visit Boreham, to be exposed to the atmosphere of rallying, but that 'No body styling is required – this will be done by Ghia' (Ford's Italian design studios). I had already concluded that a unique shape would be needed for the car for three reasons: 1) I wanted a 'world' car that could be used by Ford locations not selling European models; 2) it would be ageless and unaffected by mainstream model changes; and 3) it would be a hell of a lot easier to shift 200 cars (the number needed for motorsport homologation) if it was a unique shape rather than, say, a Fiesta with bulges and wings all over the place.

In April Mike Moreton went over to Turin to see Ford's styling consultants, Ghia. Like all motor-mad Italians, Filippo Sapino at Ghia was enthused by the idea and said that although Ghia was always busy with other Ford work, he would make time for his people to style the B200: 'It is just the kind of project we are looking for . . .'

Filippo reckoned it would take up to four and a half months, and up to £200,000, to do the job properly. On the assumption that I could raise the money, I promised mechanical package information by July, so that Ghia could complete a full-scale model by November/December. By September I had sent him a three-page brief on what we expected of Ghia in which I petitioned for 'An ageless design . . . An exciting (but unaggressive) design with a "Ford family flavour". A "Porsche Sierra", perhaps . . .'

Mind you, it wasn't all plain sailing with them. On my way back from the Italian GP in 1983, I collected a package of styling sketches from Ghia, showed them off at a meeting we held at Boreham . . . and Mike Moreton drew the short straw to go back to Turin to say that we didn't like any of them. Even less tactfully, he took with him a sketch done by Ford of Europe's design chief (and motorsport buff) Andy Jacobson, which we all liked. I gather from Mike that Ghia's designers then hit the roof. Steam came out of their collective ears as they made it clear that what we had seen were only rough roughs, concepts, ideas, call them what you will, and were in no sense final proposals.

The big argument was over the working environment for the drivers. We wanted an upright screen so that there would be no distracting reflections when flashing through forests. Ghia wanted a more raked and sporting one. Eventually, we won.

In a way, though, I think all this put them on their mettle and the result was a much more distinctive shape that they later improved, and which we soon approved. It was a shape that evolved considerably in the first few months; the first car looked rather different from numbers 2 to 6, and all the production run. The design was further refined for us at Dunton by Ian Callum – of Escort Cosworth and DB7 fame – and John Hartnell, who also designed the interior with symmetrical instrument panel.

I always tried not to get emotionally involved in my business dealings, but when I first went to Turin, along with Ed Blanch, Jim Capolongo, Ken Kohrs and Mike Moreton, to see the full-scale model, and saw the clay in the studio, I came as close to tears as at any time at Ford. Even in budget meetings.

No one was ever going to confuse the RS200 with anything else. It had an entity of its own, it looked like a thoroughly professional design, and it certainly didn't resemble an ugly kit car of the type produced by some of our rivals. It was, incidentally, not only an attractive style but also effective, because at speed there was positive downforce at the front and rear.

The designer's brief had gone to three people – Tony Southgate, Mike Loasby and Nigel Stroud – while John Wheeler of Boreham also put forward his own ideas. John was the designer of the RS1700T and also had years of Porsche design experience. I found out later that he was furious that he had not been asked to submit a design – this on top of the cancellation of his baby, the RS1700T.

Tony Southgate, who had once designed BRM and Arrows Formula 1 cars, had recently been working on the C100 (and, later, would design Jaguar's Le Mans-winning XJR-9). Mike Loasby had been the technical director of Aston Martin for a time, before working on the DeLorean sports car project. Nigel Stroud (one-time Formula 1 designer at Lotus, who had also engineered Nigel Mansell's race cars) was also invited to put up a scheme.

We wanted their proposals to be evaluated without bias, so the designers were asked to put code numbers, not names, on their submissions. Mike Kranefuss over in Detroit was beginning to take an interest, and in Germany Peter Ashcroft's opposite number, Lothar Pinske, suggested consulting a specialist racing car company like Dallara of Italy, but I thought that they were too close to Fiat

Lancia and turned that down. Even at this point Lothar, by the way, suggested that we would need at least 500bhp to be competitive ...

Each of the invited designers reported back by midsummer, and once again I asked Gordon Murray, as well as several Ford colleagues, to vet what had been suggested.

All the proposals had the BDT engine, longitudinally mounted immediately behind the cabin. One study included the engine on the centre line of the car but it fell down on other respects, while another was considered to be more of a racing car than a rally one. In fact, no single proposal stood out. From Germany, for instance, Lothar Pinske suggested that all the designs looked too complicated for rough-and-tough rally use, and wondered if we would be better with a transversely positioned engine (like the Lancia Stratos). Others didn't like the idea of offset in-line engines, and there was some resistance to the idea of using aluminium honeycomb and other 'race' as opposed to 'rally' materials in the structure.

In the end we decided to go for an amalgam of two proposals, one from Tony Southgate and one from our own John Wheeler. They were asked to get together, combine their talents, and come up with a fully engineered design. This was done, the two continuing to work in reasonable harmony ('reasonable harmony' always being a relative term where talented engineers are concerned) for the next 18 months.

At this time, incidentally, the 'B200' was still only a paper car, and I had no funds with which to have even one car built. But we pressed on, and because of the way the engine would be fitted, offset from the car's centre line and leaning over to the left, we fitted one in a Sierra at much the same attitude, to gather experience. It worked fine.

My hope was, first, to gain approval to build one car – a 'look-see' prototype – then, if that looked promising, to get five more cars built in 1984. The six cars would give us two for production development, two for rally testing and two for legal homologation; one of them would later be hurled into a concrete block at 30mph to meet the crash test. Only then would we be able to produce the balance of 194 cars, to reach the 200 needed for Group B homologation.

The critical meeting was on 20 September 1983 and was chaired by Bob Lutz, who was now running world-wide automotive operations from Detroit. The meeting took place at Ford's London office and there was some debate over whether the money would be better spent on Formula 1 or rallying; I argued that it wasn't 'either/or' but that we should do both. It all became a bit tense and I didn't help by being overly critical of my predecessor at one point; there had to be a recess while emotions cooled down and Lutz and Ed Blanch held a private conference. With a certain amount of deep breathing we got approval to spend $293,000 on a prototype (with the possibility of five more to follow). A close thing.

Finance man John Kaplan's formal request for funds stated that, 'Assuming successful completion of the initial testing, it is planned to build five more prototypes. The additional expenditure of $580,000 will be included in the 1984 Motorsport Sales Promotion Budget'.

Five and a half months later, on 12 March 1984, we had a running car to show to Bob Lutz and a few important people at Ford's garage in Balderton Street, not far from Oxford Street, where personal export cars were delivered to customers. Drawings, opinions, budgets and every other aspect of the project were considered; John Wheeler was a valuable colleague, for he and Lutz got on well and Bob was technically literate about the whole thing. The first non-Ford man to see the car there was Prince Michael of Kent, a keen enthusiast who had rallied Escorts in the old AVO days.

That prototype, which used a slightly modified RS1700T engine, had been assembled by ART, an organisation at Woolaston in which Tony Southgate and John Thompson were involved. John's company, TC Prototypes, had produced the chassis and other sheet metal. The car looked great, it worked, and everything seemed promising. By this time it had logically been christened 'RS200'.

All of which makes it sound easy. It wasn't. Southgate and Wheeler had sweated blood to refine the design, FF Developments of Coventry had produced a unique four-wheel-drive transmission and Ghia had produced the styling. And the body? That was built in Wales by Ken Atwell then elegantly trimmed by Aston Martin Tickford. Ken was the maker of the GTD40 kit car – a high-quality replica of the GT40 that I'd seen on display at various community events organised by Len Stuckey at the Ford plant in Swansea. He was initially regarded as an odd build choice for such an important product but I believed that only someone like Ken, totally unencumbered by 'systems', would deliver something in the time we needed. And let me repeat: *it took only five-and-a-half months from approval to having a complete and running car.* I rest my case.

The fact that we had managed to build one car so quickly must have impressed Bob Lutz, especially because we actually brought it in under budget and the next stage, to build five more prototypes, went ahead with little discussion. Alex Trotman, who later went on to head Ford worldwide, was on the scene by this time and he too was supportive. At this time we were still hoping to have production cars available in the first half of 1985, and to get that far would need an extra $200,000 spending on rally testing, and $400,000 on development and certification work.

Jackie Stewart drove the car, fast, at MIRA, on the handling course, and in September 1984 his letter to Walter Hayes was illuminating: 'The car I think has great prospects. Although there is still much to be done it has started off as a car with no apparent bad habits; the handling is extremely good for a first time running.'

Enter, at this stage, Bob Howe, who was fast approaching retirement in European Advanced Service Engineering. Bob, who had last worked with me at AVO in the 1970s, agreed to return to Motorsport on a contract basis, and took over the management of all the type approval/homologation work, which he eventually tackled along with Aston Martin Tickford. We couldn't avoid clearing this hurdle and didn't want to offer the car as a 'kit car' fiddle – type approval was seen as a frightening mountain we felt we had to climb. Thanks to Bob, we cantered over it.

At this time Mike Moreton and I spent a lot of time in meetings, mainly marketing and financial reviews where we had to push the project over other hurdles. Even though the total investment (originally estimated in 1984 at $9.2 million – about £7 million at contemporary exchange rates) was small by Ford standards, it was entirely proper that the financial side was being monitored. As an aside, it didn't exactly help Motorsport's relationship with the finance men that two other competition chiefs in the industry spent brief spells in jail. John Webb, then running the Brands Hatch group, helpfully offered to have T-shirts printed saying 'Turner is innocent'.

It certainly helped the lobbying process that I was Warley-based, as did the fact that we kept costs relatively within targets. A very successful compulsory crash test did no harm either.

The only real internal opposition to the car came from a few sales and marketing people because it didn't look like any car that the company was selling in the mid-1980s (I told them it used Sierra screen, windscreen pillar and front door profiles). They also felt that it was going to be administratively messy to sell a handful of oddball cars to a whole variety of Ford sales companies throughout the world, but we answered that one by agreeing to handle the sales ourselves as far as possible.

The crunch came when we had to get approval to build the 194 more cars needed to bring us up to the total of 200, for homologation. It stopped being a petty cash project at this point but, deep breaths, it was eventually signed off in the States. I think it helped that, at the time, Ford of Europe was seen as an important staging post for high-flyers within the company – that's why you may find a bewildering list of names flitting through these pages – so there were people in America who knew about European motorsport and its challenges.

We unveiled the RS200 at the Ghia premises in Turin immediately before the Turin Motor Show of November 1984. When I made my pitch, one journalist asked why I had changed my mind about Group B, and about four-wheel-drive – both of which I had scorned at one time. There was only one thing I could say, and did: 'It was one of the most damn fool comments I have ever made.'

Soon after the public announcement, a letter appeared in *Motoring News* from someone enthusing about the car and saying that a simplified rear-wheel-drive version would sell like hot cakes. This appeared in the press clips circulated within Ford and Bob Lutz scribbled me a note saying, 'He's giving *my* speech. Use 2.3-litre turbo for North America, Cosworth for Europe, "conventional" Ferguson 4WD, drop price to, say, £20,000 and sell thousands.'

As you will gather, he was a great car enthusiast. I found this out for the first time when I was in his office and saw a model Aston Martin on his desk. When I passed a derogatory comment he made clear his enthusiasm for the marque! Perhaps just as well he wasn't around when Ford bought Aston Martin – I happened to be addressing Ford dealers that day and told them not to get excited because we'd appraised the product range and decided to sell Astons through our truck dealers. I am talking about the earlier models, you understand.

A big decision remained over the RS200: where to build the 194 cars. There was no longer an AVO-style operation within Ford, Boreham didn't have the capability and it was crazy even to think of having the cars built in a mainstream factory. Although Saarlouis (the 'Escort factory') had finally agreed to attempt the RS1700T build, there was no enthusiasm for tackling our all-new car. For a mid-engined car, in any case, there was no obvious Ford plant where such cars could be built, which meant that we had to cast around for an independent factory.

Mike Moreton went to Blackpool to inspect the TVR business, reporting back that it had all manner of possibilities as a 'satellite' factory in which to build our Group B cars, but 'I think they would be stretched to manage the programme as well as run their own business'.

As a result of these and other visits, we made a short-list of people who might, just might, be able to build 200 cars – a list which, as well as TVR, included Lotus ('Expensive, and have links with several other companies'), Aston Martin Tickford ('Good image. They are expanding') and Reliant ('Possible. Need the work').

Having considered all the options, we decided that Reliant could offer much of what we needed. Not only were they ideally equipped to produce all the glass-fibre body panels, but they also had a large empty factory at Shenstone, near Lichfield (at one time it had built engines for the three-wheelers), just waiting to be used. And they had spare labour capacity.

There were reservations at Ford about asking Reliant to get involved, for those who were impressed by the Scimitar GT/E sports cars were balanced by those who knew all the jokes about Robin three-wheelers. But having seen the staff, and found them extremely practical about the whole thing, we did the deal, installed Mike

Moreton as Project Manager, with a team of Ford engineers and managers under him, and the race to build the cars began. Almost all the assembly and fitting was done by skilled Reliant people but we had serious quality control problems when getting the right parts for them to assemble. One problem was that we were working with suppliers used to producing small quantities (six or so for rally cars) and they struggled with the greater numbers we needed. Fortunately, we had an ex-mainstream Ford man, Ivor Joynes, on board; he was invaluable. On one occasion, some last-minute parts were taken hot from the press – literally so because they set the trim on fire in the delivery vehicle.

Shenstone was probably an ideal factory for what we wanted to do because there was enough space to store tubs, body panels, engines, transmissions and all the pieces – still with ample space to lay down a simple assembly line to complete the cars. In a way it was almost an AVO all over again.

We opened up the Shenstone assembly plant in April, equipped it, trained the staff, got in early component supplies, and finished the first true production car (Chassis 008) in September. Our initial plans called for 15 cars to be assembled every week, which meant that the entire batch would be completed in less than four months.

When we showed the press around the RS200 assembly lines in December 1985, the place was in bedlam for serious batch production had not begun until October/November; there were half-finished cars everywhere, lines of BDT engines in one corner, four-wheel-drive transmissions in another. To journalists (and, I have to say, to some of us), meeting our homologation deadline of 31 January 1986 looked unlikely.

But, in a great rush, we completed the build of the 194th car in time. All the cars were built, and counted by FISA inspectors, but the last few were thrown together, and I doubt if they would have made it out of the factory without bits falling off.

I felt the successful homologation deserved plugging inside the company, not least to maintain confidence in the programme, and wrote to Bob Lutz to say, '200 RS200 cars were counted by the motorsport authorities 2 years and $4^{1}/_{2}$ months from getting approval to start the first prototype, which must be some sort of Ford record. Austin-Rover took over a year longer with the Metro 6R4 ...'

The RS200's first rally victory came before the end of 1985, in a British event (the Lindisfarne, which allowed non-homologated cars to run), with Malcolm Wilson driving. Boreham had been preparing rally cars for some time before they started their first World Championship event, the Swedish Rally of February 1986, just two weeks after homologation was achieved. Kalle Grundel took third place on the event, and things looked hopeful.

With an approved budget of $14.4 million for 1986, we had a

formidable competition programme in prospect. Then a season of tragedy unfolded. In Portugal, where the crowds were enormous, our local driver, Joaquim Santos, went off the road in his RS200, to avoid spectators who were actually standing in the road, and three spectators were killed. Along with our rival teams, we immediately withdrew our other team cars from the event.

Only two months later Henri Toivonen crashed his Lancia Delta S4 in the Tour de Corse: both he and his co-driver Sergio Cresto were killed. It became obvious that the latest Group B cars were probably too fast for the events (and, frankly, the organisers), and within days FISA announced the end of Group B, to take effect at the end of the season.

Although we went ahead and sent two cars to the Acropolis Rally, where both led for a while before retiring, the heart went out of the season. We cancelled all further entries except for the RAC Rally, and started development work on Group A Sierras for 1987. I saw no point in throwing good money at a programme (and, as far as public opinion was concerned, in a dangerous formula) that would end almost immediately and would stop us being competitive in 1987.

On a wider front, the RS200 had a successful single season – winning 19 International rallies and several national rally championships (including the British, by the way). In the future, too, RS200s went on to dominate European rallycross events for several years, proving that the design was sound and its potential unlimited.

High-profile adventures were also considered – for instance, one-off RS200 entries in the Pikes Peak Hill-climb in the USA (which would cost $0.5 million) and a Paris-Dakar Rally Raid entry for much-modified RS200s ($4.9 million for two cars) – but we decided not to bother.

We were already on course to produce a faster 'evolution' car before the end of the year (once 200 cars were built you were allowed to do 10 per cent more evolution versions) and John Wheeler was already pushing ahead with a '100 + 100' car – 100kg/221lb lighter, 100bhp more powerful. We had already contracted the engine work for this to Brian Hart. After much research, he concluded that the engine ought to be expanded, from 1.8 litres to 2.1 litres (which would put the car in a different class/weight limit). But to do this, and still keep the cylinder head gasket in one piece, he would have to design and develop a new version with more space between the cylinder bores. This meant that the entire engine would need to be longer. We agreed this and Brian (not Cosworth) produced the 2.1-litre BDT-E, which delivered well over 600bhp in 1987 rallycross form and which has subsequently been boosted to even higher figures.

The day after Group B's cancellation, I had to break the news to our top finance man, telling him that we weren't able to sell any more rally cars. To his credit, instead of throwing me out of his office, possibly even out of the window, he sympathised and calmly and constructively sat down to see what we could do to minimise the losses. We estimated that these might total $5.2 million but this figure assumed that 30 cars could not be sold; the losses would be halved if we could sell off every car on the inventory.

While we had the Shenstone factory full of RS200s, in various stages of completion with many now facing an uncertain future, Reliant sold the adjacent building, which shared a common wall. Mike Moreton called me one day to say that fire had broken out on the other side of the wall, and that although there was no threat to the staff, he had feared for our own stocks:

'I wasn't quite sure whether to have the RS200s pushed *away* from the wall to save them, or to have them pushed the *other* way, so that we could claim the insurance money. I think I might have made a mistake ...'

At which point I guessed, 'You've saved the damned things, haven't you?'

'Yes, Stuart, sorry, but I have!'

Having failed with fire, and having noted that the nearest river was too far away to rely on a flood, we decided to close the Shenstone operation, put the cars in store, then, after a lot of hard work by a development team led by Bill Meade, we converted all the existing stock into road cars.

We decided to ease the task by stripping 46 cars to provide service spares, so a total of 148 cars remained, roughly split 50/50 between 'road' and 'rally' specification. To make the road cars more attractive, we found a specialist at Wilmslow, Strattons, known for customising Ferraris, who suggested also marketing luxury trim versions of the RS200. They gave me useful pricing advice too. When they said that £49,950 was wrong as a British retail price, I assumed that they meant it was too high and I stressed that it was as low as we could go. In fact, they meant it was too *low* and that in that area of the market a £50,000 car sounded far more appealing than a £40,000 one. We upped the price to £52,950 and found they were right.

For the next year, preparation for sale was carried out by JQF at Towcester, before the job went to Aston Martin Tickford (at Bedworth, near Coventry) in December 1987. In the end we got type approval for every European market except Sweden and Switzerland, and this involved conducting some remarkable tests, and adding one or two mildly silly features. As an example, for access to the engine bay the entire rear end panelling of the car lifted up on roof-mounted hinges, complete with tail lamps. To cater for German regulations, we had to put a duplicate set of rearward-facing tail lamps on a chassis bar *inside* the engine bay.

After his heroics on type approval, Bob Howe turned to selling the cars and for the next four years both he and Graham Robson (who was running an RS200 Club we'd formed, as Registrar) ran RS200s as normal high-mileage road cars so that we stayed ahead of our customers in sorting out problems. Sales were helped by the fact that we really did try to take customer care seriously and the service manual, bound in leather of course, was as good as they come. In the earlier days of the programme, I got too besotted with the road version. Was it really necessary to plan fitted luggage for a rally car, for instance? But the misplaced focus now did no harm.

The late King Hussein of Jordan had a test run and Bob even sold two to brothers in the Manchester area (when asked 'Why two?', they said, 'Well, we have two Quattros and two Cessnas . . .'), and a few even found their way to the USA.

We set a very high figure to cover warranty claims – originally estimated at $1,000 a car, but later set at $2,138 – even after allowing for the fact that at least half the cars would be rallied, where warranty no longer applied, and that some would receive virtually no use in the first year, after which warranty cover would automatically lapse.

Soon I had a call from Ford's warranty specialists, asking what sort of truck the RS200 was; the warranty provision was the highest of any current Ford model, so they figured it just had to be a truck. We were proved wrong to be so pessimistic because most of the cars were cosseted and driven so rarely that in the end warranty claims were much lower than feared, at only $400 average per unit.

One day someone – and it ought to be Bob Howe – should write a complete book about the RS200, how it was pushed through the legal homologation processes, how it came to be manufactured, how each individual car had to be demonstrated and sold, how many of them were stored at Boreham while new owners waited for them to appreciate in value, and how the project was brought to a conclusion.

For the record, seven new cars were sold in 1986, 41 in 1987, and the balance were sold (or contracted to be sold) by the end of 1988. In January 1989 I sent a memo around the sixth floor at Warley recording that 'With some relief, I am able to advise that orders, with deposits, were taken for the last cars in the dying days of 1988 . . . the "prepare for sale and delivery" programme will continue at Aston Martin Tickford until July 1989 . . . I sincerely hope the motorsport authorities never again cancel a rally category at 6 months notice, but this particular project is now completed. RIP!'

Walter Hayes replied that: 'I don't suppose anybody else will say it, but I thought somebody should congratulate you on the way you kept your nerve and handled the RS200 programme so well, right to the end.'

But for once Walter was wrong. Several other people said it; the most welcome reply of all came from the finance director, saying, in effect, 'Well done, we never thought you'd shift the damned things . . .' That was important because the value of maintaining credibility inside a company for an oddball activity like motorsport should never be underestimated. Cock-ups just hand ammunition to sceptics – and there are always some in any organisation.

I knew I'd need all the help I could get because now it was time for other cars.

Chapter 13

Final fling – Sierra and Escort

THOUGH THE RS200 was perhaps the most glamorous of the new products we studied in 1983, much more was involved in trying to put Ford Motorsport back on its feet.

The Escort RS1700T and C100 programmes were dead but there were other, smaller, projects for which I could see no future. When Ford should have been developing a new race-winning saloon, most of the effort had gone into smaller, front-wheel-drive Escorts. It made sense, I thought, to be rallying the Escort RS1600is in the short term (and developing turbocharged versions of the CVH engine). But Ford of Germany was dabbling with a long list of engine conversions for which I could see no purpose, everything from 16-valve heads for the CVH engine to turbocharged V6s for the Sierra, from high-performance Pinto engines for the Transit van, to a variety of work on the 2.8-litre Cologne V6. Then there were dress-up kits for Sierras – wheels, lowered suspensions, flared wings, spoilers, power-steering conversions and steering wheels. All took effort, and money, that I thought could be better spent elsewhere.

With so many changes needed, Formula Ford was one of the few 'constants'. So, with Kent engine supplies secure and with the formula established in most key markets, I asked Mark Deans, who had a European brief in Motorsport, to set up a Formula Ford Race of Champions in the UK. For a couple of years we bought 25 identical Van Diemens and flew in national FF champions to drive them at Silverstone and Brands Hatch. Drivers included such names as Frank Biela, Roland Ratzenberger, Bertrand Gachot and Paul Tracy. Considering the complexity, the events worked well and Mark's organising ability was such that when I made my 'have a safe journey home' speech at Silverstone and the Red Arrows shot over just as I finished, two or three drivers congratulated Mark on the perfect timing!

Back among the tin-tops, a succession of cars was used, or developed, with motorsport in mind, and perhaps I should separate them, to show just how complicated life could get at times:

ESCORT RS1600I

By the time I returned to Motorsport, the RS1600i, originally a Ford of Germany project for class wins, was in production at Saarlouis, and MCD, contractors to Boreham's works team, were already using two cars in the British Rally Championship. Although Malcolm Wilson and Louise Aitken-Walker always drove them as hard as possible in 1983, it was rather a wasted season.

In theory, this was only a holding programme to keep Ford in the limelight until the RS1700T was ready, but the publicity was mostly negative. With front-wheel-drive and only 155bhp available the cars were not fast enough, and because the transmissions were weak they broke down far too often.

By mid-season I was considering pulling the programme, but eventually let it dribble on. Malcolm Wilson's class win in the end-of-season RAC Rally was a relief, but I was glad to forget the RS1600i after that. Yes, yes, I know that they are cherished by collectors today, and rightly so because they were nice road cars. But not rally winners.

ESCORT RS TURBO

The original turbocharged Escorts, built up from engine kits evolved from XR3-type carburettor engines, were already competing in their own one-make championship when I arrived, and we soon decided that an evolution of the type, complete with fuel injection and style changes, should be added to our 'Ladder of Opportunity'.

Suitably prepared (and, for racing, Richard Longman's team got at least 270bhp out of the 1.6-litre engines) these cars looked promising. Bill Meade had cleverly developed kits for the championship cars – when he went to Cologne to do a hot test to check turbo reliability, he was told that 'a similar car [Dunton designed] only lasted 10 minutes here recently so we won't need to do any overtime'. But they did, and it was largely Bill's version that went into production although, as he told me recently, it didn't win him any friends at Dunton.

Dunton was very 'headcount' conscious and Bill Meade, John Griffiths and Terry Bradley gamely agreed to go there to SVE, run by Rod Mansfield, to help on the development side; if Boreham hadn't loaned people, the programme might well have taken longer. Mike Moreton's product planning skills were also important; he was our liaison man with SVE as well as with Dunton generally. One manager in Product Planning who had done some rallying was particularly helpful – Richard Parry-Jones who later rose to be Group Vice President of Car Development.

Happily, we were able to keep the extra-special (and expensive) RS1600i-type front suspension in the production specification and this was the first ever Ford car to use a viscous-coupling limited-slip differential.

Unhappily, 'Job One' slipped, production build-up was slow, and we did not get Group A homologation until the middle of 1985. This, and major problems encountered with the new five-speed transmission, meant that it never achieved its potential and the Group A rally cars developed at Boreham were a disappointment.

Even so, the original model of 1985/86 was a very effective 'class car', winning championship classes all over Europe, as well as Britain's Willhire 24-hour race outright. In all 8,604 cars were sold and from a tiny investment of $4 million this produced a healthy profit – quite enough for the company to approve a more refined and 'softer' version at face-lift time in 1986.

SIERRA RS COSWORTH

Way back in January 1983, in my report to Walter Hayes, I had suggested that we urgently needed a race-winning Group A saloon car; the old-type Capri 3.0-litre cars weren't competitive any longer. In fact Walter and I had spent a miserable day at the British GP, watching the Rover Vitesses – some run by Tom Walkinshaw – charging round and humiliating the Capris. The fastest of the Capris was ninth in practice and ninth in the race – consistent but not quick enough. Only a stirring performance by Richard Longman's RS1600i, in his class, eased our gloom.

Given a free hand to develop strategy, two steps were taken, one immediately, the other later in 1983. One was to produce an upgraded version of a new Sierra-based production car that was already coming along – the car that would be badged as the Merkur XR4Ti, and sold almost entirely in the USA – and the other would be a totally new model.

But it wasn't quite as clear-cut as that. By mid-1983 we were discussing the option of radically modified 3-litre V6 Sierras, turbocharged 2.3-litre Sierras, 5-litre V8-engined Sierras (which eventually went into production in Ford South Africa), and Sierras with engines that hadn't even been finalised. About the only thing we agreed on was that we needed to win, not just race to make up the numbers.

As I wrote in the Motorsport Committee minutes in July 1983: 'The end product will be seen as a European car and must be capable of winning against all opposition from Rover, BMW and Jaguar – BMW for Germany and Rover/Jaguar for Britain. This would probably need 300bhp ...

'The Sierra race car programme should only be done if the car will win . . .'

Luck then played a major part. I went with Ed Blanch and Jim Capolongo, Chairman and President of Ford of Europe respectively, to Cosworth to see what was brewing on the Formula 1 engine; I felt they needed to see what a DFV looked like.

Ed and Jim had never been to Cosworth or been exposed to Keith Duckworth's personality (everyone ought to be, at least once in their lives – the effect is like electric shock treatment, I can tell you) and they were duly impressed. While walking through one assembly shop to the Formula 1 area, we passed a 2-litre Ford Pinto engine that had been given a 16-valve twin-cam conversion; looking back I'm sure it wasn't an accidental sighting.

In passing, we asked, 'What's that?' Keith's comment was, 'We think we can find a market for 200-300 performance kits as a private venture of our own.'

Nothing more was said. After we'd seen the Formula 1 set-up, we went to a local pub for a ploughman's lunch, and sat round a rustic table in the sunshine talking about what we could do in the future. Almost as an aside, I suggested, 'If we could put that 16-valve conversion into a Sierra, and turbocharge it, Rovers wouldn't win another touring car race. But we'd have to build 5,000 of them' (the production quantity then needed for such a car to be legal in motorsport).

And so the Sierra Cosworth came to pass? Not really. Although I was always a great Tommy Cooper fan, it wasn't quite 'just like that' because many more discussions followed before the car went ahead. I am sure that exploratory meetings had even preceded the ploughman's lunch but the vital point was that the two key decision-makers were there and I'm convinced that this gave the real impetus to what became the Sierra RS Cosworth programme.

It must have struck a spark, because few people – except the manufacturing engineers, who eventually had to build the cars at Genk – found flaws in the concept. It had to be analysed, costed, designed and tested, and Rod Mansfield's SVE team had to take on most of the work. They produced a great car.

As they were still short of people, John Griffiths, Bill Meade and Terry Bradley agreed to stay on at Dunton after the Escort Turbo was finished. I suspect that they were afraid of being forgotten by Boreham but I'm glad they were prepared to stay; they took real motorsport expertise with them and without them the philosophy of the car might have been diluted, and we might not have ended up with a winner.

In the meantime, the new 'interim' Sierra was well on its way. By the autumn of 1983 we knew that the 2.3-litre turbocharged Merkur was nearing the end of its development and that its USA-designed/Brazilian-built engine was looking promising. The same engine was already scheduled for use in a special Mustang and the signs were that the Merkur could be a useful interim race car for us, although not before 1985 as production was not due to begin before the summer of 1984.

The race-prepared turbocharged engine was running by mid-1984 and produced 275bhp, much more than the Capri ever had, but still not as much as we wanted. However, well before series-production began the first race car was tested at the Nurburgring in August, progress was encouraging, and by early 1985 we had 320bhp. Homologation was finally granted on 1 April 1985 and Andy Rouse's car raced at Oulton Park just a few days later.

Although the XR4Ti's racing career was short – 1985 and 1986 only – it was successful, for Andy won the British Touring Car Championship both years, and the Swiss-based Eggenberger team won European races in 1986. Most importantly, it helped test and prove much of the chassis and running gear that we intended to use in the Cosworth-engined car.

One of the few internal problems we had with the Sierra-Cosworth was its extrovert looks. Although our designers were adamant that a big rear wing was essential to produce the downforce to get the power on the road on the race version, many non-believers were horrified with its size, and where it was placed, effectively half-way up the line of the hatchback.

Why, some said, could we not settle for the bi-plane rear wing already in use on the XR4i? It took time to convince those people that the package really worked. Wind-tunnel tests, carried out at MIRA, finally proved that we could guarantee downforce at front and rear, *and* reduce the overall drag coefficient.

The first time I saw the model I was startled, and I remember saying that it seemed designed so that if a police car was following, you would be able to see the blue light above the wing, and the main 'Police' sign below it. Three years later, on my way to a party in an RS500 Cosworth, I proved the point, as my driving licence will confirm.

Bob Lutz, in the end, approved the layout on a styling model in March 1984, and no more criticism was heard.

Even the late, great Jim Clark helped get the Sierra Cosworth approved. At one point when it was all a bit marginal, Ford of Britain's Chairman, Sam Toy, looked across at a painting on the boardroom wall of Jim Clark three-wheeling his Lotus-Cortina around a race track and asked, 'Will the Cosworth do for the Sierra what the Lotus did for the Cortina?'

'Yes,' I said, with fingers firmly crossed, 'and more.' Sam then became a supporter, which was vital because clearly Britain would have to commit to sell a healthy percentage of the cars. As an aside, Sam had a cottage splendidly positioned on the banks of Loch Ness. It was perhaps this connection that made it difficult to stop him calling the RS1700T the 'Monster'!

The Sierra Cosworth appealed to all the national sales companies, and there was little resistance to getting the cars made at Genk; maybe it was a relief after the horrors of the RS1700T manufacturing dilemmas.

I'm sorry if the numbers needed for a car to be legal for motorsport confuse you (welcome to the club) but over the years various figures have been set according to the mood at the time. When the Sierra Cosworth was planned, 5,000 had to be built, then 10 per cent (ie 500) evolution models could be produced for racing, although not rallying (evolution models were stopped in rallying after the death of the 200-off Group B cars). Once the RS200 manufacturing programme was out of the way, Mike Moreton worked with Boreham's John Griffiths to get the 500 extra Sierra Cosworths produced.

To give you an idea of the pace of the programme, Mike started working on the project in June 1986 and programme approval was given in December to build 500 extra cars at Genk, ready to be put into store at Ford's Frog Island base at Dagenham. We only got the extra 500 cars approved when Derek Barron, by now MD of Ford of Britain, phoned Bill Hayden to confirm that he would sign up to sell all the cars; we just missed the opportunity to schedule them all in black. Preparation work at Aston Martin Tickford's factory at Bedworth began in April/May 1987, and all 500 were converted in June and July 1987.

Profitable? Certainly. It cost less than $2 million to carry out the programme, and calculations showed that Ford made nearly $400,000 in building those cars. The really clever bloke was the one in Marketing who suggested calling it the RS500; for a time people were even paying above retail price to get their hands on one.

Even so, it was perhaps a prime example of the way Group A regulations could be exploited. Consider: the RS500 road cars had suspension mounts that were not used on road cars, over-large turbochargers that actually made them slower, not faster, than the ordinary Cosworth, and extra front spoilers that reduced the ground clearance – but if that was what we had to do to produce a guaranteed race-winning car, so be it.

The results speak for themselves. The RS500 Cosworth, in race car tune, when its 2-litre engine pushed out to 550bhp, was a magnificent racing car. By the end of 1987, the Cosworth, particularly the RS500 variety, had already achieved everything we hoped of it. In touring car racing, the Eggenberger team clinched the 1987 World Touring Car series in the final race of the year, at Fuji – a series that included five outright race victories by Ford. The championship was then abandoned. It won the European Touring Car Championship in 1988 – and that was never run again!

But the car wasn't without controversy. An element of xenophobia concentrated on the race cars' rear wheel arch specifications before the end of 1987, this being caused by the way the sheet metal was being folded over to give clearance for the racing tyres used. After the Eggenberger team had dominated the Australian Bathurst race, they were protested on 'wheel arch grounds' – which cannot have made much difference to their performance – and in the end the dedicated regulation readers got their way, and the win was annulled.

In a way this rebounded more on the teams who protested than on ourselves, and (as with the Mini 'lighting fiasco' of 1966) it brought publicity, most of it good, to our cause. We made minor changes to the way the body shells were prepared and the RS500s carried on winning.

I always took the view that we'd built 5,000 cars plus 500 evolution models, so if people wanted to beat us then all they had to do was the same. But I was probably wrong because only the size of Ford and the unique co-operation I got at the time made such a car possible, and you need more than one manufacturer to have good racing. Later rules making it easier for manufacturers to compete made more sense.

Once the RS200 project was cut from under our feet, we had little choice but to turn to the Sierra for rallying too, even though the RS Cosworth had never been designed with that in mind. Maybe the rear-drive Sierra wasn't the ideal car for loose-surface rallying, but it was certainly fast on tarmac and in 1987 Sierra RS Cosworths won 26 International rallies across Europe as well as six national championships.

Several star drivers – including Carlos Sainz and Didier Auriol – made their reputations in these cars; Didier won the 1988 Tour de Corse, while Carlos so nearly won more than one event in the same year. Both of them, and other drivers like Jimmy McRae and Mark Lovell, won national championships along the way.

Although quick on tarmac, the Sierra Cosworth was obviously at sea on snow and ice, for which we turned to the Sierra XR4x4. We got ourselves into a muddle over fuel injection systems and homologation for this and deserved a slap on the wrist. We duly got it plus a huge and, in my opinion, disproportionate fine of $250,000. It was out of line, and we were stupid to get things wrong, but it was hardly a hanging offence. At about the same time Lancia committed a similarly heinous 'crime' by using two different types of turbocharger to gain Delta HF 4WD homologation. They were found out, the mistake was well publicised, but they were not fined a single Italian lira.

By 1988/89 we were realistic about the rear-wheel-drive Sierra Cosworth's failings on slippery surfaces and made a conscious effort to spend money on events where the cars could win, not even competing in others. And we still stuck rigidly to our rule of not accepting sponsorship from cigarette companies for works programmes – and, believe me, multi-million dollar amounts were offered from time to time. I guess your attitude to fags is conditioned by whether you've lost smoker friends through cancer (I have). In my view the sooner tobacco sponsorship ends the better. The sport won't collapse – of course it won't. At business conferences I'm coming across more and more people who'd like to sponsor motorsport but, quote, 'we don't want to be in something so tainted by ash cash'.

But to attract major sponsorship of any kind, we needed a new car. And that brings me to the . . .

ESCORT RS COSWORTH

Patient readers will have gathered that, quite rightly, I spent a lot of time justifying budgets to people, from financial analysts up to the Chairman of the company. One difficulty was that while the financial payoff for, say, a dealer incentive programme could be easily calculated, the direct benefit of motorsport was a little less tangible (it still is for that matter).

To try to overcome this, I persuaded the company to spend quite a lot of money – from memory, I think it was $100,000 – on a major market research project. I wanted to find out if there was any truth in the American adage 'Win on Sunday, sell on Monday' because if there was, it would give me ammunition to back proposals for new and expensive rally car projects.

As too many people in our sport, perhaps understandably, overstate the case when seeking sponsors, I've always been a bit downbeat about the benefits, and I was mildly cynical about the results that would come back. Does anyone *really* watch a particular car win a race or rally then pant down to the dealers to buy that same make the following day? You do? I hope all your timeshares are doing well.

If you are such a convert then here's your starter for 10: if Mini UK sales in 1963 were 134,346, what were they in 1965 after all the publicity following Paddy Hopkirk's Monte Carlo win? 200,000? 300,000? Sorry to spoil your illusions but sales went down, to 103,147.

In 1993, Alfa Romeo had a sparkling season in British touring car races. So did their UK sales shoot up in the following year? Er . . . no, they fell. But, I hear you cry, perhaps the market as a whole fell. Sorry, but their market share fell as well.

Those are by no means isolated examples so you can see why I've always been sceptical about wild claims concerning motorsport's influence on sales. The argument that the sport is absolutely essential to help develop production cars doesn't really stand up either and is something of an insult to mainstream engineers and modern computer technology. After preliminary trials, the market research company confirmed my suspicions and said that it would not be possible to measure a direct link between success and sales.

What they *could* do was establish whether consistent and successful involvement in motorsport helped to boost a manufacturer's image. They could, they promised, establish what motorists really thought about the significance of motorsport.

We gave them the go-ahead and people were interviewed in Britain, Germany and Italy, about their attitudes to the sport. Not surprisingly, Formula 1 proved the most popular but rallies and touring car races were recognised as of more benefit to the ordinary motorist.

The research showed that over two-thirds of motorists believed that the sport benefited the car buyer and most felt that it was worthwhile for manufacturers even if their cars didn't win. Even many of those uninterested in racing or rallying believed that the ordinary motorist gained, particularly in engine and technological development.

One interesting conclusion was that companies who had once made large and successful efforts in motorsport, but had withdrawn several years previously, were still seen as having bright and sporting images. So the memory lingers on.

Ninety per cent of those interviewed across the three countries had heard of the Monte Carlo Rally, way ahead of the second best known, the Safari on 52 per cent. Other events were known in their own countries but less widely elsewhere.

Although the research did not prove a direct link between competition success and increased sales, the image-enhancing benefits were quite clear so I made much use of the figures in every presentation I made thereafter, both inside the company and to potential sponsors.

The research made my on-going task easier and also helped support the plans that I put forward. One brick in the wall was still missing – a world-beating rally car. We had built a competitive four-wheel-drive Group B car, the RS200, which was killed off by regulation changes, we had built a race-winning saloon car, the RS500 Cosworth, and we had a new clubman's RS model, the Escort RS Turbo.

But we still didn't have a modern four-wheel-drive rally car and, although the Sierra Cosworth 4x4 looked like being available in 1990, it also looked like being too big, and too heavy, to compete against the likes of Lancia and Toyota in the 1990s.

Peter Ashcroft, Mike Moreton, John Wheeler, John Griffiths and Bill Meade and I used to get together at Boreham regularly for meetings about the future. I think we were all agreed that whatever our next rally car would be, it had to be based on the platform and basic layout of an existing mainstream model. Also it would have to be built in a mainstream factory because of the 2,500-production rule for Group A homologations (by now the 5,000 stipulation had sensibly been halved).

There was one seminal meeting, early in 1988, when we concluded that we had to stop playing 'catch-up' – reacting to new regulations instead of planning ahead of them. We'd been last in the field with a four-wheel-drive Group B car, we'd not so far had a four-wheel-drive Escort of any type, and we'd never got enough power out of the Sierra XR4x4 to make it competitive.

Over time, the specialist press had given us a hard time over this, as well as pointing out that Ford took much longer than anyone else to get a new competition car into production. This time we wanted to plan well ahead, for the 1990s, and we wanted to start at once.

Mike Moreton had already been briefed to delve into Ford's forward model plan and he reported that every new-generation Ford would be a transverse-engined, front-drive car. At the same time we had got hold of drawings of cars like the Lancia Stratos, and of the current Lancia Delta Integrale, just to remind ourselves of packages that were competitive.

The next-generation Fiesta, Mike told us, would appear in January 1989 but we thought it was physically too small for our needs. We knew that the Sierra replacement (CDW27 was all we knew it as in those days – it later became Mondeo) would not appear until 1993, and would be too heavy and have a transverse engine and front-wheel-drive. The next-generation Escort (CE14), due in late 1990, was the right size but . . . it was also front-wheel-drive. So no obvious rally car shone through.

I fear that this isn't a good chapter for modesty because although I'm not trying to take on the halo of an all-knowing soothsayer, I think it was one of my comments, thrown into the conversation, that encouraged a breakthrough: 'Why don't we see if we can take the platform and running gear from a Sierra Cosworth 4x4, shorten it, then see if an Escort body will fit on it?'

I suppose it's the sort of lunatic thing a non-engineer would suggest and I can remember the laughter at the time. But the more we analysed our options the more sense it seemed to make.

We approached mainstream planners as well as SVE but they poured scorn on the idea and would not back it. I knew that when it came to convincing the hierarchy about a new project, it was always better to show them hardware, a real car, than sketches and drawings, so we found enough spare in our budget to use John Thompson's TC Prototypes as a 'skunk works' – a phrase the Americans use to indicate a place that can do clever and creative things cheaply and quickly and, above all, without getting bogged down in paperwork.

Somehow or other, Mike Moreton and John Wheeler got hold of a prototype Sierra Cosworth 4x4 (this car was still nearly two years away from series production) and, along with an Escort RS Turbo body shell, we set Thompson to work. For around £60,000 and in only four months (4 July to 31 October 1988), he built a masterpiece – a car that looked just like a white Escort RS Turbo but with wider track and longer wheelbase.

Having driven it round and round Boreham, to get the spring and damper settings about right, we then offered it to one of our contracted rally drivers, Stig Blomqvist, to try against the clock at Boreham. With only 230bhp available in what we still called the 'Escort Sierra', it proved to be faster than the current 310bhp Group A Sierra RS Cosworth rally car.

We showed it to the planners and SVE who were somewhat surprised to find that it was all physically (if not financially) feasible, then we took it to Head Office in Warley and offered it to several people, from the Chairman downwards, to take for a drive. They all went up and down the A12 and, to a man, came back with silly grins on their faces; then, I have to say, every one of them made much the same sort of remark:

'Marvellous, great fun. Now go away and think of something more sensible . . .'

Hardly surprising that to them, as Ford mainstream people, the idea of matching up one modified platform to the much-modified body shell of an entirely different car, and metamorphosing it all into a new model, seemed crazy. Even though we told them we'd been to see the independent Karmann business (who were already building Escort Cabriolets and Merkur XR4Tis, basically the two models that were to be melded together) and that they could handle production, it was still a big leap.

But we had the car. This did the rounds of every Ford mover and shaker in the next few weeks – and at the same time John Wheeler, Mike Moreton and I developed a detailed presentation that was intended to convince everyone that it should be approved. Between us we must have given the pitch at least 30 times. Without John Wheeler, who turned the original idea into practical engineering, and Mike Moreton, who shaped a superbly professional marketing and financial package, the car would never have gone ahead. It was one thing for me to say 'Why don't we . . .?' That was the easy bit.

Gradually we converted one critic at a time. Our flip charts included pictures, comparative drawings, market research and financial predictions – and the forecast that it would be a rally-winning car. We stressed that all (all!) we wanted was a 16-valve 2-litre turbocharged 4x4 CE14 with north-south engine – in other words an RS500 Sierra Cosworth with 4x4 and a CE14 body. At this stage we were confident that the new car could be more than 220lb/100kg lighter than the Sierra Cosworth 4x4, '. . . enabling us to get down to the permitted motorsport minimum weight'. We forecast that such a car could be 'competitive to the end of the 1990s', which was confirmed by events, for the Escort WRC did not actually 'retire' until the end of 1998.

It's funny how some cars get names, nicknames, or codes. Because this project featured a new-type Escort body style, that car being coded CE14, and because we needed it as a Group A rally car, it was logical that we should immediately code it ACE14. Soon we shortened this to ACE, or 'Ace' – and that was what it remained for the next two years.

One satisfying moment was to make a presentation to the managing directors of all the national sales companies in Europe, then hear from the darkness a voice saying, 'I'll take a thousand.' It was the head of Ford Italy, and when Ford France chipped in with a similar commitment, I felt the project was going to fly. It helped that many Ford locations had had success with the Sierra Cosworth and could see how much knowledge could transfer to the Escort so that their local preparation teams would not be flummoxed.

Most of the 'petrol heads' inside the company saw what we were trying to do, and backed us with enthusiasm. But there were other cautious operators (mainly sales or marketing people) who could not see how a car with four-wheel-drive and an in-line engine could possibly benefit a range that was soon to comprise nothing but front-wheel-drive cars with transverse engines. I remain convinced that people neither know nor care about such technicalities – looks are what matter and 'Ace' clearly looked like an Escort. (As an aside, in the Mini days more than one owner was found to have put a pair of snow tyres . . . on the back.)

It helped, however, that from the spring of 1989 I had the big guns – the Chairman, President and most Vice Presidents of Ford of Europe – on my side. A bit later, I must have felt weary on the day I had to brief the President before he went on a trip to the USA to campaign for the car, for I added a footnote: 'I guess what we really have to decide is whether, long term, we want to be winners or losers.'

Walter Hayes, needless to say, turned lobbying for 'Ace' into one of his last projects before he retired, and his input, and his by then Vice-Chairman status, made a noticeable difference.

In 1989 we gained pre-programme approval and Dunton Design could shape the car's extrovert aerodynamic hang-ons in the wind tunnel. John Wheeler was seconded to Dunton, so that detail design and development could be handled by Rod Mansfield's Special Vehicle Engineering department – where one or two minor projects were actually cancelled to make way for it.

Once they saw that the total investment involved in 'Ace' was less than $40 million (peanuts by Ford's new-model standards), the European Automotive Operations Product Committee approved the programme in December 1989. The Americans followed suit early in 1990, and the style, complete with that colossal rear spoiler, was signed off at the same time. Even so, the car did not reach production as soon as we would have liked, but then motorsport people always want things yesterday.

In an odd way the press reaction to the Sierra, which had caused so much anguish when I was in the Public Affairs job, actually helped 'Ace'. The adverse comments about Sierra's then unusual appearance frightened the company so much that it played safe with the new Escort and made it quite conservative. But when market research on pre-production cars came in it was discouraging, for the public's general impression was that the car was a bit dull.

By now I reported to Jack Brinkley, Vice President of Marketing, and we had a good working relationship. When Philip Llewellin interviewed me for *The Independent*, he quoted me as saying, 'My job involves everything but Grand Prix racing, for which I often kneel by my bed and thank God.' When this appeared in the press clips, Jack sent a copy to me with scribbled on it, 'There's something I've been meaning to tell you . . .' I was glad he was joking.

Anyway, concerned by the lukewarm response in market research clinics to the new Escort, Jack sent a note round asking for ideas to pep up the launch. I told him that there was an ideal opportunity to run our first prototype rally car in September 1990 in the one-day Talavera Rally in Spain, which had no homologation restrictions and where Ford Spain's regular driver, Mia Bardolet, could take the wheel.

If we took the car out there, with one of our contracted teams – Mike Taylor Developments with John Taylor running the team – and it failed, I reasoned that we could ignore the whole episode, and hope that no one had noticed. But if we succeeded – well, we could make as much noise as if we had won the Monte Carlo Rally. Even though the total cost of this exercise (which included building the complete car) was $180,000, Jack, who had a well-developed sense of irony, gave the go-ahead.

The car went to Spain and won the event against, I must admit, fairly ordinary opposition, but it proved its point. Although this was not a significant qualifying event for any rally championship, in terms of what it did for Ford it was almost as important as victory in a Safari.

When John Taylor called from Spain on the Sunday evening to tell me that the car had won, I rang Jack Brinkley at his home with the good news. Jack had a number of Ford of Europe people round that evening and when he told them I could hear the cheers in the background . . .

Three days after the win the car was on show on the Ford stand at the Motor Show in Birmingham. There was another consequence. Once the car had appeared in public and a success ad had run saying 'First time out. First', I knew that it would be almost impossible for the company to cancel the project without huge loss of face.

'Ace' then had a starring role in the media launch of the new Escort. The press, black-tied and cheerful, had enjoyed dinner at Blenheim Palace, near Oxford, and had then been ushered outside to see the unveiling of the range of mass-production Escorts. It was dark but Blenheim's courtyard was lit like a stage set, and there was a spectacular display of marching and music from military bands. Then a Motorsport van swept into the courtyard, drew up at the bottom of the steps, and out of it, in a stunning blue/grey stripy colour scheme, the Escort RS Cosworth rally car was pushed into view, its first real public appearance.

What few people knew is that, although the car looked ready to roll, it was not nearly finished, and it didn't even have an engine installed, which is why it was pushed rather than driven around. But it made the impact that we had hoped. Not that you can win them all. Afterwards I heard complaints from some quarters that the arrival of the rally car had taken attention away from the new production cars . . .

With a rally win and a formal press launch I knew that 'Ace' – or to give it its formal title 'Escort RS Cosworth' – was safe from cancellation and I could retire happy.

But I wouldn't want you to think that my second stint with Ford Motorsport was all about hardware. True, I seemed to spend a lot of time fighting to get the cars we wanted and that process was challenging but often enjoyable. In fact 'fighting' perhaps gives the wrong impression – there were no fisticuffs, no pistols at dawn, just rational and analytical debates about what were often quite expensive projects. The businesslike approach to things is one reason why Ford is such a gloriously successful company.

Slightly less rational at times but even more enjoyable was working with some great drivers, among them, to be diplomatic, in alphabetical order:

Pentti Airikkala: We first got to know him when he was a Dealer Team Vauxhall driver, but David Sutton hired him to drive Escorts from 1976. On performance he was beating Roger in the 1976 RAC Rally then struck car trouble in the last 24 hours – but Roger couldn't have caught him.

Later drove for the Rothmans Escort team (1981), drifted away to all sorts of odd cars, then unexpectedly won the 1989 RAC Rally in a Mitsubishi Galant VR4.

We signed him for 1990 and he drove development Sierra Cosworth 4x4s, then works Q8 cars in the 1000 Lakes/San Remo/RAC. Crashed badly in the RAC, hurting his shoulder, and that was really the last time he drove a competitive rally car.

Didier Auriol: Had been driving Metro 6R4s in the French Championship, but when Group B was cancelled, moved on to Sierras. Although he only drove Sierras for two years he made a big impact winning the French Championship outright in 1987. He joined the official works team for 1988 – for which I got some stick from the British press – but won in Corsica in a 3-door Sierra Cosworth, and was third in the 1000 Lakes. Won the French Championship again in 1988, then left the team, looking for 4WD, to drive for Lancia.

Stig Blomqvist: Once he had joined in 1985/6, he became one of Boreham's all-time favourite people. Did much test/development driving of RS200s, then Sierra Cosworths, then Sierra Cosworth 4x4s, then Escort RS Cosworths – but never actually won a World Championship event for Ford.

Stayed on board with Ford even when an 'elder statesman' and has won events and championships in Scandinavia. Rightly very popular there as I saw by the warmth of the welcome he got at Erik Carlsson's 70th birthday party in Trolhättan.

Roger Clark: He joined the works team in 1965, staying until the end of 1980, and we never lost touch. Supreme in UK events until the late 1970s and competitive at world level until about 1978/79.

Won well over 20 Internationals for Ford and was always a great ambassador for the company, his crowning glories being RAC Rally wins in 1972 and 1976. British Champion four times. Very useful as an 'Aunt Sally' for would-be hot shots like Russell Brookes and Co to aim at! In a way it was a shame that his RAC wins came with Tony Mason and Stuart Pegg because over 75 per cent of Roger's rallies were done with Jim Porter. However, as Jim was actually organising the RAC Rally we couldn't think of a way of getting him in with Roger at the same time. The other teams would just have nit-picked.

I don't think I was far out when I said at his funeral that if you asked enthusiasts to distil the very spirit of rallying into just a few words, most would say 'Roger Clark sideways'.

Alex Florio: After discussions with his father, Cesare, who was the Ferrari team manager, I encouraged Peter Ashcroft to sign him. Drove for Ford from the 1990 RAC Rally to the San Remo of 1991, with almost total lack of success. Quite overshadowed by Delecour in all respects, and never looked like being a winner.

Going back through the records, I see he'd driven Lancia Deltas from 1987 to 1990 inclusive, taking lots of seconds and thirds, but no victories. Yet he was third in the 1988 and second in the 1989 World Drivers' Championships – consistency in reliable cars helped.

Mark Lovell: A John Taylor discovery – winning the inaugural Ford Escort Turbo series of 1983. Drove oddities like Nissan 240RSs and Citroen Visa 4x4s, before struggling with the works Escort RS Turbo in 1985.

Won the 1986 RAC Rally Championship in an RS200 (without actually winning an individual event), then won lots of events in the next three years in Sierra RS Cosworths, including the Irish Tarmac and Dutch Championships. Shared Andrews Heat for Hire sponsorship with Russell Brookes in 1989, and was obliged to pull over (in front of TV cameras) to let Russell win the Manx of that year. Disillusioned, rather dropped out of serious rallying after that.

Timo Makinen: A full-timer at Boreham from 1970 to 1976. Won the RAC Rally in 1973/74/75, should have won in a David Sutton-prepared Twin Cam in 1968 (blown engine), many other successes. Some Boreham mechanics thought he was a pain (he was a meddler with specifications), others were ready to die for him. Some knew him as 'Why can't we . . .?' Bill Barnett hated the way he would come moaning to me if Bill wouldn't let him have his own way.

Colin McRae: First drove Sierras (Group N cars) in 1988, won and crashed a lot of other Sierras until 1990 when he moved to Prodrive/Subaru for 1991. Against all the later evidence, I *still* think it was probably right not to try to hang on to him at that particular time – the repair bills were ageing Ford finance men well before their time.

Jimmy McRae: Came to the top in Vauxhalls and Opels, winning lots of events in Chevettes and Mantas in the early 1980s (including British Championships). First drove a Sierra RS Cosworth in 1987, then won many events in cars prepared by RED in the next three years (including British Championships). By then he was well into his 40s so he drifted away to manage/encourage Colin's career – he called me at one point to suggest that he himself should campaign a Sierra, Colin an Escort and Alister a Fiesta for a season, but it never quite worked out!

Hannu Mikkola: Discovered by Bill Barnett and became a permanent member of the team in 1969, staying until 1974, then leaving (I think because Peter was no longer happy with his approach). He returned much more 'focused' for 1978-79, and drove for David Sutton in 1980, always in Escorts. Would certainly have been World Champion in 1979 if Waldegard hadn't been there first.

Carlos Sainz: Had driven Renault 5 Maxis in the Spanish Championship, was discovered by Ford Spain, and after RS200s drove Sierra Cosworth 3-doors for them in the 1987 Spanish Championship (which he won outright). John Taylor managed that programme.

Joined the factory team for 1988, but was unlucky compared with Auriol. Led San Remo for first half of the event, until gravel stages arrived. Won the Spanish Championship again in 1988 then left for Toyota at the end of the year, desperate for a 4WD car.

Incidentally, Carlos Sainz is not only a stunningly fast driver, but also a gentleman. One of the most touching phone calls I ever had came from Carlos at the end of 1988, when he had received an offer from Toyota that he simply could not refuse. Carlos called me, at home, to say he was sorry but although he loved the atmosphere at Boreham, he was going to move to a team that could offer him four-wheel-drive. I agreed he had no real alternative.

A typical note followed from him: 'This letter is to express my sincere thanks to you for being one of the first to show confidence in me. This is something that I will never forget. I hope ... that some day in the future I will be able to work together with Ford once again ...'

And so he did – he came back to drive works Escorts in 1996 and 1997, and was just as popular with everyone at Ford then as he had been in the late 1980s.

Gilbert Staepelaere: For his day job he was a PR man for Ford Belgium. Already successful with Lotus-Cortinas in the 1960s, he became the most successful driver in Escorts all over Europe, maintaining his own Boreham-built Escorts in Belgium. Certainly won more events in Escorts than anyone else in the world, and was dominant in Belgium, Holland, Germany and related countries until the end of the 1970s. Mr Nice Guy, incredibly helpful to everyone, and wished he could have gone on for more years, but lacked the money (and the free time) to do that.

Malcolm Wilson: Started rallying in a Mk1 Escort in the early 1970s, clawing his way up via the Castrol-Autosport series, Rothmans Escorts in the Open Series, etc.

Peter Ashcroft wanted him for a regular member in the 1980s, and he did much RS1600i, RS1700T and RS200 testing (he won the RS200's first event, the Lindisfarne, in 1985), but drifted away to run his own Quattro, then went into the Austin Rover MG Metro 6R4 works team for 1986. Later had stints at Vauxhall, then at Peugeot, but came back like a shot to drive Sierra Cosworth 4x4s.

Loyal thereafter, first with Michelin-backed Escort Cosworths (won the British Championship in one), built up his own preparation outfit in Cumbria – building very successful Escort Cosworths for people like Cunico in Italy, and for the Martini-backed team in Italy. Now fully and splendidly linked with Ford with Focus.

Incidentally, I haven't forgotten *Ari Vatanen, David Richards, Bjorn Waldegard* and *Russell Brookes* but they all came and went while I was running Public Affairs and Peter Ashcroft was at the helm.

Although dealing with drivers and getting competition cars into production had been a key task, there were one or two divertissements along the way in case boredom was ever in any danger of creeping in ...

ALFA ROMEO – THE MERGER THAT WASN'T

For a short time in 1986 it looked as if Ford of Europe would take over

Alfa Romeo and, even though it was still at the 'ifs, buts and maybes' stage, I was asked to look at the possibilities of co-ordinating our motorsport programme with theirs.

Corporate discussions went on for some time before the first leaks hit the financial pages in May 1986. For me this could not have come at a worse time for we were currently struggling with the RS200 problem, which had just been thrown into disarray by FISA's decision to cancel Group B at the end of the year.

Perhaps it is as well that this merger proposal did not get far – aided and abetted by the Italian government, Alfa Romeo eventually fell into the arms of Fiat – for I could already foresee huge clashes of interests and personalities.

If the merger had gone ahead, I suspect the arguments that might have developed could have been positively life-threatening.

PROCAR – THE 'SILHOUETTE' CARS

Remember those? The Procar formula was one of Bernie Ecclestone's and Max Mosley's less clever proposals – that they could build up a new form of motorsport, where so-called 'saloon' cars would race against each other. All would have to be run by manufacturers' works teams, using 3.5-litre Formula 1 engines and special chassis, but with composite body shells looking the same as those of current models of which 25,000 had been made. Some people said that this was just a way of getting rid of obsolete Formula 1 engines. You may say that; I couldn't possibly comment.

At a time when Group C sports car racing was dying on its feet, I could never understand why Bernie wanted to start up yet another formula, especially one that was likely to be horrendously expensive. It was a daft scheme from start to finish.

Even so, all the big manufacturers came under pressure from Bernie to get involved, and one meeting showed me a classic example of his legendary negotiating skills in action. Twenty or so representatives of key manufacturers were in the FIA building in Paris to discuss Procar. Bernie walked in, noted the size of the meeting and said, 'I think it would be helpful, chairman, if those here who are actually empowered to make a decision raised their hands.' Six of us did. Collapse of many of the other people in the meeting.

Bernie soon realised that almost everyone was against the Procar idea. Many of us couldn't believe that the public would be interested, nor would they turn up at race meetings to watch; purely as a comparison, notice how badly Formula 3000 fares against Formula 1.

For our part, Ford did no more than go through the motions of seeing if, how, and for how much money, we might get involved. I knew that Ford could never tackle this formula 'in house', so I cast around, reluctantly, for ideas, on the assumption that a current Ford

Cosworth Formula 1 V8 would have to be used. Having consulted the world and his wife about costs, timing and feasibility, I realised that it promised to be far too expensive. In a report of November 1987 I commented that 'Although some engineers' eyes light up at the technical challenge, in general there seems to be puzzlement at the idea, particularly in view of the high costs ...

'If we decide to enter, then I believe that it must be a "turn-key" operation, with an independent team building and running the cars ...'

Every top independent team ('all the usual suspects', as one of my staff commented) had been consulted, and 'On balance I believe the order of preference to be 1) Williams, 2) Tom Walkinshaw, and 3) March. We should perhaps ask Rory Byrne [then of the Benetton Formula 1 team] to be a consultant to the project.

'At first sight, the Sierra would appear to be the best car to base a silhouette on ... Rory talks of bolting big undertrays on to 25,000 Sierras to improve downforce – I'll leave someone else to break that rivetting news to Bill Hayden ...' [Ford's Vice President of Manufacturing].

'... everyone seems agreed that, as structured, *"silhouette" will cost more than F1*. There would be additional body costs and 4x4 and/or active suspension would be needed. Bizarrely, there would probably not be one Ford part on the cars.

'My own view is that silhouette is simply not cost effective ...'

Fortunately for me, almost everyone in the motorsport business came to the same conclusion and the proposal died for lack of support. It was one of the few occasions when Bernie misjudged motorsport's mood, and lost a battle.

MOTORSPORT AT ASTON MARTIN AND JAGUAR

Ford took control of Aston Martin in 1987 and of Jaguar in 1989, and in each case Motorsport was asked for comments on their motorsport programmes.

At Aston Martin, right from the start I recommended that we operated on a 'hands off' basis from their Group C programme, especially as 'If an Aston wins, the reaction will be "good old Astons", but if it loses it may be "Ford fail again in sports cars".'

Ford's John Grant was Vice President Business Strategy and therefore co-ordinating director of new acquisitions, including Aston Martin, and he was also cautious but cheered up a lot when Victor Gauntlett, the Executive Chairman, told him that Peter Livanos (at one time a major shareholder in Aston Martin) was willing to fund the race programme for three to four years.

No one thought that the Group C programme could ever match rivals from Porsche, Mercedes-Benz and Jaguar, and there was general agreement that we should not pump any money into it.

Nevertheless, and even without any financial commitment from Ford, Aston Martin went ahead with their programme, got Callaway of North America to develop 6-litre and (later) 6.3-litre V8 engines, and eventually finished seventh in the Manufacturers' Championship of 1989.

Jaguar, in the meantime, were subcontracting all their sports car racing programme to Tom Walkinshaw's TWR company in Oxfordshire. Tom's cars, partly engineered by Tony Southgate (who had been one of our stars in the RS200 programme) and later by Ross Brawn (who would go on to Benetton, then became technical director of Ferrari's Formula 1 team), were already outright winners, and a real credit to that marque.

For 1991 the FIA imposed a new set of Group C regulations, where cars would have to use normally aspirated 3.5-litre engines, which meant, incidentally, that suitably modified Formula 1 engines would be eligible. This, of course, is what Bernie Ecclestone always intended although I don't think it occurred to him that such engines would have to be re-developed to turn them into endurance units.

Suddenly, therefore, both Jaguar and Aston Martin turned to Ford and asked for Ford-Cosworth HB Formula 1 engines for their new cars.

Because I thought that Cosworth could too easily be diverted from its Formula 1 efforts, I was worried by this and in November 1989 wrote to Vice President Jack Brinkley:

'It would be understandable for both Jaguar and Aston Martin to look to our new F1 unit for their cars. We should resist this for 1990 and probably 1991, because Cosworth *must* concentrate on Formula 1 if we are to have a hope of beating [McLaren] Honda. Even when Cosworth feel they can cope with more, it would be wiser to supply a second Formula 1 team rather than spread their efforts to another category. As this season has shown, there is still life in the DFR and the sports car teams should be steered to this ...

'If John Barnard [who was connected with Benetton at the time] pushes us into a V12 for Formula 1 then, when that is proven, the HB could go into sports cars.

'There are enough DFRs to go round to cover both teams but if we ever face a choice between Aston Martin and Jaguar it really is no contest – it must be Jaguar ... properly handled, a Ford-Cosworth-Jaguar link in sports cars would be a very powerful (and quick) illustration of the benefits of Ford owning Jaguar.'

In any case, I added, 'I foresee this whole area becoming a bit emotional – for instance, although the Aston team is not Ford funded, do we really want two of our companies racing against each other?'

Not everyone agreed with me. Bruce Blythe, who was the key Ford Vice President in the Aston and Jaguar negotiations, recommended that both should get supplies but that neither team should get any other financial commitments.

In the end it was a lack of availability that stopped the DFR from being supplied to either team for 1990 (even for testing), for Cosworth was already committed to a winter manufacturing programme by this time, and could not boost it further. For 1991 the problem sorted itself out, as Peter Livanos pulled the plug on his Aston Martin programme and left the field open to Jaguar.

Honour was then satisfied, and I was relieved when Jaguar XJR 14s, with the latest Ford-Cosworth HB engines for 1991, went on to win the World Sports Car Championship.

COSWORTH

Although Ford finally took control of Cosworth Racing in 1998, this came as no surprise because it was a project that had surfaced several times in previous years.

Ever since Keith Duckworth designed the original DFV Formula 1 engine in 1966/67, Ford and Cosworth had been close. Along with the FVA (Formula 2) and BDA (16-valve road car) engines, the fortunes of the companies had been interlinked for many years.

Even so, except that they were major customers, Ford never had any financial control over Cosworth, and were quite relaxed about who owned them, except that they wanted to be sure that any specific-to-Ford knowledge would not be shared with rivals.

By 1987 Ford was consulting Yamaha of Japan about new road-car engines, Yamaha were co-operating with Cosworth on final five-valves-per-cylinder developments of the venerable DFV, and Ford certainly considered making a bid to buy Cosworth from their owners, UEI. Walter Hayes, however, was ever practical, writing in February 1988 that 'I still don't believe UEI will sell Cosworth to us, but I think a frank interchange of views between ourselves and Keith Duckworth is overdue and might generate some form of association which would erase some emerging misgivings . . .'

At that time, however, I told Walter and Alex Trotman that 'Buying Cosworth or putting in our own management probably wouldn't work – but perhaps we should offer them advice on re-organising. . . While they have undoubted talents, Cosworth are human, not perfect, and not quite as good as they think they are . . .'

There was a distinct feeling at Ford that at this time we were over-burdening Cosworth, not only with a demand for new Formula 1 engines, but for work on Indycar projects and because of the way the Sierra Cosworth and 24-valve V6 road-car engine programmes were developing.

For a few weeks, at least, desultory talks went on as to how to bring Ford and Cosworth closer together, but nothing came of this – UEI would not sell any of Cosworth's equity to Ford, and would not even consider selling the entire business.

Everything then went quiet until May 1989, when the entire UEI business was taken over by Carlton Communications. That was all very well, except that Carlton immediately admitted to the financial media that Cosworth was not a good 'fit' to the rest of their conglomerate. Although chairman Michael Green insisted that 'No companies are for sale', Ford, along with other companies, soon concluded that Cosworth was once again 'in play'.

When rumours of approaches from General Motors, Mercedes-Benz and Fiat all began to circulate, we at Ford got very alarmed. With the brand-new Ford Cosworth HB Formula 1 V8 just coming on stream, we did not want to see our partners in Grand Prix racing slip away.

By the end of 1989 Ford was definitely considering making an approach – or at least getting involved with another company (maybe Porsche, Mercedes-Benz or VW, perhaps as a minor shareholder) – and if another company had stepped in first, to take over, we were already considering withdrawing our business from Cosworth, dropping the name from models like the Sierra Cosworth, and setting up links with other racing specialists.

I became concerned by all the rumours and counter-rumours about Cosworth and sent a paper to key people suggesting that in case an 'unfriendly' buyer took over Cosworth '. . . we should have a contingency plan to give, say, Brian Hart enough support for him to tempt away the four to six key people from Cosworth (perhaps as partners in a new venture with him). . . If Fiat buy Cosworth we should on no account believe any promises to keep a Ford F1 engine competitive with Ferrari . . .'

(So young, yet so cynical . . .)

Most importantly, Jack Brinkley put his finger on an important problem: 'If we do not acquire Cosworth we would probably have to find an alternative manufacturing source which can be run economically at volumes of 5,000-7,000 units-per-annum – or *abandon our saloon Motorsport programme*' (my italics).

All in all, we put the value of the business at not less than £100 million – substantial money, even by Ford's worldwide standards – and if Fiat had put in a serious bid, I believe that Ford would have tried to see it matched.

Cannily, though, the company concluded that a 'neutral third party' should also be encouraged to buy Cosworth, although if it came to a hostile bidding battle, then so be it.

This, in fact, is what happened, for in March 1990 Cosworth was actually sold to Vickers, which was in no way a competitor to Ford. Ford's own relationship with Cosworth was not damaged, nor were personal friendships affected.

But it certainly gave us something to mull over in the winter months...

TIME TO GO ...

Climbing a mountain to get the Escort RS Cosworth was probably the hardest work – certainly the most concentrated lobbying work – that I had ever tackled. It didn't help that a debate over whether or not to close the Boreham facility rumbled on through most of the 1980s and took up quite a lot of nervous energy.

Once I knew that 'Ace' had been signed off in the USA, and was firmly committed for production, its progress was out of my hands and I began to feel under-employed.

In fact I'd already started thinking of retirement in the late 1980s, and I was not the only Ford manager to make the break at the same time. Walter Hayes retired in 1989 (though 'retirement' didn't last long, as he was soon drafted in to be the brilliant Chairman of Aston Martin in the early 1990s), which was, in fact, the impetus for Motorsport to become the responsibility of Marketing not Public Affairs.

Once he had urged the Escort RS Cosworth project over its most important obstacles, Mike Moreton could see that his life might never again be as exciting, so he also moved on, to join Tom Walkinshaw's team as project manager on the XJ220 project.

There were many reasons for my own decision to go, but apart from making all the usual financial calculations, there was certainly another important factor – that the Turner 'seven year cycle' was looming up again, and seven years from when I was persuaded back to motorsport in 1983 would take me up until 1990.

It was, in any case, the right time to go. Ford of Europe was going through a boom period, but their far-sighted planners were already looking ahead, and starting to ask for head-count reductions at all levels. As I knew from the AVO days, I hated cutting heads, so this time I thought I would ease the pain by chopping off my own instead. In any case, according to my detailed analysis, most of what I had set out to do in 1983 had now been achieved.

My decision to retire early was influenced by the fact that various packages were on offer as part of the headcount reduction programme and one of these looked so good that I grabbed it; that a key finance man retired under the same scheme simply confirmed that my decision was right because Ford finance men *never* get their sums wrong.

Once Jack Brinkley and I had agreed that I would go at the end of 1990, I suggested that Peter Ashcroft should take over from me. In my opinion he thoroughly deserved the career boost and I was delighted when Jack took my advice. The announcement was made in November 1990 and the end of my Ford world, therefore, came at Christmas in

1990, when I was not quite 58. I had already moved my office out of Warley into an unused conference room at Boreham, so I was able to slip quietly away from there.

Amidst all the cheers from drivers who, over the years, I hadn't picked (contrary to their expectations), the first letter of good wishes came from Stirling Moss, while Jackie Stewart wrote, 'There are so few people one can genuinely abuse with feeling on a continuing basis, whether it be by telephone, in writing, or even in front of a live audience . . . I am afraid I have to admit that I enjoyed working with you very much over the years . . .'

The much respected Leo Mehl of Goodyear wrote to thank me for saving his company millions of dollars by totally failing to persuade him that he should support our rally cars. He said, 'It's been great not working with you all these years. I figure since 1971 we have saved $100,000,000 ($5,000,000/year x 20 years).' (The commission never did reach my Swiss bank account, Leo.) He added, 'I know you're really not retiring. What kind of ploy is this?'

He was right – another side of my life was already opening up.

Chapter 14

Tale end

FORD THREW A great party when I left (or so I heard) and I was delighted to receive a Gregor Grant Award from *Autosport,* over 30 years after I'd won their navigator's trophy. This time there was the extra joy of sharing the stage with Mario Andretti who collected a similar award. Then I got a trophy from the RAC MSA 'to recognise the contribution over many years in the field of motor sport', but any tendency to swollen headedness was firmly squashed when I spoke at a Ford Yorkshire Dealers Association dinner and was mercilessly roasted in the speeches, then presented with an engraved trowel 'to mark my entry into gainful unemployment'.

But was I to be unemployed? The only firm decision I'd made was that I wasn't going to keep popping back in to the office 'just to say hello'. General de Gaulle, I believe, had a colourful French phrase for that sort of thing . . . something about 'not crapping in other dogs' kennels' is roughly what he said, although I think he probably put it more poetically.

But would I suffer from withdrawal symptoms? Would I spend hours crouched in front of Ceefax, waiting for updates of rally positions? Would I be tempted to call Boreham, at regular intervals, to ask what was going on? Well, except for the annual agony of wondering when the Escort RS Cosworth would finally win the Monte Carlo Rally, I never did.

Anyway, before idleness could set in, what had started as a 'hobby' was starting to keep me more than busy. Public speaking.

Standing up in front of an audience, 'singing for my supper', was not new to me because I'd been doing it at motor clubs since the 1960s, and I was used to making management presentations (if you think that is easy, you try standing up in front of a roomful of sceptical top brass to 'sell' them a way-out project like an RS200 or an 'Escort Sierra'). I was speaking at 15-20 functions every year, mainly motor clubs, but it was all ad hoc and fairly low key.

The turning point came in 1988 when, out of the blue, I got a letter from a PR company telling me that as a promotion, Benedictine was sponsoring some annual 'After Dinner Speaker of the Year' awards. They enclosed a list of nominees in various categories and I was surprised to find myself included among the dozen or so finalists in the 'business' section. The list had been drawn up following nominations from leading opinion formers, but how I got on to it I simply don't know, for there must be hundreds of worthy business speakers.

The PR company asked nominees to send any tapes or videos of speeches to help the judges decide. I sent some round and forgot all about the award. Then in November Margaret and I were invited to a dinner at the Savoy Hotel, in London, where the prizes were to be presented. I was at a meeting in Germany that day and was in two minds about rushing back, but it promised to be an interesting evening so I made the effort and we scrambled in just as the meal was starting.

Sir Clement Freud, gourmet and one-time Liberal MP, was the chairman of the judges and, during the meal, one of the PR people found me and said that Sir Clement wanted a word. I left it until the coffee then went over to his table and, to my surprise, he said, 'I'm getting up in a few minutes to announce the awards. You have won the "business section", and we'd like all four category winners to make 2-minute acceptance speeches which I will weave into mine'.

That gave me all of 5 minutes to think up something. I recall that the actress Patricia Routledge was there and made some flattering remarks afterwards, but I doubt if my piece was all that good. Nevertheless, I walked back to the car on air afterwards.

The next morning I got a call from Annie Hallam, who was then one of the partners in a speaking agency, the Right Address. Having won the Benedictine award, she said, would I be interested in them representing me more fully? With the help of Annie and her partner, Jane French, the momentum began to build and, since then, that trophy – a Benedictine logo'd wine coaster that probably cost no more than £60 – has generated an enormous amount of income for me simply because of the difference it made to be able to put 'Benedictine After Dinner Speaker of the Year' on my cv. A bit like having a *Good Housekeeping* seal of approval if you like, because booking a speaker is always something of a hit or miss affair and anything to reassure an event organiser helps.

That award transformed something that until then had been a mild diversion into a new career. I'm now making around 80 speeches a year – half of them conventional after-dinner speeches, the other half on management subjects like team building, drawing on experiences, good and bad, that I have been involved in over the years.

In the last couple of years alone, this has taken me to North America, South Africa, and many European countries. But it isn't just the money that keeps me talking – I enjoy meeting new people and at dinners I usually end up sitting next to a chief executive or two, and how else am I ever going to sit next to ex-Prime Ministers, even Bishops, for a meal? As a result I'm prepared to tackle almost anything. I have actually spoken at a function where 11 people were promised, two were ill and couldn't make it, and one was called away to a business meeting. On another occasion there were 23 different nationalities in an audience of 48.

That is one extreme, the other being that I have spoken in the Great Room at the Grosvenor House in front of 1,500 people, which I thought was impressive enough, until the head waiter said, 'By the way, there are 500 more in the ballroom on a loudspeaker extension.'

One of the most bizarre engagements I ever had was to fly to Phoenix, Arizona, to speak to 30 people from the insurance world who had flown in from Australia on an incentive trip. No, I didn't understand it either. Some of the locations are unexpected, and awe-inspiring, such as speaking to an IBM group in the motor museum near Geneva airport, in front of one of the most expensive displays of Ferraris I have ever seen. Not that I see that many.

Then I was talking to a Licensed Premises Surveyors' dinner recently, where I sat between two top brewers and as a result now probably know even more about trends in beer consumption than I did when working with rally drivers. And while his name may well be forgotten by the time this book appears, having sat next to Geoffrey Robinson at a dinner added another dimension for me to the Mandelson affair when it blew up later. 'Self satisfied' is the description I'm looking for I think.

Whether the strain of speaking does anything for your health is another matter, of course. Some people are paralysed with fright at the prospect of speaking, and stay frightened when on their feet. I was – and still am – nervous *before* I start speaking, but once the first words are out, then I'm usually OK. I rarely sleep well afterwards because of the adrenalin high I suppose – there's quite a thrill in getting a standing ovation. I got one recently and I only said a couple of words. Mind you, they were 'The Queen'.

Conversely, there is no worse time than driving home after giving a speech that has flopped. And I know, believe me. Sod's Law can also be relied upon to operate and if anything can go wrong, it will. While I was speaking at one dinner, a cat strolled across the dance floor. Foolishly, instead of ignoring it, I pointed out to the audience that the committee had gone to great expense to get an animal act to appear for them. The cat must have had a sense of occasion because as everyone looked at it, it sat down in full view and started licking its backside. Some things a speaker can't follow; that was one of them.

Then, of course, there are other opportunities that could not otherwise come my way other than by being on the speakers' circuit. As an example, as a result of speaking at the same function as him, I had the joy of having a long discussion about comedy with Eric Morecambe, the greatest of them all. That was a privilege, as it was to speak at the Cambridge Union and also at various times alongside Peter Ustinov and Les Dawson. Being asked to speak at Stirling Moss's 60th birthday with Rob Walker and Innes Ireland gave me a kick too.

A year or so ago I spoke at a lunch at Goodwood and was then involved in a question-and-answer session with Stirling and Tony Brooks. That, in itself, was fascinating, but after lunch Stirling invited me for a few laps round the circuit with him, in the same Ferrari 250GT Berlinetta in which he had won the Tourist Trophy race in the early 1960s. Why am I telling you this? Believe me, I've told *everybody*. In fact Margaret says that for days afterwards I was stopping complete strangers in Chipping Norton to tell them about the experience. Magic!

Apart from all the public speaking (I nearly wrote 'spouting' which I suppose wouldn't be that far wrong really) I found that I still had many links with motorsport, and new ones cropped up.

I wrote an irregular column for *Autosport* for about a year until I ran out of things to say (always a good time to stop, I feel) and I was pleased to hear that one piece campaigning for a replacement for Jean Marie Balestre as the head of the FIA was quoted at more than one meeting of national bodies. I hope it helped because I thought it was high time JMB was ousted. I got a call from Howard Strawford, then chairman of the British Racing & Sports Car Club, inviting me to join the Board of that club, and at the time of writing I am still a director. That led to becoming a trustee of the Motorsport Safety Fund (which had been started in the 1970s after Roger Williamson was killed at Zandvoort). That Fund had become fairly moribund, but a group of us managed to rejuvenate it by supplying regular information via *Rescue and Resuscitation*, a magazine that I edit for doctors and paramedics. The Fund also organises the annual Watkins Lecture on safety matters, the first of which was given by Prof Sid Watkins, the second by Jackie Stewart.

Over the years I'd had a good relationship with the Motor Sports Association and although, like many on the 'outside', I'd gently taken the mickey out of the Blazer Brigade, I recognised that no national organising sports body can please all of the people all of the time – watch the turmoil that afflicts other sports if you don't believe me. The MSA must have forgiven any mickey-taking because I was co-opted on to the Council, with the specific brief of helping the grass roots of motorsport.

In many ways this was almost like going back to my own grass roots in the North Staffs Motor Club and Stafford and District Car Club. For such clubs I helped the MSA produce a 'Motor Club Manual', giving advice on everything from keeping a club's finances straight to organising a dinner dance. In addition, our dining room table is laden every month with the *Wheels* supplement – pages of 'oven ready' copy sent free to 400 or so clubs for them to photocopy and include in their own magazines. I cheerfully acknowledge a debt to a Bishop in Essex because I cribbed the idea from an insert he sent round to all the churches under his control; I think I noticed the publication when I was on my knees praying for a particular budget to be approved.

I also got involved as a member of the committee of the MSA's Club Development Fund – which makes grants to clubs, mainly on safety items – and for a brief period chaired the MSA's Historic Rally Group. I've even judged the odd concours d'elegance. I use the word 'odd' advisedly because, ye gods, the entrants are so fiercely competitive that they make Formula 1 constructors look effeminate. One concours left me so traumatised that when judging at a pet show the following week I played safe and gave the cup to someone who turned up with a tin of salmon.

I still get invited to speak at ten or so motor club dinners every year, although this may simply be because I don't charge! Having had an enjoyable life through motorsport I feel it would be obscene to demand payment. If the FIA wanted to help the grass roots of the sport, it would introduce 'plough back' days, making it compulsory for a driver to give one day to his national club for every ten or so points scored in a world championship – the days to be used to project the sport to sponsors, schools and politicians and, not least, to talk at motor club functions. Look through old motor club magazines and you'll find that Formula 1 drivers, legends like Graham Hill, would regularly turn up at club dinners. Today? Don't ask.

Yes, yes, I recognise of course that today's stars are busy with their fitness trainers, financial consultants, sports psychologists, Feng Shui advisers, floral arrangers and tarot readers, but it's still a pity because the sport needs a strong base. The sad fact is that in spite of every initiative by the MSA, and in spite of massive TV coverage of motorsport, membership of traditional, locally based clubs is steadily *declining*. We may be heading for a significant drop in the number of clubs around, an implosion if you like, because we have a downward spiral of fewer members meaning more work being done by fewer (ageing) committee members who, sooner or later, may, almost certainly will, say 'stuff it'.

Through doing the *Wheels* supplement I see 50 or so club magazines a month and there is a depressing pattern of pleas for people to please take on this or that job in a club. All too few clubs, for instance, have anyone trying to promote their activities with the media. And as for getting enough marshals to run events . . . oh dear. It's only a small consolation that this decline is part of far wider social changes – talk to other specialist-interest groups and you'll find that they face similar challenges.

Curiously, forums or question-and-answer sessions devoted to the Old Days seem to fare better with clubs than anything featuring more recent events. Among the questions I get asked most frequently at these are:

Who is your favourite rally driver? Has to be Timo Makinen because of his amazing Monte win and his RAC Rally hat-trick. (Incidentally, when I saw him recently he said that ambitious rally drivers should cut their teeth on *two*-wheel drive cars before leaping into 4x4s.)

The most nervous time with him was when he was going for his hat-trick on the RAC Rally. He was convinced that the stages were going to be very rough and asked for 15-inch wheels for his Escort. I told him we'd just get mixed up with the 13-inch used by the other team cars. He insisted and I gave way because he was up for three-in-a-row.

The inevitable happened: he got to the end of one stage and I told him he'd done it on two 13-inch and two 15-inch. He said it didn't matter because the car had handled well . . . whereupon I took delight in pointing out that the 15-inch were on the offside, the 13-inch on the other.

Carlos Sainz ranks high on my list as a rally driver too, not least because of his approach to the sport. I once held a crisis meeting before the Corsican Rally to sort out a problem he was having with Ford over his national programme in Spain. Before the discussion began, Carlos asked for the floor so that he could stress that he could not support any changes that adversely affected an old friend of his to whom he had given his word about something. I think it's called honour, and you don't see enough of it in motorsport today.

Favourite race driver? Well I get starstruck easily so pick any one you like from Stirling Moss – and remember he had a *rally* career most would envy – Graham Hill, John Surtees, Jody Scheckter, Jackie Stewart and Gerry Birrell. I've probably had most to do with Jackie over the years, not least via a regular exchange of rude letters. The Tyrrell days with Jackie and François Cevert were good days indeed.

A few years ago I saw JYS hold an audience of hard-nosed Swiss bankers enthralled as he spoke after a dinner in Geneva; more recently, when giving the 1999 Watkins Lecture, he captivated an audience for an hour on safety issues. A great ambassador for our sport. Pity he has such a blind spot about rallying.

How competitive have women drivers been over the years? Very, very competitive in the case of Pat Moss – and I saw her in action both as her navigator and team manager. Val Domleo was always a serious threat as a navigator on rallies.
Christabel Carlisle was braver than most men in her Don Moore-prepared Minis; her 'English rose' beauty bowled over the Americans when we took her to Sebring to race an MGB with Denise McCluggage. (Gillian Fortescue-Thomas later raced an Escort with Don Moore under a similar arrangement to Christabel.)

One of the most successful programmes ever run for women drivers was the Fabergé Fiesta Ladies Championship. This stemmed from a throwaway remark I made when a journalist asked at our annual motorsport press conference what we were doing to encourage women drivers. I said, 'Nothing at the moment but if any of your lady readers out there are interested, tell them to write in.' I expected 20 or so letters but the Post Office nearly had to put on extra deliveries because hundreds replied – some even sent very revealing photographs of themselves, as if that could ever influence a team manager. The very idea.

John Taylor ran a series of elimination sessions in quarries around the country using RS2000s, then the 15 finalists did six races and six rallies in 1979, each in yellow Fiesta 1300Ss owned by Ford RS Dealers. Jackie Stewart helped us launch the series to the dealers and TV presenter Dickie Davies was involved on the press side.

Louise Aitken (the -Walker came with her marriage later), who was 19 at the time and had *no* motorsport experience, was so outstanding in the testing stages that John Taylor and Charles Reynolds wanted me to back her there and then, but I felt that we were too far down the road with plans for the championship. Louise finished close behind the championship winner, Guenda Eadie, and was outstanding in the six rallies and of course went on to great things. It did no harm with the press that her then co-driver, Anne Kidd, was very young and journalists had photographs of her with a satchel because she was still at school!

There is usually a follow-up question: *Will a woman ever win a Grand Prix*? Some panellists bob and weave and never answer the question but I prefer the honest approach and say, 'Not a hope in hell.' Mind you, I check where the exit is first.

Which is the best rally car you have ever worked with? The TR2 and TR3 did more for rallying than they're now given credit for, but maybe my favourite has to be the Escort, almost any Escort. If you think about it, over its 30-year life in motorsport *thousands* of drivers have won awards in one and *hundreds* (maybe thousands in fact) of tuning and preparation shops have been founded on the back of it.

What were the differences between BMC and Ford? Well, if you've waded this far, you'll probably have noticed that the Ford chapters have many more references to finance in them than the BMC ones. But the proof of the pud and all that is that Ford is still a strong company, BMC is long gone.

What do you think of the changes that have happened to motorsport over the years? As this is the last chapter, I guess I'm allowed to be a Self-opinionated Old Fart just once and say that today's World Championship rallies are not as challenging as the old Alpines and Lièges were. But, in fairness, they can't be – society quite rightly won't allow cars to go charging around nowadays on public roads at high speeds.

In addition, the growth of sponsorship (no decals in the BMC days) means that events have to be tailored more closely to the needs of the media. Changes in that media itself have played a part too and while Formula 1 is all-triumphant, rallying still struggles to find its proper niche. Thirty-five years ago, Monte wins put Minis on to prime-time TV shows; today a Monte win will be buried in some newspapers below a change of manager for a Third Division football team.

One irritating change: there was a day (what do you mean, oh Lord, here he goes again?) when if a driver crashed he put his hand up and admitted the mistake. Today, it seems, it's either the tyres at fault or 'the car hit a tree' as if it had a mind of its own.

One sad change: the loss of major 'brand names' over the years – events like the Targa, Alpine and so on. With the relentless drive for standardisation, even once famous events like the Monte are now little more than 'Round 1 of the Championship'.

Anyway, things are *never* what they were. Those of us who moan about the lack of atmosphere at today's major events should be reminded that John Langley, the former *Daily Telegraph* motoring correspondent, once complained about the blandness of a Monte he was watching – and he was writing in 1967!

One question I hate, and so do most panellists, is *What was your funniest moment?* Funny moments tend not to sound all that good when told for the nth time. Mind you, I relish the memory of the time Timo Makinen was asked to walk along a line in the road by a State Trooper in Florida to check his sobriety. Timo pretended not to understand the word 'stop' and was nearly in the next state before they halted him.

And when I was with Ari Vatanen when he was stopped on the M1 in the early hours, we both made out that he couldn't speak English, although I nearly burst out laughing when the patrolman radioed to the police station to ask if there was anyone on duty who spoke Finnish. At 1.45am . . .

Forums and chat shows sometimes produce their own funny moments. Some years ago I chaired a panel in Leeds where Ford driver John Taylor mentioned that whenever he got behind the wheel of a rally Escort, he grew horns. I turned to Roger Clark and without thinking asked, 'Do you get a horn when you are in a rally car, Roger?' It was several minutes before we could continue the forum.

On the domestic front, although a lot of nonsense is talked about Essex and its so-called lack of visual charm (explore some of the villages north of the A12), Margaret and I wanted to move back towards the Midlands, and because we had always been happy at Abingdon, we naturally gravitated towards that part of the world.

Over the years, almost accidentally, we'd acquired, renovated, and subsequently sold a series of other houses, cottages and flats while our main home was in Essex. First of all there was a cottage near Thirsk in Yorkshire (where I was hugely impressed to find that 'James Herriot' was the vet who looked after the pony belonging to the lady who kept the key for us), then cottages at Long Melford in Suffolk, a flat in Cambridge, houses in Leeds (full of medical students, which is how I know why it is said that most doctors don't smoke – they're usually too drunk to light the things) . . . activity that led to the book *Buying and Renovating a Cottage* (now available from all good charity shops).

After all that, coming across some land in Oxfordshire and building a third 'Penny Farthing' was a pleasure and if anyone is contemplating retirement with dread – on the basis of 'What on earth am I going to do?' – I can recommend building a new house and supervising its construction. Never a dull moment, especially when I was later able to buy more land and build an equestrian centre – not from any great love of horses (I'm afraid of them and deeply suspicious of what can happen at either end) but because it was all that the planners would allow. The conservation awards I was involved in while Director of Public Affairs at Ford must have struck a lasting chord because I had 250 yards of Cotswold stone wall round the land renovated . . . and was pleased to get an award in 1999 from the Dry Stone Walling Association as a result. (So people who described me as a 'wallie' over the years weren't that far out, although I suspect their spelling was usually with a 'y'.)

I genuinely thought that by moving to Oxfordshire I would get away from motorsport, geographically at least. But when I asked a new neighbour if our village was always quiet, he said that it was 'unless Tom Walkinshaw is flying over in his helicopter'. I then realised that the Benetton Formula 1 factory was only a short distance across the fields in one direction, while Tom Walkinshaw's HQ was not far away in another. Further, our house has been built on the edge of what was once a very large estate, where motor car speed trials had been held by the Oxford Motor Cycling Club (the then President was William Morris, no less) as early as 1912. So, clearly, there was to be no escape from motorsport. As an aside, someone sent me a Route Card from the Oxford Motor Club's Non-Stop Trial of 1923 – it had space on the back for competitors to sign whether they'd made a non-stop run. Their word was taken on trust . . . Ho hum.

Looking back, I was lucky to be able to do all the property transactions because at one point I came very close to going bankrupt. That I didn't was mainly due to public speaking.

I went to speak at a Lloyd's function, where I knew the audience would be wealthy brokers or underwriters and, I assumed, well-behaved. Not so; it was like performing in a bear garden. The master of ceremonies couldn't get the room quiet even to say grace, while the chairman was heckled from the beginning of his speech to the end. I was the last speaker and, believe me, I was already in a state of panic when, just before I stood up, the head waiter whispered to me that he would be grateful if I could signal him when I was about one minute from the end of my speech. Very odd, I thought, but I did so and I was glad I had because as I walked off, the exotic dancer (a charming lady and a natural blonde) walked on. One more sentence from me, and I would have had a personal lap dance.

Anyway, a few weeks later my accountant invited me to a reception where someone from Lloyd's was present, giving us a sales spiel and inviting us to become 'Names'. At the time this was highly profitable and looked like a licence to print money. I was on the margins and probably shouldn't even have been invited to the meeting, but I chortled along with everyone else and thought how witty the man from Lloyd's was when he said, 'Of course, I have to tell you that you could lose everything . . .' I drove home impressed, talked it over with Margaret, and went to bed convinced that I should sign up.

Mercifully, I had a 20-minute drive to Ford's Head Office and on the way the next morning I suddenly thought of the mayhem at that earlier dinner and realised that *they* would be the people looking after my money. I decided to forgo impressing my in-laws by becoming a Name and phoned my accountant to say 'No thank you' instead.

Reader, if this page is damp as you read it, it is perspiration, because even as I type this now I break out into a cold sweat remembering how close I came to penury. Several good friends, including famous rallying personalities, were dragged into the same net and lost a great deal of money.

So-called retirement gave me more time to maintain my interest in the theatre and even to discover a belated interest in jazz. Don Moore, from my BMC days, regularly invited me over to the Farmers' Club in Cambridge where, along with John Ogier, I sat and listened to a series of great jazz musicians brought there by Brian Lister who sat in on the drums. All I had to do in that company was throw the names Archie Scott Brown and Lister-Jaguar into the conversation, then sit back and listen, spellbound.

At long last, too, I found time to indulge myself, by going to Edinburgh every year for the Fringe Festival when the whole place is buzzing with shows. Margaret maintains it's undignified at our age to be running down Princes Street late in the evening to get from one show to another and won't come, but I usually manage to cram in 14 or 15 shows in a couple of days every year. Highly recommended.

There was also the joy of having more time to stay close to Jill Summers who, although not a blood relative, was the closest of what I came to call 'family' for most of my life. Jill had an astonishing career boost in the 1970s when she became Phyllis Pearce in *Coronation Street*; and the part could have been written especially for her – a strong, formidable, always quotable matriarch. She was a character, a warm and friendly character, who richly deserved the tributes paid her by many celebrities when Michael Aspel sprang a *This is Your Life* on her.

Towards the end of her life she spent much time in hospital, but one of her friends and a working colleague from 'The Street', Roy Barraclough, brought laughter to her funeral by recalling one particular hospital visit when Jill had about 15 people around her bed, all helpless with laughter, under a sign saying 'Only three visitors at a time'.

Whenever I visited her in hospital I always came away with a list of things to do and people to contact. It was only after making consecutive calls to 'Lily Savage' and then Dame Thora Hird that I realised what a wide range of friends Jill had! She worked regularly on *Coronation Street* until she was 85 – that she remained so alert convinced me there must be something in the theory that the brain is just another part of the body that needs regular exercising, in Jill's case by memorising scripts. I'm told that if you don't keep active, you spend a disproportionate amount of time reading articles in life-style magazines about 'flatulence in the over-50s' and the like. And apparently you worry a lot about your feet.

I suspect it is a mistake to buy a house with too much garage space, which is what I did in Danbury when I was with Ford. During that time, after a spell charging round the garden in an 1172cc 1953 Underwood Special I owned for a while, I had four Austin-Healey Sprites, an XK120 and XK140, then an MGA – all of which I sold at a loss, which requires skill in a rising market.

Maybe I'll fare better with my latest acquisition, a Dellow. Why a Dellow? Well, partly because I met Ron Lowe (the 'low' of Dellow) at motor club functions in the 1950s and liked his down-to-earth approach and partly because I'd seen one advertised. But it was really Jim Porter's fault. He was the organiser of the 1997 Norwich Union (later Guardian Insurance) Classic Car run and, along with Cliff Gaskin, I had gone to Silverstone to watch all the cars streaming in – Ferraris, Jaguars, Aston Martins, Triumphs, MGs, etc. As a Rolls rolled by, Cliff remarked, 'You won't see anything like a Dellow at an up-market event like this. . .' and at that moment, out of 1,600 cars in the event, we turned and saw the next car to arrive – which was the only Dellow entered. We followed the car to where it parked and discovered that the lady driver was Jim Porter's daughter, Jim of course being Roger Clark's long-time co-driver. I reckoned that odds of 1,600 to 1 on that happening meant Someone was trying to tell me something, so I followed up the ad for a red Dellow and went down to Devon to buy it.

Donald Morley was quick to phone soon afterwards to point out that it had been said on the Terry Wogan radio show that the male menopause is not complete until you have owned at least one small red sports car!

It was a joy to potter round the Guardian RAC Classic the following year in the Dellow. The best thing was that at the end *Dellows were parked with Rolls-Royces and Bentleys*. Well, if you want to be pedantic, they were lumped under 'others' but let's not spoil the memory.

I traced the widow of an early owner, Bob Parsons, a Cornwall-based vet, and learned from her that my particular car, MLJ 928, in the 1950s did the Land's End Trial, club rallies, driving tests and sprints. And Mrs Parsons said that she still had the equipment that her husband put in the Dellow on a Monday morning, when he used it as everyday transport for his vet's practice. We need similar low-cost ways into our sport today if it is to stay strong.

There needs to be more than just a clutch of Formula 1 races and World Championship rallies, tailored – some would say neutered – for television; the base of the motorsport pyramid is just as important at the exotic apex, at least it is if the 'sport' in motorsport is to mean anything.

But enough pontification. What else is there for this final lap? Well, for the book to be really complete I suppose I should tell you about the struggle I had to build up my collection of cigarette cards of world-famous upholsterers, but I don't want you getting over excited so I guess we'd better make it chequered flag time. Thank you for joining me in my anecdotage. If you've made it this far, I reckon that you, in turn, deserve an *Autosport* award. For perseverance.

William Shakespeare, when he discussed the seven ages of man, wrote:

'... Last scene of all,
That ends this strange eventful history,
Is second childishness ...'

Well, I reckon Will knew what he was talking about.

I used to write a motor club magazine called *The Wheel*, now I write for the MSA's *Wheels* supplement for motor club magazines.

I used to sit and watch comedians in music halls, and be the odd one out as the youngest in the audience; now I sit and watch comedians at the Edinburgh Fringe and am the odd one out as the oldest in the audience.

I used to be involved with 1172 specials, now I own a Dellow, which is really only a thinking man's 1172 special (although don't tell the Dellow Registrar I said so).

So, as you can see, I am clearly regressing to Will's second childishness. If you see me roaming the streets in short trousers with a lollipop, you will have a quiet word with my care worker, won't you?

In the meantime, would you like to come round and play with my new train set?

Index